MAINE FOREVER

A GUIDE TO NATURE CONSERVANCY PRESERVES IN MAINE

SECOND EDITION

WRITTEN, EDITED AND ILLUSTRATED BY

Ruth Ann Hill

DESIGN BY

Michael Mahan Graphics

PHOTOGRAPHS BY

*Thomas Arter, Lee Carbonneau,
Mary Droege, Richard Forrester,
Julie Henderson, Alan Hutchinson,
David Muench, David Smiley,
Barbara Vickery,
and Susan Woodward.*

MAINE CHAPTER, THE NATURE CONSERVANCY
122 MAIN STREET, POST OFFICE BOX 338
TOPSHAM, MAINE 04086, TELEPHONE: (207)729-5181

Acknowledgments

This second edition of *Maine Forever* illustrates the collective achievements of the members of The Nature Conservancy's Maine Chapter. Without their support, none of the outstanding natural areas described herein would be protected as nature preserves.

A goodly number of people merit particular recognition and thanks for their contributions to the book. Chapter Board chairperson Sherry Huber and Development Committee chairperson Carol Wishcamper took the idea of a second edition and turned it into reality. All of the photographers whose work graces this edition generously offered to forgo their usual fees and donate use of the images instead, allowing the Chapter to use color to bring its lands and their denizens to life on the printed page.

I am grateful and forever indebted to Mary Minor Lannon, author and editor of the first edition of *Maine Forever*. My special thanks and gratitude also go to the Maine Chapter Board of Trustees Communications Committee, led by Cherie Mason, which could be counted on for its wise counsel, creative ideas and patient support. Without the careful reviews, criticism and support of the Chapter staff, especially Mason Morfit, Kent Wommack, Barbara Vickery, Julie Henderson and Deb Clark, this book would not be. Simple thanks are not enough for them. And, to the stalwarts of Michael Mahan Graphics, I simply say, "I owe you one." Finally, for me, this book is dedicated to my parents, who have always encouraged me to explore the wild places, and to John, who now explores with me and who kept me going when she needed just a bit more fairing-in.

Ruth Ann Hill
July 1989

Corporate Support

Publication of the second edition of *Maine Forever* was made possible in part by the support of Maine's corporate community. Contributions from Maine companies paid for printing costs of the book, allowing the Maine Chapter to keep that amount in its operating account, at work protecting land. The corporations' generous support has also enabled the Chapter to devote all profits from sale of *Maine Forever* to protecting more land.

Corporate Donors

Underwriter
Casco Northern Bank

Benefactor
Anonymous
Bath Iron Works Corporation
Blue Rock Industries
CYRO Industries
Dead River Company
Ellsworth Builders Supply, Inc.
G & S Commercial Brokers
J. M. Huber Corporation
Kennebunk Savings Bank
The Knowles Company - Insurance
Liberty Group
Peoples Heritage Bank
Tom's of Maine
Wishcamper O'Neil Properties, Inc.
Voyagers Whitewater

Patron
Barton, Gingold, Eaton and Anderson
Consolidated Hydro, Inc.
Harborside Graphics
Hinckley Insurance Agency
Moss Inc.
Prentiss & Carlisle
Quality Tree Growth, Inc.
James W. Sewall Company
Sunkhaze Stream Chapter, Trout Unlimited
Union Trust Company of Ellsworth
Wood Structures Inc.

Sustainer
Advest, Inc., Charles P. Harriman
Allen Agency
Atkinson Contract Services, Inc.
Bangor and Aroostook Railroad
Bar Harbor Banking & Trust
Deering Lumber, Inc.
Guilford Industries
Hancock Lumber
Life Sports of Maine
Morton Lumber Inc.
Thos. Moser Cabinetmakers
Murray, Plumb & Murray
Michael L. Ross, Esquire
Rufus Deering Company
Sunshine Group Broadcasting

Sponsor
Anonymous
Anonymous
Blue Hill Books
C. E. Environmental
Cascade Woolen Mill Inc.
Castine Conservation Trust
First NH Bank of Maine
First National Bank of Bar Harbor
Robert G. Gerber, Inc.
Great Northern Paper
Maine Boats & Harbors
Moody & Company
Park Row Associates
Peat Marwick Main & Co.
Prime Tanning Co., Inc.
Proprietors of Union Wharf
J. T. Rosborough, Inc.
Charles W. Sawyer, Jr.
Small Hydro East
Wasco Products, Inc.
X-press Copy Service

Casco Northern Bank

(Thomas Arter)

**Rachel Carson Salt Pond Preserve
(Thomas Arter)**

(Rick Forrester)

Visiting the Preserves

We ask that you observe the following guidelines when visiting the preserves:

Preserves are open to the public for careful day use only. Camping is not allowed.

Fires are not allowed on mainland preserves. On islands, fires are allowed only with town and/or Maine state fire permit(s) and must be built below the high tide line.

Please do not explore "bird nesting preserves" between March 15 and August 15. Human disturbance during this period can seriously jeopardize the nesting success of bald eagles as well as great blue herons, common eiders and other colonially nesting birds.

Ecologically sensitive preserves have restrictions that limit or prohibit unguided public access. These places deserve special respect, and are best visited only on Chapter field trips.

To protect the preserves' wildlife and as a courtesy to other preserve visitors, please leave your pets at home.

Please stay on the trails, using marked trails wherever they exist.

On coastal preserves where trails are nonexistent, please walk on the rocky shore.

Please leave plants, rocks and other natural features where you find them in the preserves, but remember to take your trash home with you.

If you would like to visit a preserve with a group of more than 12 people, please contact the Chapter office for permission first.

Please respect private property adjoining the preserves.

Be careful. Your safety is your responsibility. Enjoy your visit!

Bird's-eye primrose, Mistake Island Preserve (Thomas Arter)

In search of amphibians (Thomas Arter)

How to use this book

This book is designed to be used, whether it dwells upon the coffee table or has a permanent place in the scramble of useful items kept in the car.

For the sake of easier navigation through the book and around the state, the directory is divided into eight regions. Each regional section begins with a locator map showing the general location of the preserves, keyed to page numbers. There is also a table of contents and an index.

The preserve listings

Each listing contains a general summary of the preserve's features, including its topography, plants, animals, geology and human history. The text is a useful, but rather bare, outline. The preserves speak for themselves far more eloquently.

Access

Four symbols indicate the kinds of access and activities that are appropriate for each place:

 Visitors welcome; access by land.
The Conservancy maintains very few "improvements" on its nature preserves. Signs and other intrusions are kept to an absolute minimum. Trails can be very rudimentary (often maintained by wildlife as much as humans) or nonexistent. There are no visitor centers, porta-johns or picnic tables. There is, however, the kind of serenity and joy that only wild places can give.

 Visitors welcome; access by small private boat.
Many Conservancy preserves can or must be reached by water. With one exception, there are no docks or facilities for landing. Landing sites vary from sheltered beaches to exposed rock ledges. A good chart, local knowledge and common sense are essential, especially if anchoring offshore.

Nesting sanctuary; access restricted to protect breeding birds.
Preserves with sensitive nesting birds are usually closed from March 15 to August 15. Please obey the restrictions noted for each preserve; ignoring them in order to satisfy curiosity can have devastating effects on the birds. For example, one well-meaning couple stopped on an eider nesting island to "see the birds." Their walk across the small, open island took less than 15 minutes. But their presence caused the parent eiders to flee the island, allowing predators to destroy more than half of the nests.

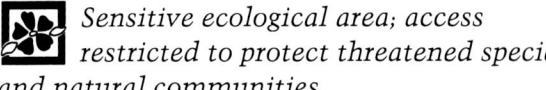 *Sensitive ecological area; access restricted to protect threatened species and natural communities.*
A number of preserves protect plants, animals and natural communities that are exceptionally rare and threatened. Many of these areas simply cannot tolerate too many visitors, however appreciative and careful. The restrictions noted in the preserve listings are designed to allow these special places the privacy they need. The Conservancy does offer occasional guided field trips, which allow people to enjoy these preserves while also limiting human impact as much as possible.

Maps

Maps are provided for preserves that are especially suitable for visiting. The maps are meant to be used for basic reference only; although they are accurate, they are are also illustrative, and are therefore no substitute for the appropriate USGS topographic quad or NOS navigational chart. A good state map or gazeteer is also invaluable for finding the preserves in the first place. Conservancy preserves keep an extremely low profile, but the explorer provided with the information in this volume and several more detailed maps, together with a little patience and a fair sense of direction, should have no problems.

Table of Contents

Maine Chapter, The Nature Conservancy

The Nature Conservancy is an international, nonprofit private conservation organization committed to the global preservation of biological diversity. It devotes its resources to identifying, protecting and managing biologically significant natural areas and the variety of life dependent upon them. Nationwide, the Conservancy and its members have been responsible for the preservation of more than 3.5 million acres of forests, marshes, prairies, deserts, mountains and islands. The Conservancy maintains more than 1,000 nature preserves open to the public. Virtually all of the Conservancy's support comes from private, tax-deductible contributions.

Since its founding in 1956, the Maine Chapter of The Nature Conservancy has protected nearly 60,000 acres of Maine's finest natural lands. With the help of its 13,000 member-families, the Maine Chapter has assembled the largest system of privately owned nature preserves in the state, a network comprised of more than 75 separate sanctuaries.

La Verna Preserve (David Muench)

Origins

It began in 1956 with a postcard bearing a picture of a holly forest on Fire Island, New York.

The postcard's recipient, Dorothea Marston, made a contribution to help save the forest and thereby became a member of the group that had sent the card, a five-year-old private land conservation organization called The Nature Conservancy. "Then came a nudge from the national office," she later recalled. "Why not form a Maine Chapter?"

The Maine Chapter, chartered in the same year, was the fourth Conservancy chapter in the country. Nine people, including conservationist and author Rachel Carson, who served as honorary chairman of the Chapter until her death in 1964, attended the first meeting. The volunteers found that they had plenty to do: researching potential land acquisitions, recruiting new members, and raising money to buy preserves and provide for their care.

In 1962, Rachel Carson published her book *Silent Spring* as a warning of the need to stop the desecration of the natural world before it was too late. In its newsletter, the Maine Chapter echoed her message: "What we have saved and what we may save in the next few years will be all the true wild nature that will remain to pass on from generation to generation. Land is what they are not making any more of."

The Chapter volunteers had already begun the work of saving Maine's beautiful and trea-

The Maine Chapter's first preserve, Step Falls, was acquired in 1961. The falls tumble more than 150 vertical feet in less than an eighth of a mile. (David Smiley)

sured natural lands. In 1961, one such place, a cascade of sparkling waterfalls in Newry called Step Falls, became the Chapter's first preserve.

During the next 13 years, the all-volunteer group acquired nearly three dozen preserves, including Damariscove Island (Boothbay), Rachel Carson Salt Pond (New Harbor), Indian Point-Blagden (Bar Harbor), and The Hermitage (T7R10 NWP).

In 1969, the Chapter trustees hired their first executive director, Charles Bradford, a dedicated conservationist who had also served as Chapter chairman and trustee. For the next

decade, Brad *was* the Maine Chapter to many people. During his tenure, the Chapter acquired many more gems, including Douglas Mountain (Sebago), Crockett Cove Woods (Stonington), Great Wass Island (Beals) and Crystal Bog (Crystal/Sherman).

By the end of its second decade, the Chapter had protected more than 10,000 acres.

Now into its fourth decade, the Chapter has protected almost 60,000 acres of Maine's finest natural lands, thanks to the support and commitment of its members. In just over 30 years, the Chapter membership has grown from a handful of individuals to more than 13,000 families.

In a letter to friends, Rachel Carson expressed her thoughts about conservation: "I think you understand this in me...my feeling for whatever beautiful and untouched oases of natural beauty remain in the world, my belief that such places can bring those who visit them the peace and spiritual refreshment that `civilization' makes so difficult to achieve, and consequently my conviction that wherever and whenever possible, such places must be preserved...."

Rachel Carson devoted her life to teaching about and helping to preserve the natural world. The Nature Conservancy appealed to her, she said, "because it was the only group doing something practical about actually preserving areas."

How The Nature Conservancy Works

One of the world's largest populations of the endangered small whorled pogonia was saved from inadvertent destruction by information provided by the Conservancy's Maine Natural Heritage Program. (Thomas Arter)

The spotted turtle was once fairly common in small ponds and wetlands throughout southern Maine. Today, much of its habitat has been filled or drained, and the turtles are listed as state threatened. (Thomas Arter)

Being practical

The primary goal of the Maine Chapter of The Nature Conservancy is simple: to protect the full array of Maine's natural diversity, starting with its most threatened plants and animals, together with the best examples of its natural ecosystems.

In the last century, at least 11 species have been eliminated from Maine's fauna. As many as 90 plants may have been lost as well. Scientists believe that at least 50 animal and 140 plant species are now sufficiently rare or threatened in Maine to warrant concern. Without immediate action to protect the habitats—the natural communities—on which the state's most imperiled plants and animals depend, experts predict that we will witness the extirpation of many species within our lifetimes. Twenty-five of Maine's natural communities also are considered rare or threatened.

To protect threatened flora and fauna, it is necessary to know the basics: which species and natural communities are in trouble; where they are; how many there are; and what kind of threats exist. In 1974, the Conservancy started looking for a way to make this kind of information readily available. The lack of comprehensive, up-to-date and easily accessible biological inventory data was a perennial headache for scientists and conservationists concerned with critical habitat protection.

The Conservancy's answer is a nationwide system of state Natural Heritage Programs. These continuing, systematic ecological inventories use an integrated network of computer, map and manual files to identify significant natural features and to help establish protection priorities.

There are now Heritage programs in all 50 states, as well as similar, Conservancy-developed programs in several Latin American countries and Canadian provinces.

The Maine Chapter launched its Maine Natural Heritage Program in 1983. After five years of developing the program, the Chapter entered into a cooperative agreement with several state agencies that gave the program a permanent place in state government, inspiring cooperation and information exchange among all those concerned with threatened species.

The Heritage Program data system includes historic and current information on more than 400 species of threatened plants and animals, as well as specifics on more than 70 types of natural communities. The system currently pinpoints more than 2,000 individual occurrences of rare species and natural communities in Maine.

One of the greatest advantages of the Heritage approach is its predictive ability. For example, the small whorled pogonia (*Isotria medeoloides*) is one of the state's rarest plants. It is listed as endangered by both federal and state governments. By taking all the information known about places where the plant has been found, Heritage botanists have been able to describe a typical habitat (topography, exposure, soils, vegetation) for the species.

Field researchers begin with maps and target likely sites with appropriate habitat, greatly increasing the odds of finding plants that by definition are very difficult to locate.

The Maine Natural Heritage Program advises state and town governments as well as developers and others on the confirmed or suspected presence of threatened species on their lands. In 1988, a standard request to review a subdivision proposal resulted in a find that increased the world's known population of the small whorled pogonia by nearly 10 percent. When informed of this, the developer generously agreed to donate the land to the Conservancy to protect the plants.

Getting down to business

Armed with the latest information about Maine's threatened natural features, the Conservancy is prepared to go to work.

The primary tool in the Conservancy's collection of land protection devices is outright acquisition. The Maine Chapter owns and manages a system of more than 75 nature preserves totaling approximately 17,000 acres. The preserves include grasslands and river shore in the south; mountains and waterfalls in the west; old-growth forests and bogs in the far north; and islands along the coast. The Chapter also helps other public and private conservation agencies acquire lands; in this way it has directly assisted with the protection of an additional 35,000 acres.

The Butler and Marshall Preserves protect more than a half-mile of unspoiled shore along the tidal Kennebunk River. (Thomas Arter)

The Chapter's protection staff works with the owners of properties that have critical habitats to find the best possible ways to preserve the areas. Frequently, landowners are as anxious as the Conservancy to see their special places protected. Generous Conservancy supporters have donated more than 75 percent of the Maine Chapter's preserves, including Butler and Marshall (Kennebunk), Upper Goose Island (Harpswell), Crockett Cove Woods and Barred Island (Deer Isle), Perham Bog (Perham) and Long Island (Lubec).

Corporations have also protected some of the state's finest natural areas by donating them to the Conservancy. Crystal Bog (Crystal and

The threatened showy lady's slipper grows at Woodland Bog and Perham Bog preserves in northern Aroostook County. (Barbara Vickery)

Sherman), Seboeis River Gorge (T5R7, T6R7 WELS), and several other major acquisitions were corporate gifts.

Many landowners are interested in having the Conservancy acquire and protect their properties, but are unable to donate them. Bargain sales (properties sold at less than fair market value), land exchanges, reserved life estates, joint ownerships, and other creative approaches provide landowners with an opportunity to participate in the process of conserving their lands and to contribute to the Conservancy.

When an area faces an imminent threat, the Conservancy can move very quickly to protect it. The Maine Chapter maintains a revolving, internal loan fund that allows it to buy land immediately, then repay the loan once permanent funding has been secured through fund-raising or by transfer of the property to another conservation organization.

As the largest private owner of islands in Maine, the Conservancy is steward of more than 20 nesting sanctuaries for seabirds such as these common eiders. (Thomas Arter)

Conservation easements protect seven islands in the Great Wass Island archipelago, including the group known as The Cow's Yard. (Julie Henderson)

Maine Chapter members have shown their commitment to the preservation of Maine's natural lands through their generous donations to the campaigns that allowed the Chapter to acquire and protect some of its most important preserves: Big Reed (T8R10, T8R11 WELS), Great Wass Island (Jonesport), Kennebunk Plains (Kennebunk), and many islands, including Mistake Island (Jonesport) and Great Duck Island (Frenchboro). The Chapter depends entirely upon private donations to pay for the acquisition and associated long-term stewardship costs of lands in its statewide preserve system.

Being able to act rapidly, to negotiate creative real estate transactions, and to raise significant amounts of money have become increasingly important as Maine's natural lands have become prime targets for speculation and development.

Acquiring wild and unspoiled lands is not necessarily a simple matter of finding the owner and striking a deal. For example, the acquisition of the Big Reed Forest Reserve, a 3,800-acre sanctuary that contains New England's largest remaining old-growth (or "virgin") forest, required more than three years of negotiations. The final agreement was as complex as it was innovative, involving a three-way exchange among the Conservancy, the timber company landowners, and the state Bureau of Public Lands.

Big Reed is also an excellent example of the rapid growth in demands upon the Maine Chapter's limited resources. Projects of this scope and complexity require a long-term, concentrated effort. They also require a tremendous commitment on the part of the Chapter's supporters. The price tag for the Big Reed Forest Reserve's acquisition and long-term management was $1.1 million. Thanks to generous gifts from thousands of people, as well as major grants from several foundations and Maine corporations, the Chapter met its goal after a two-year-long campaign.

Creative ideas

The need to protect whole habitats, combined with rapidly rising land prices, makes tools other than ownership an important part of the Conservancy's land protection repertoire. Conservation easements; transfer to other conservation organizations; management leases; voluntary landowner agreements; and strategic technical assistance are essential approaches to getting the job done.

Short of outright ownership, a conservation easement is the highest level of land protection available. Easements are legally enforceable agreements that restrict development and other activities incompatible with protecting the natural environment. Properties with easements remain in private ownership, and the owner continues to exercise all rights of ownership except those specifically affected by the easement.

By holding a conservation easement, the Conservancy accepts responsibility for monitoring the property in perpetuity to make certain that the terms of the easement are upheld. The Maine Chapter holds conservation easements on more than 30 properties totaling nearly 3,000 acres. They range from inland rare plant habitats to isolated coastal islands.

The Chapter also acquires natural lands on behalf of other conservation interests. Conservation restrictions are often imposed when land is transferred to the care of another organization, and such lands continue to be monitored by the Chapter.

Lands acquired for others by the Maine Chapter include: thousands of acres in Maine's federal and state-owned wildlife refuges, including the newly formed Sunkhaze Meadows National Wildlife Refuge; lands along the Allagash Wilderness Waterway and the Appalachian Trail; a peatland used for research by Colby College; the largest undeveloped lake (and surrounding forest) in the White Mountains; a major stop in the Gulf of Maine for birds migrating on the Atlantic flyway; and a dozen sanctuaries owned and managed by towns or local land trusts.

The Conservancy also helps with land protection projects by resolving conflicts and negotiating agreements. For example, the Chapter negotiated the complicated transaction that resulted in the Maine Bureau of Public Land's acquisition of a 7,200-acre "wild land" recreation area at Donnell Pond/Black Lake/ Tunk Mountain, just east of Ellsworth. Two major parties in the negotiations, the state and the developer/timber company partnership that owned a key parcel, broke off talks repeatedly during a period of several years, but were able to reach a workable agreement with the Conservancy's assistance. Meanwhile, the Conservancy began simultaneous negotiations with other landowners to acquire several large adjacent parcels. The final result: a treasured natural area protected despite the long odds against its preservation.

As Maine's largest private conservation organization, and as a specialist in the protection

The Kennebunk Plains is home to the world's largest population of the northern blazing star and at least four other threatened species. (Mary Droege)

The Conservancy has helped state and federal governments protect thousands of acres of wildlife refuge lands. (Susan Woodward)

of endangered and threatened species through land conservation, the Conservancy's Maine Chapter regularly provides technical advice and assistance to other conservation groups, government agencies, local officials and private individuals.

Since the Conservancy is focused on direct protection of threatened habitats and the plants and animals they shelter, it very rarely becomes involved in public policy issues. However, when it is clear that legislative matters will affect Maine's threatened species and natural lands, the Conservancy does offer its expertise and assistance. For example, Chapter science staff helped establish Maine's official lists of endangered animals and plants. In addition, the Maine Chapter was the leading organizational sponsor of a $35 million public lands acquisition bond issue passed overwhelmingly through public referendum in 1987.

The Conservancy has since become an active participant in the process of acquiring new state lands with bond issue funds. The first area selected for purchase was the Kennebunk Plains, based on a proposal submitted by the Conservancy. The state agreed to acquire a 1,450-acre wildlife refuge at the Kennebunk Plains for $2.9 million, less than two-thirds of the land's original asking price. In the deal negotiated by the Conservancy, the state's expense will be matched by contributions from the Conservancy and local groups of money, land (a bald eagle nesting site in Hancock County) and land management services.

The Plains shelters at least five state endangered or threatened plants and animals and is also a highly valued recreation area in a part of Maine experiencing a particularly rapid loss of open space. This project is a wonderful result of cooperation among multiple public and private agencies.

Careful study of the vegetation of the Kennebunk Plains helps the Conservancy staff develop the best approach to protect and manage the area and its threatened species. (Barbara Vickery)

Piping plover (IF&W)

Taking care

When the deeds are in, the job is far from over. The Maine Chapter is responsible for looking after its irreplaceable natural areas for generations to come. To do this, the Chapter's stewardship program depends upon the latest biological information and management techniques, provided by Conservancy staff and consultants, along with invaluable assistance provided by those who know and love the preserves best: scores of local volunteer land stewards.

The Chapter is caretaker for some of the state's best and last remaining populations of rare and threatened species. These plants and animals have very few secure habitats; in many instances, Conservancy preserves are vital to their continued well-being, or, in the case of an unfortunate few, to their hoped-for recovery.

Chapter biologists periodically visit the preserves to assess and record the health of the resident rarities.

Each preserve is managed according to its own special requirements. Inventories and other ecological studies provide essential information needed to develop management plans. The stewardship of each place continues to evolve to meet changing circumstances and to make use of improved techniques, especially in the case of seriously endangered species such as least terns or piping plovers.

Seawall Beach in Phippsburg has always been a stronghold in Maine for nesting least terns and piping plovers. In recent years, however, predators such as foxes, crows, skunks and raccoons have taken many of the birds' eggs and young. Increasing use of the beach by people has also added to the stresses on the birds.

Maine Chapter staff, in cooperation with the Maine Audubon Society and the state Department of Inland Fisheries and Wildlife, have acted to protect the terns and plovers. String and electric fences erected around the tern colonies have successfully kept out dogs and people; recent efforts to completely enclose piping plover nests seem to be effective in preventing crow predation. However, the search continues for ways to protect these beleaguered birds.

Volunteers are essential to the Chapter's stewardship program. Dedicated volunteer stewards are the eyes, ears and hands of the Maine Chapter. They sail out to the islands, hike the trails, snowshoe into the bogs, and spend hours counting rare plants. They also do much of the yeoman work on the preserves, marking boundaries, clearing trails and monitoring use.

Volunteer work crews have repaired the observation tower and trails on Douglas Mountain, hauled rubbish off Great Duck Island and built a boardwalk through a bog on Great Wass Island. School groups have also volunteered to help; students from the Chewonki Foundation in Wiscasset designed and built the trails at Fernald's Neck (Camden), and members of the Boothbay Region High School shop class built and installed a weatherproof bulletin board on Damariscove Island.

In addition to handling the day-to-day responsibilities of managing its lands, the Chapter must look ahead toward improving its ability to protect its preserves against future threats. The Chapter has an active research program aimed at learning more about the needs of the threatened species and natural communities under its care.

Biologists and botanists sponsored by the Conservancy have added to the knowledge of old-growth forests in Maine by comparing the lichens of Big Reed Pond Preserve to those of other forests; documented the relationship between herbicide use and the breeding populations of the endangered grasshopper sparrow at the Kennebunk Plains; and investigated the role of fire in controlling shrubs competing with the rare flora in the Crystal Bog fen.

Since virtually all of the Maine Chapter's preserves are open to the public, stewardship also involves thoughtful consideration of the balance needed to protect the preserves' natural features while providing opportunities for human visitors. On the whole, people who visit the preserves are good stewards themselves, content to enjoy the peace and beauty of these sanctuaries without demanding the amenities they might find in a park or recreation area. This makes the Chapter's job easier, of course, but it also reflects an underlying respect that people have for Maine's land.

To help people understand and enjoy the preserve lands, the Chapter offers field trips led by experienced naturalists. Participants have done everything from investigating mosses and

lichens in coastal forests to rafting a river while searching (successfully) for rare shoreline plants.

The goal of the Maine Chapter of The Nature Conservancy is simple: protecting Maine's most biologically threatened lands. Attaining this goal requires the hard work and financial support of thousands of people. In the most direct sense, the Chapter *is* its members. To learn more about the Conservancy's work in Maine—and to support that work—please contact the Maine Chapter, 122 Main Street, P.O. Box 338, Topsham, Maine 04086; telephone: (207) 729-5181.

Contributors to this section: Mason Morfit, Kent Wommack, Barbara Vickery, Julie Henderson.

The Conservancy's legion of volunteer preserve stewards do much of the caretaking work on the Chapter's lands, such as construction of boardwalks to protect boggy places. (Thomas Arter)

Every year, the Conservancy offers guided field trips to explore its preserves and learn about their natural features. (Barbara Vickery)

Conservancy and Maine Audubon researchers count endangered least terns nesting at Seawall Beach in Phippsburg. (Barbara Vickery)

Kennebunk Plains Preserve (Thomas Arter)

Southern Region

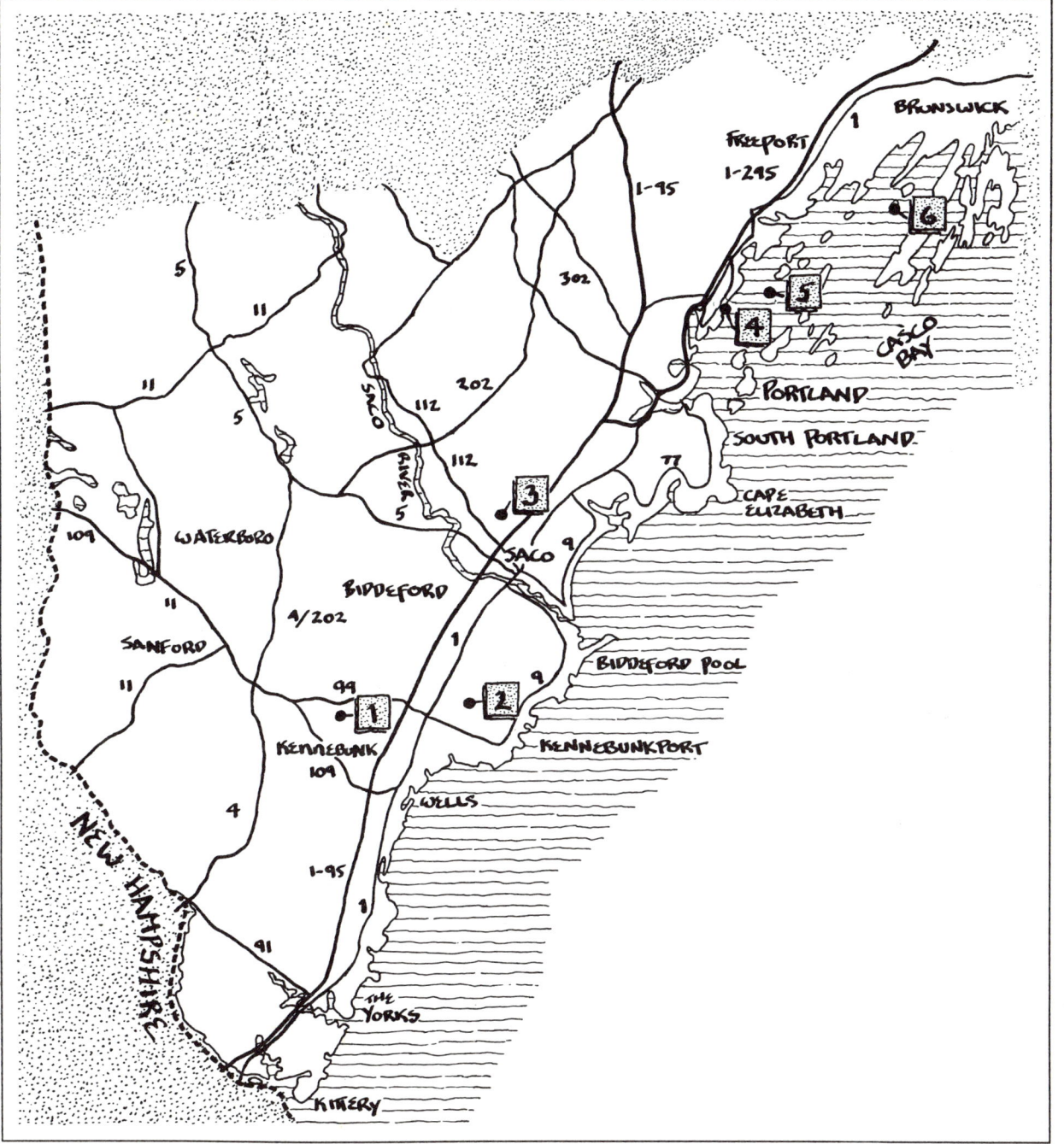

Southern Region

Many plant and animal species reach their northern frontier in southern Maine. A significant number of these are considered rare or threatened within Maine; many are declining throughout their entire range. Loss of habitat is probably the single most important reason for their dwindling numbers: the plants and animals are being forced to give up their home grounds to a growing population of human residents.

The most visible example of the Conservancy's efforts to preserve southern Maine's threatened habitats, and the species that depend upon them, is the Kennebunk Plains. At least five species and two natural communities considered endangered or threatened in Maine are found at the Plains.

Southern Maine is also the southern limit for some species and natural communities usually found much farther north. Saco Heath Preserve is a good example of this north-south overlap. The heath is believed to be the southernmost raised bog in North America. It also contains one of North America's most northerly stands of Atlantic white cedar.

Conservancy biologists and volunteers searching the state for its rarer inhabitants trek throughout southern Maine, hoping to hear the sheeplike bleat of a Fowler's toad or to catch a glimpse of a basking box turtle or black racer snake. They scour the countryside looking for new populations of rare wildflowers, obscure sedges and other plants, and investigate remaining examples of natural communities like freshwater wetlands, pitch pine/scrub oak woodland, and naturally flooded river shore.

The pitch pine/scrub oak woodland natural community is a good example of the subtle forces that threaten southern Maine's natural areas. The woodlands are found on top of glacially derived sand and gravel deposits. The demand for sand and gravel for construction has never been higher; consequently, these relatively scarce deposits are being mined as fast as possible. The natural woodland they support is the most threatened natural community in New England.

Conservancy preserves in southern Maine protect habitats for common species as well as the most threatened members of the region's flora and fauna. Upper Goose Island (Harpswell) supports New England's largest nesting colony of great blue herons. The Butler-Marshall Preserves (Kennebunk) and Mill Creek Preserve (Falmouth) are home to many breeding birds and other life of the water's edge.

With the exception of Upper Goose Island, which is closed during the March 15 to August 15 nesting season, the Conservancy preserves in this region are open year-round for varying degrees and types of recreation.

Saco Heath, a fragile, wet place that is not easy to visit in summer, becomes a perfect place to ski in winter. Although the Kennebunk Plains is home to some very endangered nesting birds and other threatened species, for generations they have co-existed well with people enjoying quiet recreational pursuits. Basket Island (Cumberland) is one of the most popular spots in Casco Bay. Picnic Rock, the most renowned feature of the Butler-Marshall Preserves, has been a favorite spot to relax for countless summers.

Town governments own and manage properties protected with the help of the Conservancy, including an environmental education site on Cousins Island in Yarmouth and a park in Falmouth. Land trusts are also active in the region. River Bend Woods on the Mousam River (Kennebunk), and Vaughn's and Redin's islands (Kennebunkport) were protected with the help of the Conservancy and are now owned and managed by local land trusts. Part of Maine Audubon's East Point Sanctuary (Biddeford) was also protected with the Conservancy's assistance.

In addition to working with local groups, the Conservancy has assisted the federal government with several key additions to the Rachel Carson National Wildlife Refuge, which stretches from Kittery to Kennebunk.

For more information on The Nature Conservancy's preserves in southern Maine, please contact the Maine Chapter stewardship office in Topsham.

Kennebunk Plains

Kennebunk, 123 acres

Vital habitat for the grasshopper sparrow and four other animals and plants considered endangered or threatened in Maine, the Kennebunk Plains is also a highly valued open space and recreation area.

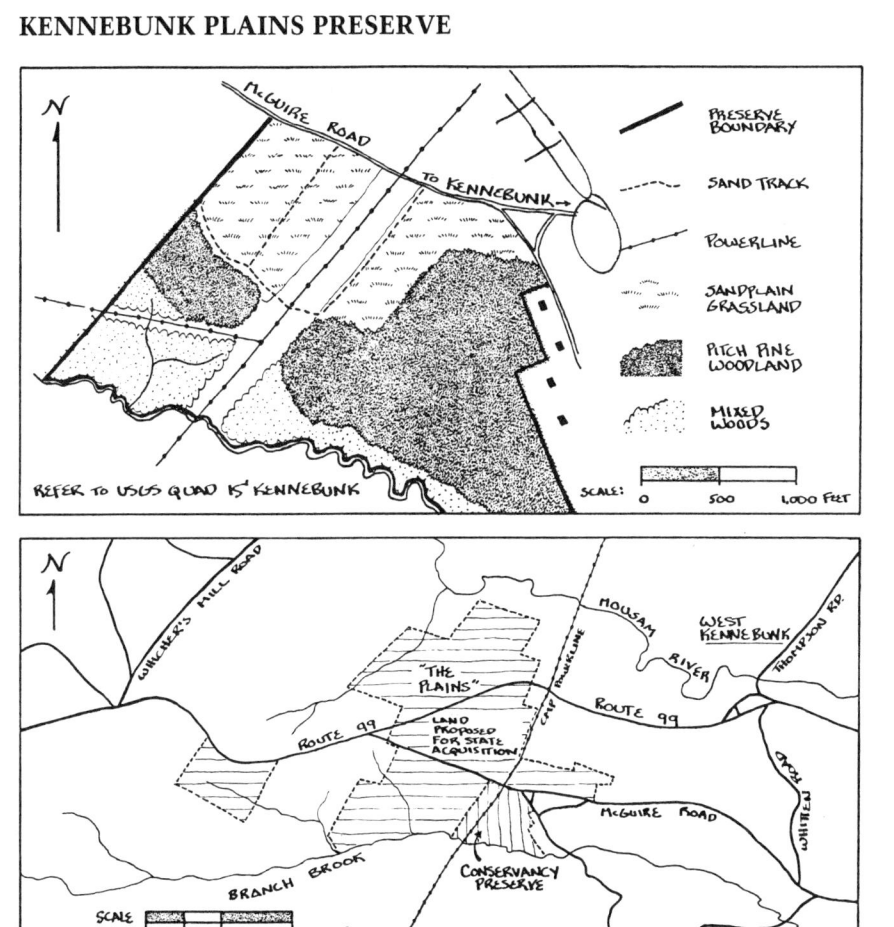

KENNEBUNK PLAINS PRESERVE

On a hot summer's day, the rustling grasses of the Kennebunk Plains provide background for the sounds of what appears to be a collection of very musical insects. The buzzy trills emanating from the cover of the tussocks of grass are made not by insects, but by one of Maine's most endangered birds: the grasshopper sparrow (*Ammodramus savannarum*).

The Kennebunk Plains is a coastal sand plain grassland that has also been managed for many years as a commercial blueberry barren. It supports one of the largest known grasshopper sparrow breeding populations in New England, and is one of only four nesting sites for the species in Maine. The tiny, reclusive sparrow prefers dry grassland habitats with bunchgrasses such as poverty grass and little blue stem. Its numbers are declining due to loss of habitat through its U.S. range.

In 1984, there were 26 pairs of grasshopper sparrows nesting on the Plains. Then the herbicide Velpar was sprayed on most of the grassland, eliminating essentially all of the vegetation except blueberries. By 1987, there were only a dozen breeding pairs left, many of which had settled on the Conservancy's 123-acre preserve because it had never been sprayed.

The Conservancy acquired its preserve in 1987, protecting a core of undisturbed habitat for the birds and the Plains' other threatened species.

In 1989, the state, acting with the support of the Conservancy and local groups, agreed to acquire nearly 1,500 acres at the Plains as its first purchase with the money from the 1987 $35 million public lands bond issue. The land to be acquired includes the threatened grassland and adjacent woodlands. Fortunately, Conservancy studies show that Velpar-treated areas will return to natural condition after several years.

Sand plain grasslands are threatened natural communities throughout the Northeast coast because they are ideal for development: flat, well

drained and near the sea. The Kennebunk Plains is one of the largest sandplain grasslands left in New England.

Three plant species considered threatened in Maine grow in the Plains grassland. In late summer, the area becomes a sea of purple when the northern blazing star (*Liatris borealis*) is in bloom. Rare and declining throughout its range, this striking wildflower is relatively resistant to Velpar and continues to thrive at the Plains. The Plains is the only viable site for the species in Maine and its population is believed to be the largest in the world. The second rarity, toothed white-topped aster (*Aster paternus*), also prefers open sandy areas and is found at only one other site in the state. The third, upright bindweed (*Convolvulus spithamaeus*) was discovered at the Plains in 1988. The Velpar has apparently affected it severely, but it is hoped that the plants will recover once the grassland is restored.

The Plain's open, low vegetation is also attractive to many other grassland birds, including upland sandpipers, vesper sparrows and horned larks. Wild turkeys, reintroduced in the mid-1980s, feed on the barrens in the spring. More than 87 other bird species breed in the Plains area; another 50, including occasional wanderers like sandhill cranes, have been seen during migration.

The grassland is surrounded by pitch pine/scrub oak woodland, another natural community that is suffering a decline rangewide. Several rare moths depend upon the trees for part of their life cycles. The only documented population of the state endangered northern black racer snake inhabits these open pine forests.

On the moister slopes, the forest grades into white pine and white oak, then into the mixed hardwoods typical of southern Maine. Hemlocks grow in the cool ravines.

Up to 70 feet of clear sand left by the glaciers lies under the Kennebunk Plains. This glacio-marine delta outwash deposit forms one of the most important aquifers in southern Maine. Countless springs flow out of the edge of the sandy plateau; four brooks meander through the surrounding woods, offering fine fishing for brook trout.

The sheltered woods are habitat for white-tailed deer, moose, otter, beaver, bobcat, gray fox, red fox, coyote, long-tailed weasel, mink, skunk, raccoon and black bear.

LAND FOR MAINE'S FUTURE In 1987, roughly two-thirds of Maine's voters approved a $35 million bond issue to buy natural lands. Six private citizens and five public officials appointed by the governor make up the Land for Maine's Future Board, the group responsible for selecting the lands. The board invites proposals of lands suitable for acquisition. Criteria for selection include preservation of threatened species and natural habitats; protection of public access and recreation opportunities; and community and private support.

The Kennebunk Plains is one of the last large open spaces remaining in rapidly developing southern Maine. Although the blueberry company posted its land against trespassing, it allowed activities that did not interfere with its operations. People have enjoyed birdwatching, botanizing, fishing, hunting, snowmobiling and cross-country skiing on the Plains for many years.

The Conservancy purchased its preserve after a year-long fund-raising campaign. It conducted the initial scientific research, handled the land negotiations and submitted the final proposal to the state for the public land purchase. The proposal was strongly endorsed by many local interests, including the Kennebunk Board of Selectmen; Kennebunk Conservation Commission; Kennebunk Fish and Game Club; Kennebunk, Kennebunkport, Wells Water District; Kennebunk Planning Board; Ramanascho Land Preservation Trust; Wells Conservation Commission; and Wells Planning Board.

A network of sand tracks offers access to the Conservancy preserve and adjacent wildlife refuge. Please stay on the tracks to avoid disturbing the nesting birds.

DIRECTIONS: From Kennebunk, take Route 9A west turning right onto McGuire Road just past the interstate. The Conservancy preserve is on the left at the beginning of the grassland and is bisected by the powerline.

The Butler Preserve and the Marshall Preserve

Butler, 14 acres, Kennebunk;
Marshall, 181 acres, Arundel

The Butler and Marshall preserves protect more than a half-mile of Kennebunk River shore, including Picnic Rock, a popular spot for swimming and picnicking on summer afternoons.

The quiet, tidal lower Kennebunk River flows through more than a half-mile of undeveloped shore protected by the Butler and Marshall preserves. On one side, the Butler Preserve hugs the shore, while on the other the Marshall Preserve extends well back from the river.

The approach by water from Kennebunkport is a pleasant trip. Picnic Rock, a large glacial boulder on the Butler shore, is a favorite spot for picnicking and swimming.

The Butler Preserve is covered with red and white pine interspersed with spruce, hemlock and balsam fir. Canada mayflower, moccasin flower and clintonia are scattered throughout the woods.

Across the river, the Marshall Preserve shore is also forested with white pine. The shore along Arundel Swamp Brook is a band of salt marsh.

Former Maine Chapter board chairman and trustee G. Robert Butler and his sister Jane Butler donated the Butler Preserve over a 15-year period beginning in 1972. In 1985, Mr. and Mrs. Donald Buttfield donated an additional two acres along Old Pond Road. The Marshall Preserve was donated in 1973 by Mrs. Lewis Keith Marshall in memory of her husband.

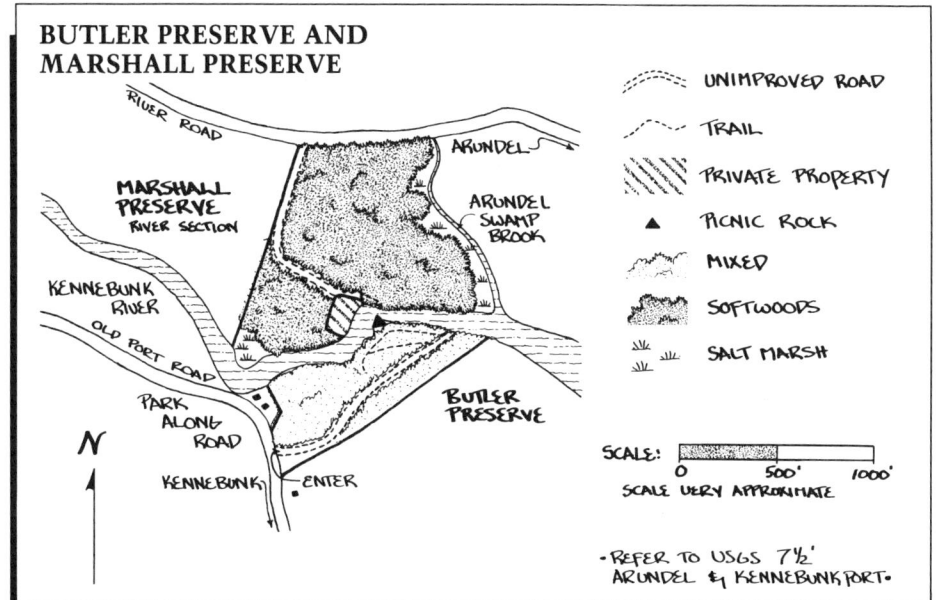

BUTLER PRESERVE AND MARSHALL PRESERVE

RIVER ROAD
ARUNDEL
MARSHALL PRESERVE RIVER SECTION
ARUNDEL SWAMP BROOK
KENNEBUNK RIVER
OLD PORT ROAD
PARK ALONG ROAD
BUTLER PRESERVE
KENNEBUNK
ENTER
N

UNIMPROVED ROAD
TRAIL
PRIVATE PROPERTY
PICNIC ROCK
MIXED
SOFTWOODS
SALT MARSH

SCALE:
0   500'   1000'
SCALE VERY APPROXIMATE

• REFER TO USGS 7½'
ARUNDEL & KENNEBUNKPORT •

  Both preserve shores are easily reached by canoe. On the Butler Preserve, a short trail begins at Picnic Rock and joins up with an old logging road to make a loop through the forest. There are no trails on the river section of the Marshall Preserve, but it is possible to walk along the shore. Please do not land on the shore in front of the house; this is private property.

DIRECTIONS: *By land:* Take the Old Port Road about 1.7 miles from Kennebunkport to a woods road on the right, just before the road bends close to the river. The woods road is marked with a TNC sign and blocked with a pile of gravel. Park along the Old Port Road and walk in. *By water:* The landing at Picnic Rock is about a mile and half upstream from Kennebunkport.

Saco Heath Preserve

475 acres, Saco

Critical habitat for the globally threatened Atlantic white cedar and a butterfly found nowhere else in Maine, the Saco Heath is also a treasured open space and natural area in one of the fastest growing parts of Maine.

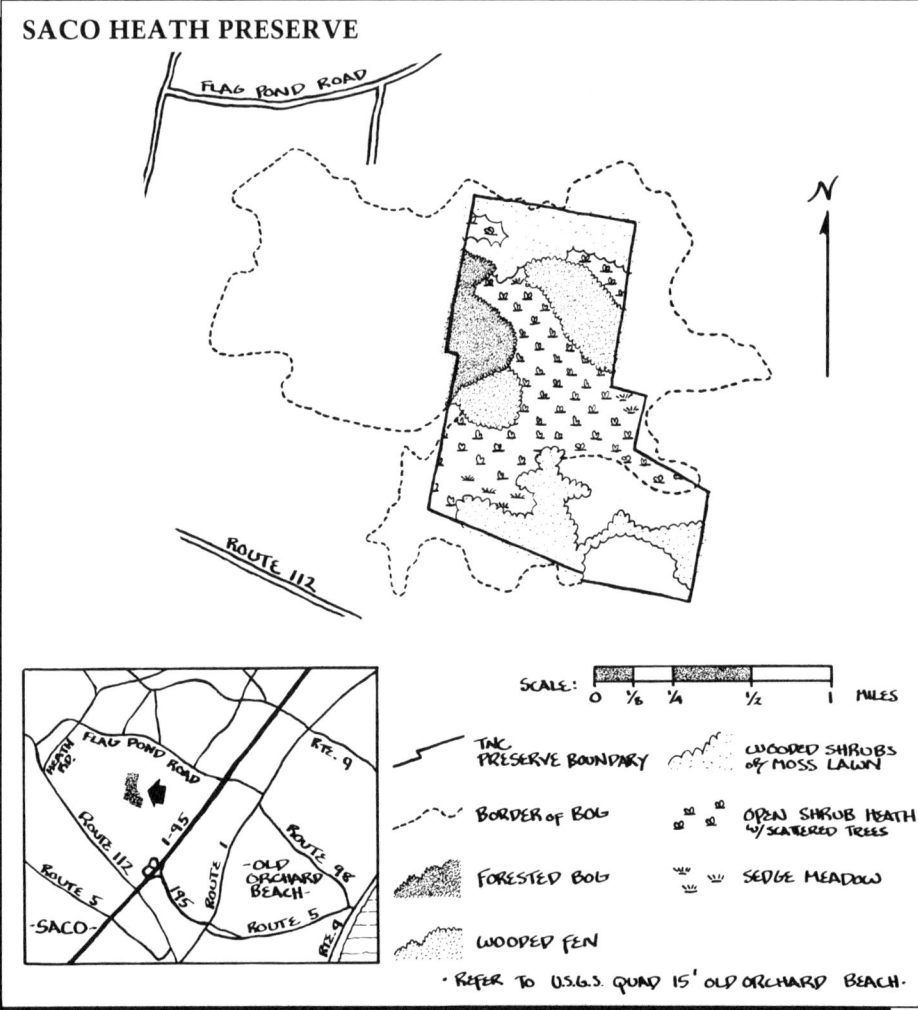

An undeveloped wild land in the heart of southern Maine, Saco Heath is a sanctuary for Maine's largest stand of Atlantic white cedar (*Chamaecyparis thyoides*) and its rare associate denizen, the Hessel's hairstreak butterfly (*Mitoura hesseli*). Discovered by Conservancy Natural Heritage Program director John Albright in 1987, the population of Hessel's hairstreak at the heath was the first ever recorded in Maine.

Saco Heath is a special type of peatland known as a raised coalesced bog. In other words, the bog's domed surface has grown above the influence of the local water table (raised), and the bog as it appears today formed when two domes that began separately in adjacent basins gradually joined together (coalesced).

Raised bogs are found throughout Canada and the northern United States, where cool temperatures and steady precipitation maintain plenty of moisture, creating conditions ideal for their formation. Saco Heath is the southernmost example of a raised coalesced bog known to occur in Maine, possibly North America.

The Saco Heath is the sole known example of Atlantic white cedar growing on a raised bog in North America. The heath is a kind of ecological crossroads: Atlantic white cedar nears the northern extent of its range here; raised bogs their southern limit.

Due to logging and wetland alteration, the extent of Atlantic white cedar has declined dramatically and undisturbed stands have become increasingly hard to find. Hessel's hairstreak, which feeds only on Atlantic white cedar, is globally threatened.

The cedars grow most densely on the higher, drier parts in the center of the bog, along with other trees such as tamarack and black spruce, and heath

shrubs including sheep laurel, labrador tea, bog laurel, leatherleaf and blueberry. A series of ponds form a flowage along the central section where the two domes meet. Beyond the domes, the heath begins to slope noticeably down toward the southeast.

On the downslope, the cedars become more widely scattered. Distinct bands of rhodora, leatherleaf and wet sedge meadows outline the sloping edge of the heath, where pitch pine becomes more common. The bog is bordered by a lagg, a narrow trough filled with open water.

The heath has a large winter deer yard and moose are frequently in residence.

More than a million tons of peat could be harvested from the Saco Heath. Since 1918, various interests have tried, largely unsuccessfully, to commercially exploit the northern part of the heath. In 1984, the heath was listed on the state Register of Critical Areas. In 1985, strong public support for the protection of the area prompted the town of Saco to zone the entire heath as a resource protection area.

Joseph Deering and his family donated nearly half of Saco Heath to the Conservancy in 1986. In 1988, Saco residents and the Conservancy proposed the acquisition of up to 700

RAISED PEATLANDS Saturated sphagnum mosses, which make up the peat "soil" of Saco Heath, can hold up to eight times their weight in water. Although the bog is raised above the surrounding water table and is completely dependent upon atmospheric sources for moisture, the its surface is watery and disconcertingly yielding.

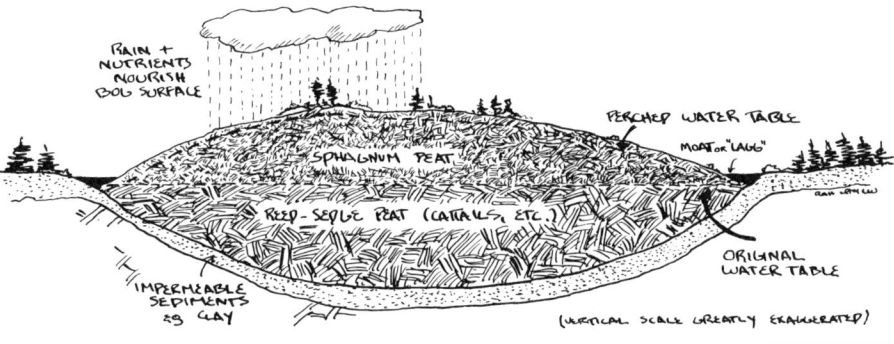

additional acres of the heath and adjacent uplands to the Land for Maine's Future Board, the group responsible for spending the state's $35 million public lands bond issue.

 There are no trails, but it is possible to carefully explore parts of the heath. Please use discretion when wandering on the bog; excessive trampling will compress the spongy soils and destroy the bog

vegetation. Also be careful—although most of the bog will easily support your weight, there are some very wet places lurking beneath deceptively firm mats of red sphagnum and other plants. Don't forget a compass. With few memorable landmarks, the heath is easy to get lost in.

Winter is the most popular time of year to visit the heath, since it is easiest to explore on skis or snowshoes.

DIRECTIONS: The Conservancy preserve is in the eastern half of the heath. The local snowmobile club maintains a trail through the woods around the heath. The open heath can be reached from this trail, but access to the snowmobile trail is across private property. Please ask permission first.

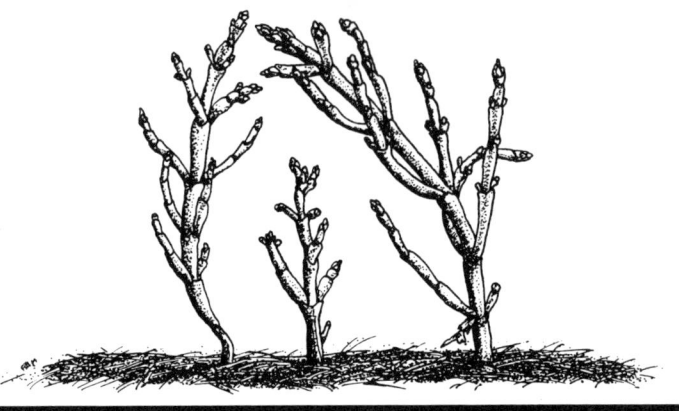

Mill Creek Preserve
20 acres, Falmouth

Mill Creek Preserve is an unexpected oasis in the midst of a highly developed area, and part of an expanding greenbelt protecting both public access and threatened species.

Mill Creek meanders quietly down to Mussel Cove, a large area of tidal flats on Casco Bay. The lower portion of the creek is flanked by salt marshes. The Conservancy's Mill Creek Preserve and its neighbor, the Falmouth Foreside Preserve, protect more than 50 acres of the marsh and adjacent uplands. The Falmouth Foreside Preserve was acquired by the Conservancy and transferred to the town of Falmouth. Both areas are taken care of by the Falmouth Parks Department. They are separated by a narrow private lot.

Along the creek, tall cordgrass grows within reach of the daily tides. Higher up, salt marsh hay covers the marsh in fine cowlicks. Tumbled-down sheep fences crisscross the marsh, a reminder that salt hay was once highly valued pasture.

Above the marsh, the land rises gently to low ridges on both sides. The uplands are wooded with white pine and other conifers that have grown up in the fields of the farm that was once here. The farm's apple trees are now dying out in the shade of the pines.

Patient watching will reveal great blue herons and snowy egrets in the marsh, and woodland songbirds in the uplands.

The two Mill Creek preserves are the core of a cooperative effort to expand the protected greenbelt. The

SALT HAY High salt marshes, those that are flooded only by spring tides and storms, are not common along Maine's largely exposed, rocky shore and in fact peter out near the Kennebec River. Salt marsh hay (*Spartina patens*), the dominant species in the high marsh, was once highly valued as pasture. In mid-summer, the hay was scythed and forked onto pole racks, where it stayed until it could be hauled off by team and wagon over the frozen marsh.

Conservancy is working with nearby landowners to protect *Carex polymorpha*, a globally rare sedge that grows in three places in the immediate area. The Falmouth Land Trust and Town of Falmouth are also exploring ways to protect additional acreage.

Mill Creek Preserve and Falmouth Foreside Preserve were protected by gifts of Charles Whitney Payson in 1971.

  Although there are no trails on the Conservancy's Mill Creek Preserve, it is possible to walk along the upper edge of the marsh. The town preserve has a well-marked trail system. Tidal Mill Creek is a short, but pleasant, canoe trip.

DIRECTIONS: Coming from the south, turn off Route One onto Route 88 (Foreside Road) and go about one and-a half miles to the Falmouth town pumping station. Go past the road to the station and park in the town preserve's parking lot on the west side of Route 88. The town preserve's trails begin at the lot. To explore the Conservancy preserve, walk back down the main road and in on the pumping station entrance road. This is also the easiest place to put in a canoe.

Basket Island Preserve

9 acres, Cumberland

This well-known Casco Bay landmark is a popular summer port of call. The island was scarred by fire in 1979; although full recovery will take years, it is already well under way.

Picnics on Basket Island are a summer tradition in Casco Bay. Lying close to the Falmouth shore and protected by Cousins and Chebeague islands, the small, low island's sheltered location and several gravel beaches make it an inviting stopping place.

In 1979 a camp fire got out of control and destroyed the understory vegetation and most of the island's spruce and fir. The efforts of the Cumberland Fire Department and Maine Forest Service confined the most intense fire to a few acres in the center of the island. The larger trees on the island escaped serious damage.

On the northern end of the island, there is a clearing with staghorn sumac, quaking aspen, rugosa rose and cherry scattered throughout. Poison ivy also thrives here. Although the fire helped keep this area open, all of these species are characteristically found on lands that have been grazed heavily by sheep, as Basket was during the 19th and 20th centuries. The southern part of the island is wooded with mature red oak and white birch. Red spruce, beech, elm and basswood grow on the island's higher western side.

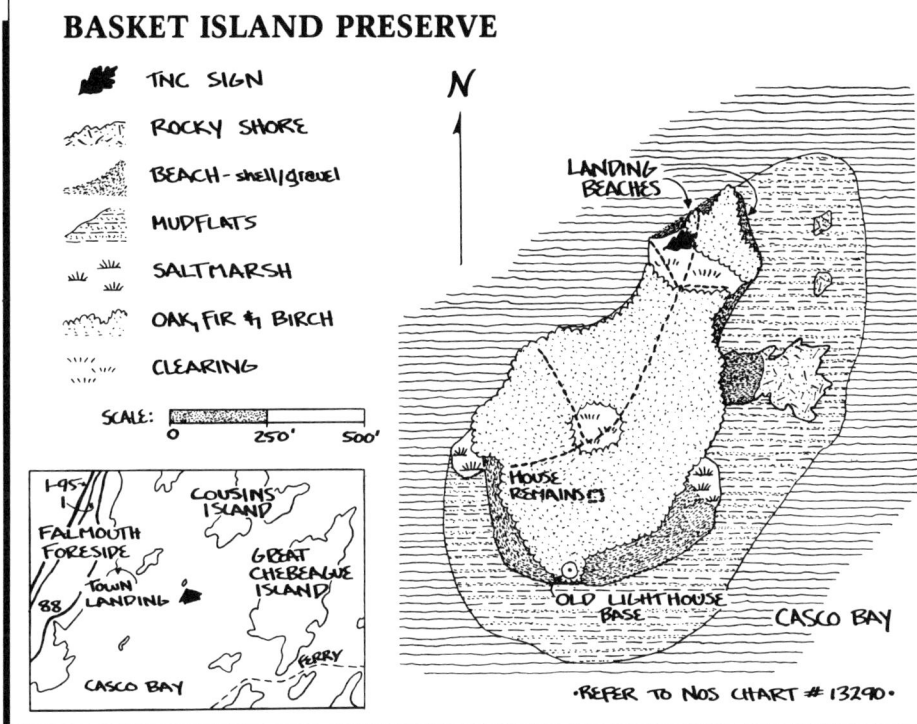

BASKET ISLAND PRESERVE

- TNC SIGN
- ROCKY SHORE
- BEACH - shell/gravel
- MUDFLATS
- SALTMARSH
- OAK, FIR & BIRCH
- CLEARING

SCALE: 0 250' 500'

N

LANDING BEACHES

HOUSE REMAINS

OLD LIGHTHOUSE BASE

CASCO BAY

·REFER TO NOS CHART # 13290·

I-95 FALMOUTH FORESIDE COUSINS ISLAND GREAT CHEBEAGUE ISLAND TOWN LANDING 88 FERRY CASCO BAY

Basket Island's intertidal zone is extensive, particularly on the southern shore. Shell and gravel beaches slope gradually into sandy and muddy subtidal flats. The flats are covered with eelgrass, an ecologically important plant that stabilizes the bottom sediments and provides food and shelter for countless small fish and invertebrates. Blights periodically decimate large areas of eelgrass, causing serious problems for animals that depend upon it, like young bay scallops. Most of the eelgrass died off in this part of Casco Bay in the early 1970s. The Basket Island flats recovered before those of the other islands.

Unlike most of the larger islands in Casco Bay, Basket Island has not been inhabited for decades.

Basket Island was donated to the Conservancy in 1967 by the Dessau family. The Portland Yacht Club monitors the island, and its junior members organize trips to pick up litter and check for other problems.

EELGRASS One of only two seed-producing plants found in marine waters along this coast, eelgrass is a relative of the pondweed. It is the primary winter food of brant, a small, dark, arctic goose that can be seen in Casco Bay during spring and fall migrations, and occasionally during the winter. In 1931, disease destroyed most of the eelgrass along the East Coast, causing a decline in the brant population. The brant eventually adapted by eating sea lettuce and similar plants.

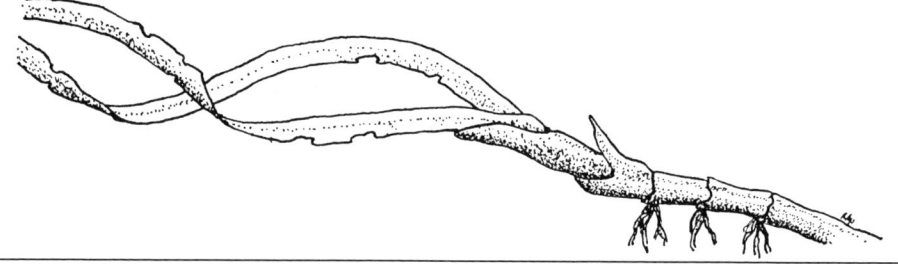

Since it is so near Portland, Basket Island receives considerable use. Careful day use is welcome, but overnight stays are not permitted. Fire has already taken its toll; please build fires only on the rocks below the high tide mark on the lee shore. The town of Cumberland requires fire permits for all open fires.

DIRECTIONS: Large boats can be anchored off the island's western shore. Small boats can be pulled up on the gravel beaches.

Upper Goose Island Preserve

94 acres (partial ownership), Harpswell

Renowned as New England's largest great blue heron rookery, heavily wooded Upper Goose Island also shelters nesting ospreys and basking harbor seals.

For more than 30 years, great blue herons have returned each summer to nest in the safety of the dense forest of Upper Goose Island.

The Upper Goose heronry, the largest in New England, is included on the state Register of Critical Areas. Biologists have counted more than 250 nests lodged in the hemlocks, beeches and yellow birches in the island's interior. Some trees are weighed down with as many as 10 nests. The colony moved to the island from nearby Whaleboat Island in the 1950s and shows no sign of leaving.

Located in the upper reaches of Casco Bay between the Freeport shore and Harpswell Neck, Upper Goose is sheltered from the winds and seas of the open bay. The northern end of the island is forested with hemlock and hardwoods, including a 30-acre stand of mature trees, some of which are at least 200 years old. The hemlocks and hardwoods gradually merge into a forest of red and white spruce on the island's southern shore.

The shore is rocky ledge alternating with gravel beach. A gravel bar connects Upper Goose Island to Lower Goose Island (not part of the preserve). Seals frequently haul out on the ledges off Upper Goose's southeastern shore. At least four pairs of ospreys nest in the trees near the water. In the winter, common eiders and other sea ducks regularly raft up offshore.

The Abnaki Indians visited Upper Goose. Although it may have been used for pasture and was partially logged, there is little evidence of any later inhabitants.

The Conservancy preserve includes all of the island except two lots of four and 10 acres, respectively, both of which are protected by conservation easements. The preserve and easements were donated to the Conservancy in 1980 by Mr. and Mrs. C. Frederick Kaufholz and Mr. and Mrs. Dickinson R. Debevoise.

 Nesting island: Closed to the public during the March 15 to August 15 nesting season. Please do not harass the nesting great blue herons and ospreys by landing on the island or lingering offshore. Disturbance can cause serious nest losses.

During the rest of the year, it is possible to land a small boat on one of the gravel beaches and walk along the shore. Please avoid landing or walking on the two inholdings. One is on the western shore. The other is on the southern shore and includes the small cabin and dock. The boundaries of these properties are marked with small blazes.

GREAT BLUE HERONS Great blue herons construct rather flimsy stick nests, usually nesting together in the larger trees in island interiors or at the edge of swamps. Each pair usually produces four eggs; the young are able to fly after a couple of months.

Nature Conservancy preserves protect more than a third of the great blue heron nests along the Maine coast.

DIRECTIONS: Upper Goose Island is approximately two miles west of the Harpswell Center town landing.

Douglas Mountain Preserve (Thomas Arter)

Western Region

1. Step Falls Preserve/31
2. Sucker Brook Preserve/33
3. Douglas Mountain Preserve/35
4. Indian and Fowl Meadows
   Islands Preserve/37

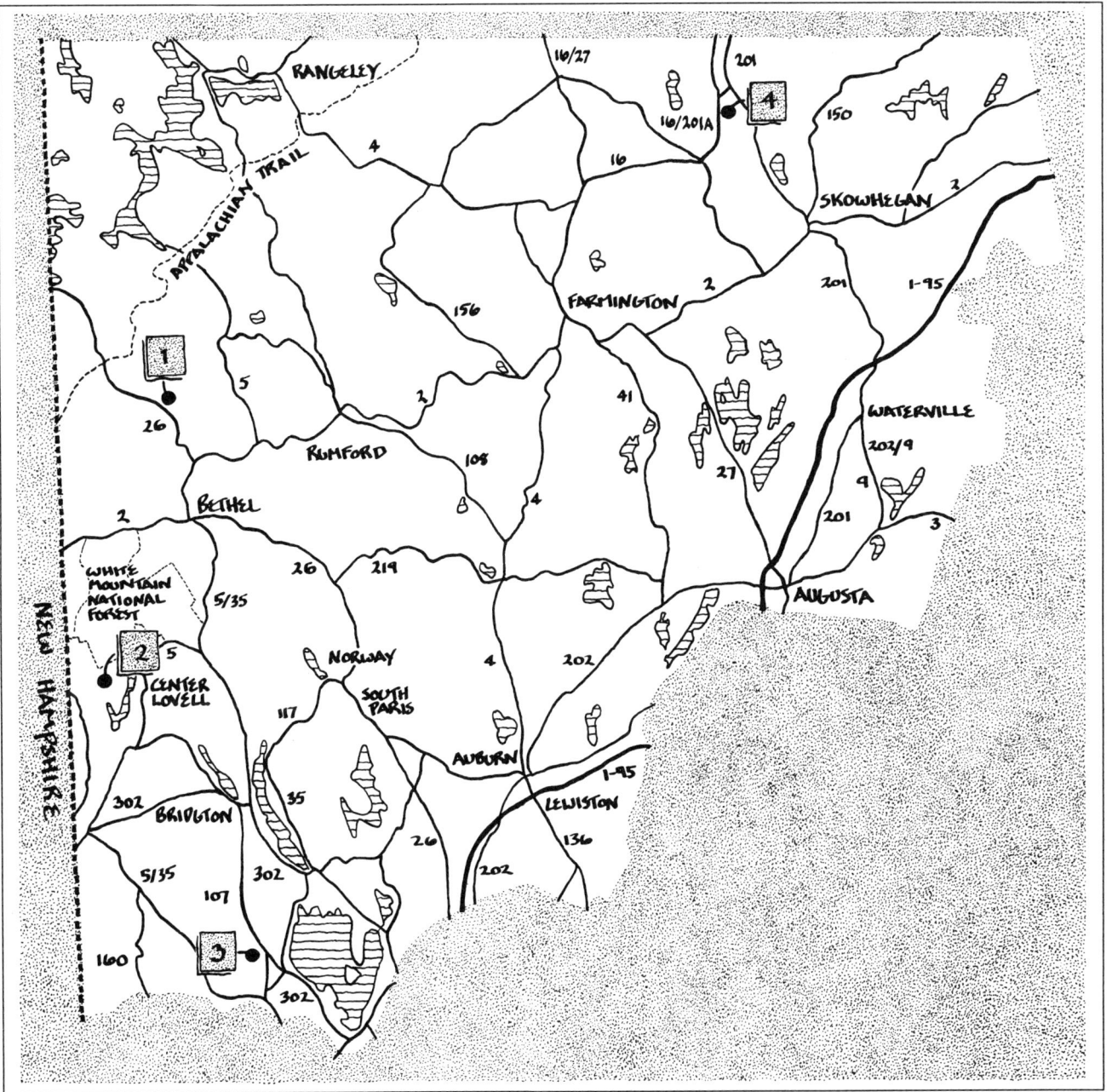

Western Region

With its level floodplains, gently sloping hills and mountains, the western Maine region tends toward pastoral. In fact, during the 19th century most of the land was cleared for animals and crops. Although there are still plenty of pastures and fields left, the majority of the region's farms were abandoned by the early part of this century, if not decades before. The land has returned to forest that is mostly hardwoods, white pine and hemlock.

One of Maine's rarest species, an unassuming pale orchid known as the small whorled pogonia, lives on wooded hillsides, often in places that were once farmland. The orchid is listed as endangered by the federal and state governments. The Conservancy is involved in all aspects of its preservation, from initial field searches to monitoring and acquisition of habitats.

Because the small whorled pogonia is a certified rarity, it attracts all kinds of interest, including that of people who want to possess it as a mounted specimen or doomed plant in a backyard garden. Therefore, the exact locations of the orchids must be kept confidential.

Freshwater wetlands are an integral part of the landscape in this region. Sucker Brook Preserve (Lovell) and Sabra's Creeper Hill Preserve (Stow) protect acres of marsh and swamp near Kezar Lake, as does another property in Lovell donated to the Conservancy but now in the care of a local land trust. Farther east, in the middle reaches of the Kennebec River, Indian and Fowl Meadows Islands Preserve is a fine, unspoiled example of floodplain islands, with their typically lush vegetation. Western Maine contains some of the Maine Chapter's best-loved preserves. Step Falls (Newry) and Douglas Mountain (Sebago) are short hikes offering spectacular views, especially in the fall. Both have been popular with local people and visitors alike for generations.

The Conservancy helped the U.S. Forest Service with two major additions to the White Mountain National Forest: nearly 1,700 acres of forest surrounding Virginia Lake (Lovell, Stoneham) and another 1,400 acres in the Great Brook watershed nearby.

Several volunteer stewardship committees and one seasonal caretaker watch over The Nature Conservancy's preserves in the western Maine region. For more information, please contact the the Maine Chapter Stewardship office in Topsham.

Step Falls Preserve
24 acres, Newry

The Maine Chapter's first acquisition, Step Falls Preserve protects a series of waterfalls and pools near Grafton Notch State Park. The drop is dramatic: more than 150 feet in less than one-eighth of a mile.

The dramatic scenery of Grafton Notch near the New Hampshire border provides the backdrop for Step Falls Preserve, where Wight Brook cascades down the side of Baldpate Mountain over granite ledges. The preserve's gentle, steplike falls and quiet pools offer an interesting contrast to the cataracts of Screw Auger Falls and Mother Walker Falls, both located in Grafton Notch State Park.

Despite its relatively gentle appearance, Wight Brook moves swiftly through the falls; in the last eighth mile of its descent, the brook tumbles more than 150 vertical feet. It then crosses beneath Route 26 before joining the Bear River. The preserve includes both shores of the brook.

Massive amounts of rocky debris carried by torrents of water beneath the melting glaciers carved and polished the granite bedrock, creating impressive potholes and gouges.

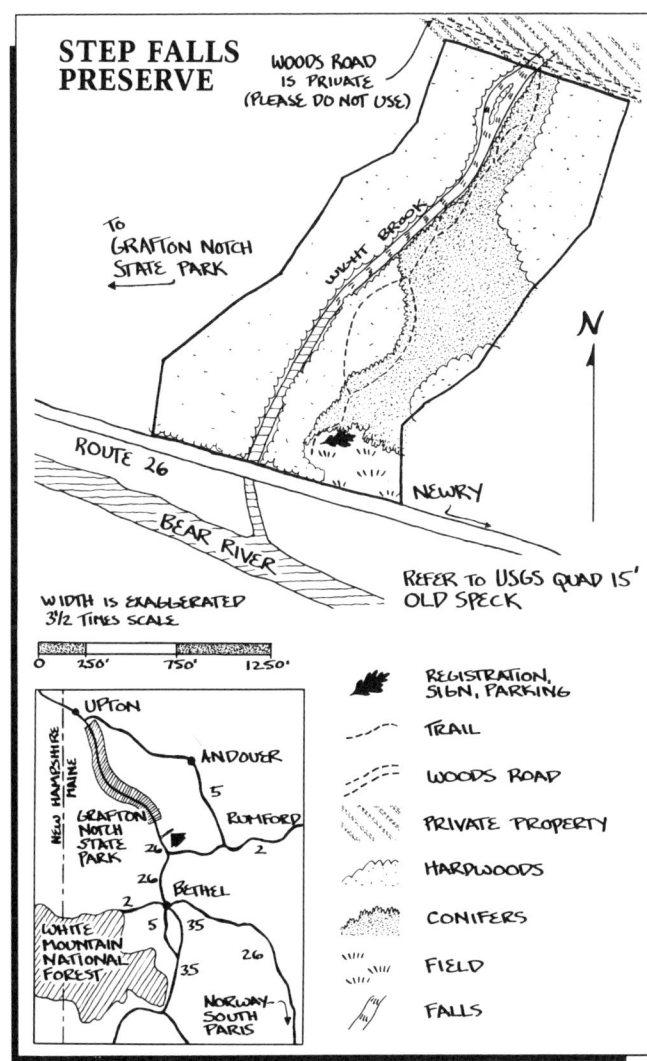

STEP FALLS PRESERVE

WOODS ROAD IS PRIVATE (PLEASE DO NOT USE)

TO GRAFTON NOTCH STATE PARK

WIGHT BROOK

ROUTE 26

BEAR RIVER

NEWRY

REFER TO USGS QUAD 15' OLD SPECK

WIDTH IS EXAGGERATED 3½ TIMES SCALE

0   250'   750'   1250'

UPTON
ANDOVER
NEW HAMPSHIRE / MAINE
GRAFTON NOTCH STATE PARK
RUMFORD
BETHEL
WHITE MOUNTAIN NATIONAL FOREST
NORWAY-SOUTH PARIS

REGISTRATION, SIGN, PARKING
TRAIL
WOODS ROAD
PRIVATE PROPERTY
HARDWOODS
CONIFERS
FIELD
FALLS

The granite is crisscrossed with pegmatite dikes and veins of milky quartz. The preserve's impressive falls and striking geology have earned it a place on the state Register of Critical Areas.

At the base of the falls, the forest is dense red spruce and balsam fir, which gradually give way to hardwoods at higher elevations. On the western side of Wight Brook the woods are predominantly birch, beech and maple.

The preserve is inviting at any time of the year: the falls are particularly dramatic during spring run-off; the cool, splashing waters are restorative in mid-summer; and the scenery in the autumn is spectacular.

Step Falls was the Maine Chapter's first preserve. The property's owners turned to the newly formed group to help protect the area. The all-volunteer Chapter launched a fund-raising drive and acquired the land in 1961. In 1983, the preserve was dedicated to Charles E. Heywood, Chapter board chairman from 1961 to 1965.

Step Falls Preserve has clearly marked trails and is a fine spot for a family hike. It is only a short distance to the falls, yet the more adventuresome can go on to the top.

The trail begins in the grassy parking area, and climbs up along the eastern side of the brook for about a half mile, offering good views of the cascading waters and the distant mountains. Near the top of the falls, a logging road crosses the trail. The road is not on Conservancy property; please use the trail and return to the parking lot. There are several alternate trail sections to add variety to the return trip. A trail brochure is available at the preserve entrance.

The broad, rounded boulders in the falls are inviting, as are the pools, but please be careful when venturing into the brook. The rocks are very slippery and the current is surprisingly strong.

DIRECTIONS: The preserve entrance is on Route 26, but there is no sign on the road. From the east: take Route 26 toward Newry, about eight miles from the junction with Route 2 in Bethel. The preserve is on the right, just before Wight Brook. From the west: go about three miles past Grafton Notch State Park. Please park in the area near the brook. A welcome sign and registration box are located just inside the woods.

WATERFALLS In areas where the granite bedrock breaks into evenly spaced, parallel cracks, or joints, streams tend to transform steep slopes into steplike falls by gradually, steadily plucking off whole blocks of stone. The angular blocks are then rounded and smoothed by the flowing stream.

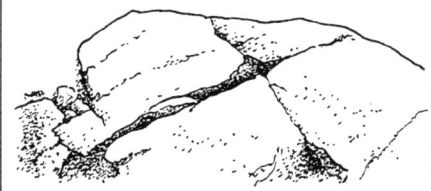

Sucker Brook Preserve

32 acres, Lovell

In the shadow of the White Mountains, Sucker Brook flows through the marshes of Moose Pond on its way to Kezar Lake. In late summer, cardinal flowers bloom among the rocks at the water's edge. Moose frequently browse along the pond shore.

Lying at the eastern edge of the White Mountains, Sucker Brook Preserve protects a half-mile stretch of Sucker Brook, including Moose Pond and bordering marsh lands.

Sucker Brook changes character several times within the preserve, creating a variety of habitats with diverse plant and animal life. Beginning as a rocky, tumbling stream at the outlet of Horseshoe Pond, the brook slows and widens at the site of an old beaver dam. It regains its rocky character for a short stretch, then flows into a broad marsh surrounding Moose Pond. The pond and marsh are maintained by a colony of beavers.

Cardinal flowers and watercress grow in abundance among the rocks bordering the faster sections of the brook. In the quieter areas, sensitive and royal ferns form emerald bouquets along the water's edge.

Moose Pond is largely open, with water lilies, pickerelweed and other water plants growing in the shallows and along the shore. The back shore is a dense swamp of speckled alder, sweet gale and button bush.

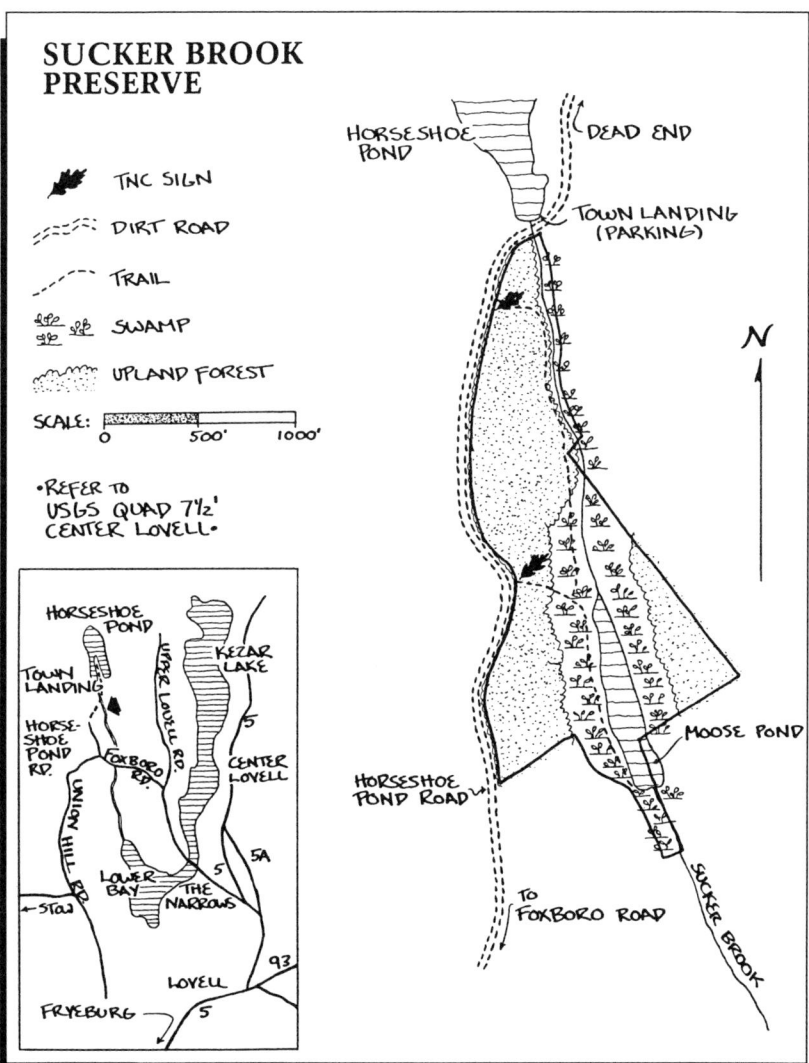

SUCKER BROOK PRESERVE

- TNC SIGN
- DIRT ROAD
- TRAIL
- SWAMP
- UPLAND FOREST

SCALE: 0   500'   1000'

• REFER TO USGS QUAD 7½' CENTER LOVELL •

The higher, drier elevations are forested with hemlock, white pine and mixed hardwoods. In 1980, a severe windstorm caused many blowdowns, providing several large clearings throughout the preserve.

The Conservancy acquired Sucker Brook Preserve largely through the efforts of an active local volunteer Stewardship Committee whose members raised the money to acquire the two parcels that form the preserve. In 1974, almost 21 acres encompassing most of Moose Pond were acquired and dedicated to Dr. Wilson Wing. Three years later, a 12-acre parcel to the north was added and dedicated to Charles Parker III, Margaret Anderson and John Halford, Sr.

FERNS Ferns do not bear seeds, but reproduce by alternating between the familiar asexual fronds that release spores and a tiny, heart-leaved sexual form that eventually grows into a new set of fronds. This fact was not discovered until the mid-1800s.

During the Middle Ages, people believed that fern seeds were invisible, and had the power to make anyone who collected them also invisible. Optimistic souls gathered in fern colonies on St. John's Eve, when the plants were supposed to produce blue flowers and—for the briefest of moments—magical golden seeds.

A mile-long trail marked with red circular markers winds along the brook to the edge of the pond. A loop can be made by walking a short stretch on Horseshoe Pond Road.

DIRECTIONS: Coming from the east, cross The Narrows of Kezar Lake and bear left at the first major fork after a mile and a half. Within another mile and a half the main road bears left; continue straight ahead on the gravel road past several houses for another half mile. Turn right on Horseshoe Pond Road. Go about a mile, past two TNC signs marking the preserve entrances, to the town landing parking lot on Horseshoe Pond.

Douglas Mountain Preserve

169 acres, Sebago

For generations, hikers have climbed to the summit of Douglas Mountain to enjoy the panoramic view from the Atlantic to the mountains of New Hampshire.

Situated in the lakes region of western Maine, Douglas Mountain is the highest point of land for several hundred square miles. From the 1,415-foot summit there is a spectacular panorama encompassing Sebago Lake and the White Mountains. On a clear day, the view extends as far as the Atlantic Ocean. Visitors with good eyes report that it is possible to see the Green Mountains of Vermont.

At the summit, a 16-foot stone tower ascended by an interior staircase offers the best vantage point. The tower was built in 1925 by the land's previous owner, a surgeon who found relaxation in stone masonry. Maine Chapter volunteers recently continued the tradition, repairing the tower to keep it useable for many more years.

The slopes of Douglas Mountain are littered with glacial erratics, boulders left by the retreating glaciers. In 1921, one large boulder on the summit was inscribed with the proclamation *Non sibi sed omnibus*— Not for one, but for all. This still reflects the philosophy of the preserve.

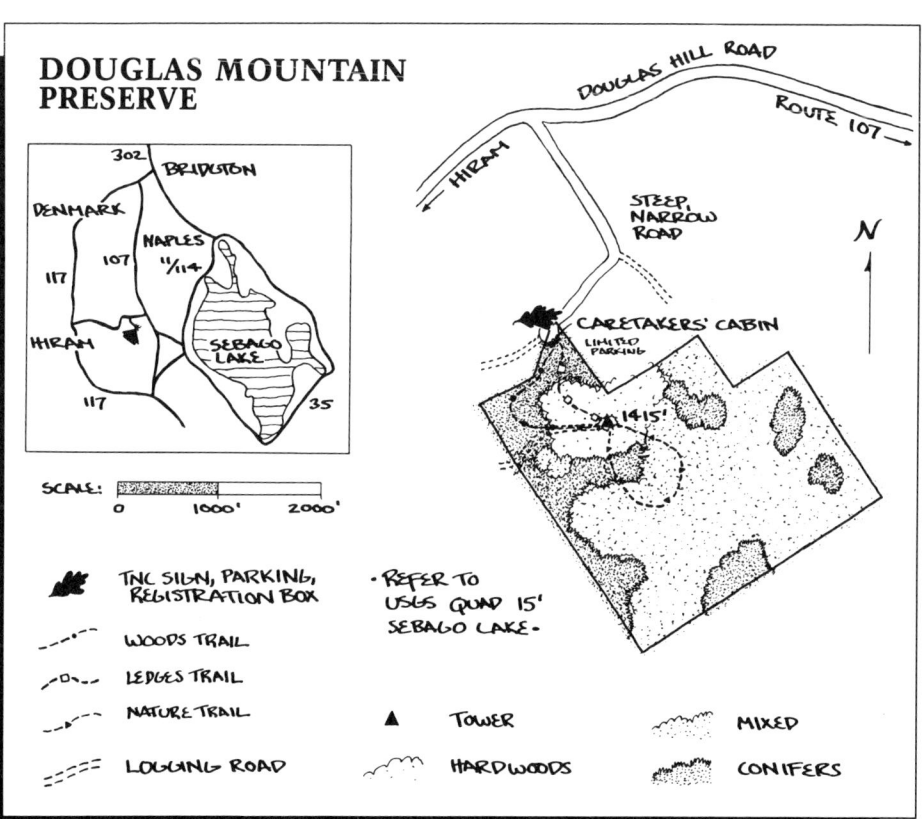

DOUGLAS MOUNTAIN PRESERVE

SCALE: 0 1000' 2000'

TNC SIGN, PARKING, REGISTRATION BOX

- - - WOODS TRAIL
- - - LEDGES TRAIL
- - - NATURE TRAIL
===== LOGGING ROAD

· REFER TO USGS QUAD 15' SEBAGO LAKE.

▲ TOWER

MIXED

HARDWOODS

CONIFERS

Mature hemlock and mixed hardwood forests dominate the northern part of the preserve, in contrast with the more open stands of beech and oak on the protected southeastern slopes. The soils are shallow, and there are many open ledges. Blueberries, blackberries and juniper abound.

In addition to stonework, the former owner had another hobby: collecting trees. Only one fir species, balsam fir, is native to Maine. The doctor brought two western species, douglas-fir and white fir, to the mountain. The Douglas-fir, with drooping branches that resemble bottle-brushes, is quite easy to find at the base of the mountain before the trail forks.

Like much of western Maine, Douglas Mountain was cleared and farmed in the past century. Photographs taken in the 1890s show the mountain, and most of the surrounding countryside, in use as fields and pasture. After the turn of the century, the land was allowed to return to forest, although it was selectively logged.

People have enjoyed the view from Douglas Mountain for generations. It received permanent protection when the Conservancy purchased the land in 1971.

Douglas Mountain receives more than 6,000 visitors each year. The help of every visitor is needed to keep the area unspoiled. Please stay on the trails. Thin soils and steep slopes make erosion a recurring problem that is only partially alleviated by control measures such as water bars. Careful use is very important. As at all preserves, for the sake of the resident wildlife and other preserve visitors, please leave your dog at home and pack out your trash.

The summit is a half-hour hike from the base of the mountain. The trail begins just past the registration box and stone pillars; it is clearly marked with white blazes. After a short distance the trail forks and two routes lead up the mountain to the tower. The Woods Trail is gently sloping and easily negotiated at any time of the year. The Ledges Trail is shorter and provides excellent views, but has several steep sections near the summit which cross bare ledge. This trail is dangerously icy in winter.

On the top, a three-quarter-mile loop nature trail heads down from the tower into the woods on the southeastern slopes for a look at the preserve's different forest types. Be sure to follow the trail markers, since old roads lead off the preserve onto private property.

Visitors are welcome at any time of the year. It is a fine place to watch fall hawk migration or to snowshoe in winter.

School and camp groups should contact the Chapter office for permission before visiting the mountain.

DIRECTIONS: Take Route 107 in Sebago, turning west onto the Douglas Mountain Road. Follow this road for approximately three-quarters of a mile, then take the first paved road to the left. Follow this to a small turnaround which provides parking for several cars. Please do not block the road and adjacent driveways.

Indian and Fowl Meadow Islands Preserve

32 acres, Emden

Flooded regularly by the waters of the Kennebec River, Indian and Fowl Meadow islands support a rich variety of wildflowers and ferns. The islands are also an important resting and feeding stop for migrating waterfowl.

Indian and Fowl Meadow islands are small floodplain islands lying mid-channel in the upper Kennebec River.

Annual flooding gives the islands a distinctive flora at two levels: an easily flooded lowland and a higher terrace. The terrace is especially distinct on Indian Island.

Blue vervain, cardinal flower and sundew grow on the cobble shore, backed by a band of wetland shrubs. The lower floodplain is forested with red maple, ash, paper birch, willow and beech. Jack-in-the-pulpits grow more than two feet high.

Red oak, paper birch, ash, hop hornbeam, red maple and basswood make up the terrace forest. The rich woodland soil supports many herbs, including wild leek, blue cohosh, bloodroot and scouring rush.

The wetter areas on both islands have lush growths of ferns, including nearly pure stands of head-high ostrich ferns.

In the spring and fall, migrating waterfowl stop here to rest and feed. Deer are frequent visitors, and there is a large beaver dam at the southern end of Indian Island.

At one time, the islands may have been used for pasture, since the river is shallow and easily forded. Loggers also came across in search of timber, especially oak.

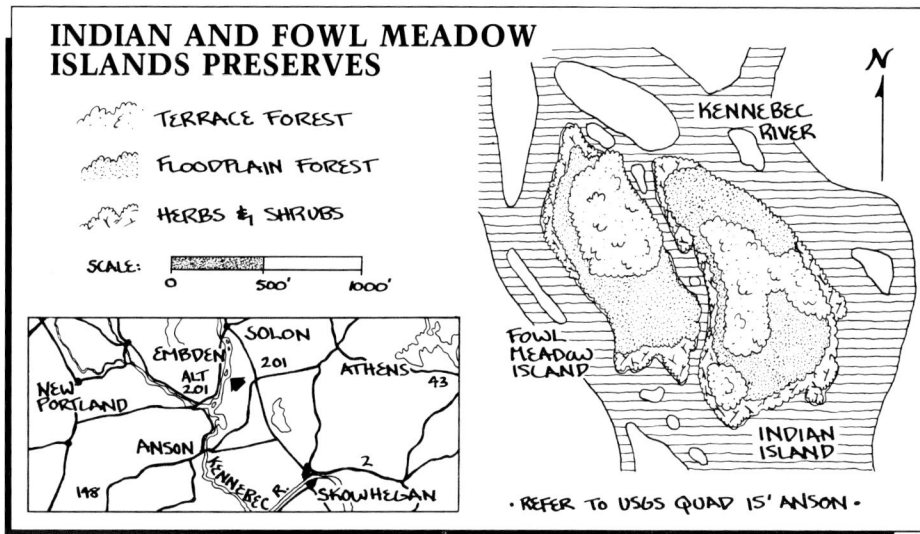

INDIAN AND FOWL MEADOW ISLANDS PRESERVES

- TERRACE FOREST
- FLOODPLAIN FOREST
- HERBS & SHRUBS

SCALE: 0 — 500' — 1000'

NEW PORTLAND · EMBDEN · ALT 201 · SOLON · 201 · ANSON · ATHENS · 43 · KENNEBEC R. · SKOWHEGAN · 2 · 148

KENNEBEC RIVER · FOWL MEADOW ISLAND · INDIAN ISLAND

· REFER TO USGS QUAD 15' ANSON ·

Pulp logs were driven down the Kennebec River every year until 1976. The men responsible for keeping the long logs from jamming in the shallow, obstructed channel were stationed in a cabin on Indian Island's northern end. The ruins of their cabin and several pulpwood deadheads remain.

Indian and Fowl Meadow islands were donated to the Conservancy in 1967 by Clinton and Louise Townsend, who have retained a life interest.

 The preserve is open for quiet and careful day use. There are no trails, but walking is possible.

DIRECTIONS: The closest launching area is upstream, on the east side of Route 201/8 in Solon.

Damariscove Island Preserve (Julie Henderson)

Mid-coast Region

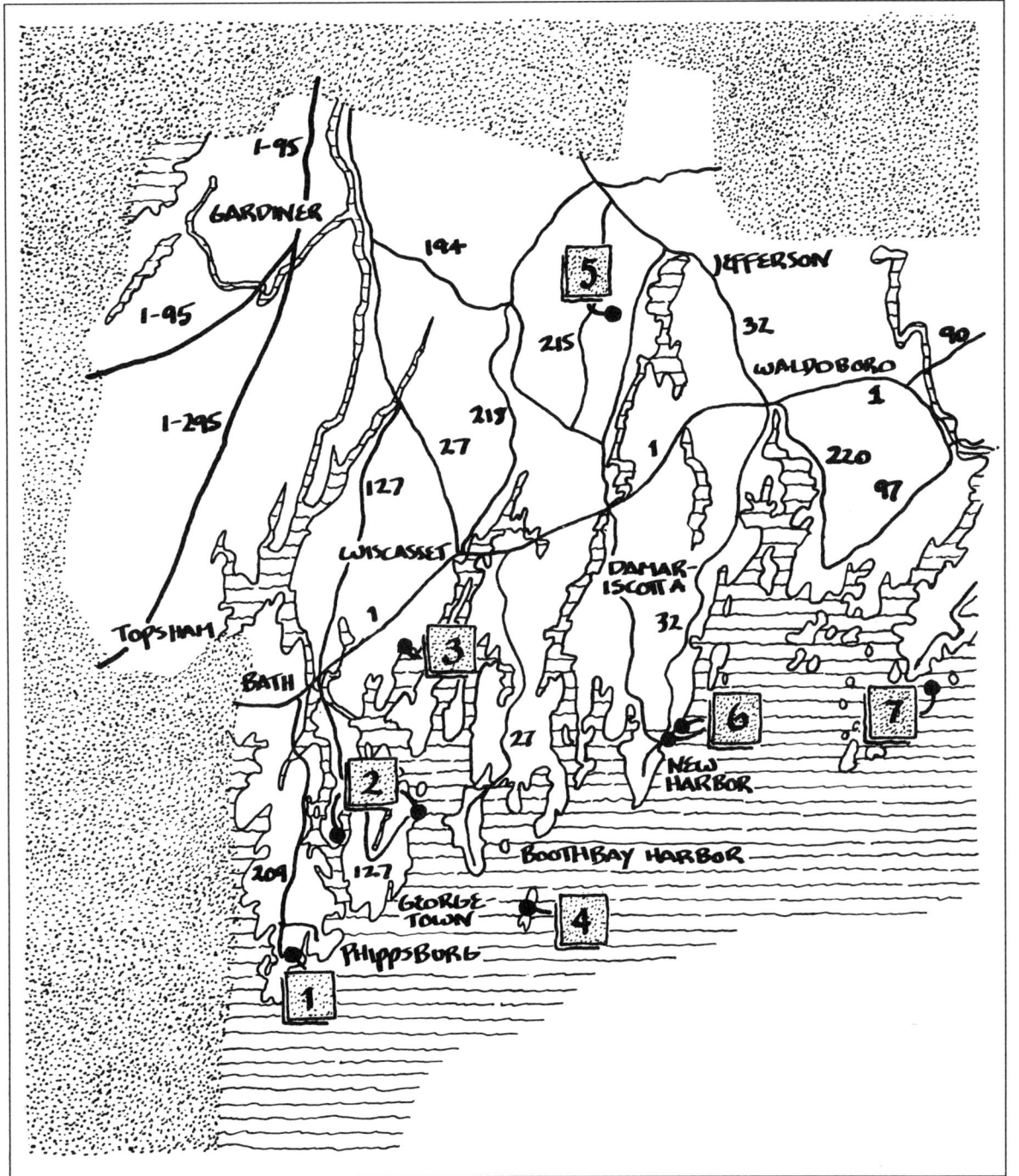

Mid-coast Region

Beginning in Casco Bay, the Maine coast becomes a series of long, narrow peninsulas and chains of islands divided by equally long, narrow bays. Several of the state's largest rivers empty into these bays, forming productive estuaries where their waters meet the sea.

At Morse Mountain/Seawall Beach, at the mouth of the Kennebec River in Phippsburg, the Conservancy helps protect the state's last sizable unspoiled barrier beach/dune/salt marsh complex. The chain of beaches and salt marshes that stretches along the East Coast ends in mid-coast Maine. North of Seawall and its immediate neighbors (Popham, Half Mile and Mile beaches), the coast is nearly all rocky shore. Beaches hide in little pockets or are part of glacially deposited bars; salt marshes perch wherever there is shelter from the waves.

Since most of the country's sand beaches disappear every summer under blankets, picnic coolers and supine bodies (if they have not already disappeared under the foundations of cottages), there is precious little room left for nesting birds seeking peace and quiet. Seawall Beach is one of the few places where the needs of nesting endangered least terns and piping plovers take priority.

Upriver from Seawall Beach, at the confluence of the Kennebec and Back rivers, Bald Head Preserve (Arrowsic) hosts a gathering of bald eagles each winter. The preserve and its salt marshes are part of the extensive estuarine ecosystem of the Kennebec, Back and Sheepscot rivers. Two other Conservancy preserves, Montsweag (Woolwich) and Ledgewood (Georgetown), also protect uplands and intertidal areas in this system.

Nearly four centuries ago, European explorers took home tales of the mid-coast region's productive fishing grounds. By 1600, fishermen had settled on what is now the Conservancy's Damariscove Island Preserve (Boothbay) and were shipping home boatloads of freshly dried cod.

Farther east, the Conservancy has several preserves on the Pemaquid peninsula. Plummer Point Preserve (South Bristol) and an adjacent easement protects an entire peninsula on the Damariscotta River. The Osborn-Finch (Waldoboro), Bass Rock (Round Pond), LaVerna (Bristol), and Rachel Carson Salt Pond (Bristol) preserves front on Muscongus Bay, offering access to the bay's western shore.

Inland, in the upper Sheepscot River watershed, Musquash Pond Preserve (Jefferson) includes a variety of wetlands that are popular with waterfowl and other wildlife.

Local groups own and manage many natural areas within the region, including three protected originally by the Conservancy: Stover Point Marsh (Harpswell), The Tracy shore (South Bristol) and Meadow Mountain (Waldoboro). The Conservancy collaborates with other local groups, as well as the state, educational institutions and other conservation organizations, in efforts such as the research and recovery program for least terns and piping plovers.

The Nature Conservancy's preserves in the mid-coast region are taken care of by several local stewardship committees and a pair of seasonal caretakers. For more information, please contact the Maine Chapter stewardship office in Topsham.

Morse Mountain, Seawall Beach and the Heron Islands

Morse Mountain Preserve, 28 acres;
Morse Mountain Easement, 580 acres;
Heron Islands Preserve, 9 acres;
All in Phippsburg

Seawall Beach-Morse Mountain is an integral part of Maine's last large undeveloped barrier beach system. The quiet beach is a vital breeding area for least terns and piping plovers, species that are steadily declining due to harassment and loss of habitat.

Morse Mountain-Seawall Beach, together with adjacent Popham Beach, is Maine's last large undeveloped barrier beach system. The Morse Mountain complex includes more than 700 acres between the Sprague and Morse rivers.

An innovative, somewhat complicated arrangement protects the area and its ecosystems. The Conservancy owns three small preserves, two on the marshes of the Sprague and Morse rivers, the third encompassing the Heron Islands lying just off Seawall Beach. The Conservancy holds a conservation easement on 580 acres, including the backdunes, most of the uplands and more than 150 acres of salt marsh. The land under easement is owned by a nonprofit corporation and leased to Bates College in Lewiston. Bates manages it as a research site known as the Bates-Morse Mountain Coastal Research Area. To further protect the nesting least terns and piping plovers, the Conservancy and Bates College have a management lease with the Small Point Association, the owners of Seawall Beach. In addition, the Maine Audubon Society is an active partner in the monitoring and management of the endangered birds. The Seawall Beach nesting colonies are listed on the state Register of Critical Areas.

At low tide, Seawall Beach stretches 400 feet from dune ridge to ocean waves. The piping plovers and least terns nest from the very edge of the storm tide mark up into the dunes.

Many of the plants growing in the dunes are at the northern edge of their ranges, including the largest expanse of undisturbed beach heather (*Hudsonia tomentosa*) left in Maine.

Behind the dunes lie salt marshes that were once harvested for salt hay. The marshes and their tidal creeks are an important nursery for shell fish and fin fish.

Between the marshes are wooded uplands rimmed by high, imposing granite ledges. Mature spruce and pine make up much of the forest, but there are extensive sections of open pitch pine woodland. The pitch pine grows in association with broom crowberry (*Corema conradii*), and abundant lichens and mosses, as well as blueberry, huckleberry, golden heather (*Hudsonia ericoides*), mountain sandwort (*Minuartia glabra*), and bastard-toadflax (*Commandra umbellata*). This pitch pine-broom crowberry natural community is found only along the north Atlantic coast, and is considered threatened throughout its range. It is also beautiful; the gnarled pines growing on ledges carpeted with subtle greens and grays create an elfin forest that is especially appealing in the fog.

More than 70 bird species nest in the protected area; nearly 300 species have been spotted in the vicinity. Birders visit the preserve year-round to enjoy everything from spring warblers to wintering sea ducks. Deer, porcupines, red foxes and raccoons are seen regularly; moose, beavers and coyotes have also been sighted.

The Heron Islands, five small ledges close to the beach, are home to nesting double-crested cormorants, herring gulls and greater black-backed gulls. The birds' presence has reduced the islands' vegetation to orache, ragweed and a few grasses. The islands had trees until around 1920; their disappearance may have been the result of winter storms or a legacy from nesting great blue herons. In later winter, brants rest on the Heron Islands during migration.

Morse Mountain lies at the heart of a nationally significant historic region. Nearby Popham was settled in 1606. During the 1800s, the Morse Mountain area was farmed by two Morse families, who cut salt hay and lumber, sold cream and eggs, and harvested cranberries for the Boston market.

Surprisingly, Seawall never became populated with cottages like most of Maine's sand beaches. However, at least one attempt was made to develop the property into a resort. In 1892, the Mountain, Farm and Seashore Company advertised 200 little house lots laid out from the beach over the dunes up the mountainside. Fortunately, the company's flowery brochure attracted few buyers.

Although the summer colony idea failed, the property was divided up into many ownerships. It remained so until George St. John, Sr. began reassembling the pieces in 1938. This slow process was interrupted during World War II, when a submarine tracking radar station was installed on the mountain.

In the 1950s, the St. John family set out to find a way to protect the entire area permanently. Protecting the largest section involved 19 family members and was completed in 1976.

An additional 175 acres were donated in 1983 by Mr. and Mrs. George St. John, Jr. The Morse Mountain-Seawall Beach sanctuary is a tribute to the perseverance and dedication of the St. Johns, who are still actively involved in its management.

Three of the Heron islands were donated to the Maine Chapter by Mrs. Frances Fickett in 1973. The other two are leased from the state of Maine and managed by the Conservancy.

Additional information about the research area can be found at the entrance during the summer or obtained by writing to the Biology Department at Bates College, Lewiston, Maine 04240 or the Conservancy's Maine Chapter office.

  Please be aware that the Seawall Beach-Morse Mountain area is managed primarily for research and protection of its natural resources. For recreation, consider nearby Popham Beach State Park, which has a fine view of Seawall.

The beach is a two-mile walk or ski from the main road. Stay on the access road or beach, and avoid the fragile dunes and marsh. Please leave your dog at home during the nesting season.

During the least tern and piping plover breeding season (May 15 to August 15), string and electric fences as well as signs mark the nesting areas. Pass as far away from the colonies as possible and do not linger. During most summer days, a Conservancy plover-tern warden will be on the beach monitoring the birds and will be available to answer questions.

The Heron Islands are nesting islands and are closed to the public during the March 15 to August 15 nesting season. At other times of the year, it is possible to land on the islands, but the ledges make it difficult.

DIRECTIONS: Take Route 209 to Route 216 in Phippsburg. The entrance road is on the left, about a mile past the junction of the two routes. There is a small parking lot just off the road. If the parking lot is full, please do not park on the main road but return (earlier) another day.

HOW NOT TO BE SEEN Piping plovers blend so well into the surrounding beach shore that they usually are heard (*peep!*) and not seen, at least until they move. Plover chicks and eggs are equally well-disguised. This adaptation, known as cryptic coloration, is effective against most predators, but has its drawbacks, since frisbee-chasing beachgoers can easily trample hidden plovers.

Bald Head Preserve and Ledgewood Preserve

Bald Head, 296 acres, Arrowsic;
Ledgewood, 28 acres, Georgetown

Rising above the Back River, the steep cliffs of Bald Head Preserve are crowned with pines that are favorite roosts of wintering bald eagles. On Sheepscot Bay in Georgetown, the Ledgewood Preserve protects more than a mile of shoreline.

Bald Head

The southern tip of Arrowsic Island, known as Bald Head, divides the waters of the Kennebec and Back rivers. Steep cliffs rise nearly 100 feet from the Back River, giving the point its name and offering fine views down the Kennebec.

Bald Head is located in the middle of one of Maine's four major bald eagle wintering areas.

Eagles regularly roost in the pines at the top of the preserve's cliffs. Historically, eagles also nested here, but the breeding population of the lower Kennebec was decimated by DDT, which was sprayed over the marshes to control mosquitoes. The eagle population is recovering more slowly here than elsewhere in the state.

The preserve includes 75 acres of salt marsh, which essentially divides the cliffs and uplands from the Arrowsic mainland. The salt marshes are a continuation of the extensive marshes found on Arrowsic and Georgetown islands, with typical plants such as cordgrass, salt marsh hay, and bulrush. Seaside gerardia (*Agalinis maritima*), a species at the northern limit of its range, also grows here.

The wide mudflats on the Back River are important feeding grounds for great blue herons, snowy egrets and many waterfowl. Flounder, striped bass, shad, sculpin, sturgeon, alewife, salmon, herring, and smelt are all found in the Kennebec and Back rivers. Short-nosed sturgeon (*Acipenser brevirostrum*), a species currently listed as federally endangered, is thought to breed in this estuary.

Although there were settlements nearby in the 1600s, no cellar holes have been found on the preserve. The marshes were cut for salt hay and the peninsula cleared for pasture. Major logging operations ceased in the 1950s.

Neighboring landowner Julian Sobin donated Bald Head Preserve to the Conservancy in 1980.

To see bald eagles at Bald Head without disturbing them, look out over the marsh on the right just before the Arrowsic-Georgetown bridge on Route 127. Bald Head is in line with this vantage point, and eagles often circle over the marshes and rivers.

Access to Bald Head Preserve is from the water. The Back River is a pleasant canoe trip, but watch the tides and currents, especially near the Kennebec and at the narrows between Arrowsic and Georgetown. There are old logging roads on the preserve, but they are overgrown and not maintained as trails. The salt marsh mosquitoes are fierce; come prepared.

The small camp at the northern end of the peninsula and a lot at the southern end are privately owned. Also, the Squirrel Point light is not part of the preserve.

DIRECTIONS: Take Route 127 to Arrowsic, turn right at the last road before the Arrowsic-Georgetown bridge. At high tide, it is possible to put in a canoe at the first small creek.

Ledgewood

The unspoiled shore of the Ledgewood Preserve extends for more than a mile on Dry Point south of the small village of Five Islands. The preserve also includes Wood Island, a two-acre island connected to the tip of the point at low tide.

Most of the preserve is woods dominated by red and white spruce, with some white pine and balsam fir. Under the trees the ground is a green blanket of mosses and lichens. Blueberry, huckleberry, juniper and ferns fill in the openings. The entire point is exposed to the full energy of winter winds, making blowdowns an annual occurrence. White birch, quaking aspen and raspberries are common in the clearings left by the fallen trees.

The preserve's quiet woods and shore are excellent shelter for wildlife. Ospreys nest here, along with ovenbirds, white-throated sparrows and other forest birds. Raccoons, porcupines, snowshoe hares and foxes are regular visitors.

During the 19th century, most of the land in Five Islands was cleared and farmed. Traces of old stone walls and wire fencing remain from the days when the preserve land was used as a cattle pasture.

Mr. and Mrs. Warner Eustis donated Ledgewood to the Conservancy in 1966, subject to a life tenancy. After their deaths, the Conservancy sold the two lots containing the main house and boat house, subject to conservation restrictions. The proceeds were used to help identify and protect Maine's threatened wildlife, as the Eustises wished.

 Aside from the access road, there are no real trails on the preserve, but it is possible to walk along the shore. It is also possible to land a boat on the flats near Wood Island. Please avoid walking or landing on the private property: two cottages near the preserve entrance and the estate at the tip of the point. The beach near the entrance is kept for the use of Five Island residents through the wishes of the Eustises.

EAGLE DINING One of the "sea eagles," bald eagles feed mostly on fish that they either catch themselves or steal from ospreys. They also eat injured waterfowl, carrion and small mammals. One of the major hazards eagles face is extra "seasoning" in their meals, including lead shot in waterfowl, and pesticides and other toxins concentrated in fish inhabiting polluted waters.

DIRECTIONS: Take Route 127 south to Five Islands, then the last road on the right before the town wharf. Park in the small lot before the gate and walk along the shore, turning back at the private property and returning on either the shore or the access road.

Montsweag
Preserve 45 acres, Woolwich

A coastal ecosystem in miniature, the Montsweag Preserve offers ideal learning opportunities for school groups studying ecology and others interested in the life of estuaries and the land bordering them.

The Montsweag Preserve protects 1,500 feet of ledgy shoreline along tidal Montsweag Brook. On the preserve's northeastern shore, a small tidal creek drains a large area of freshwater swamp and salt marsh. The uplands are a mixed growth of hardwoods and softwoods, bordered by fields and thick bands of white pine. The varied habitats of this coastal ecosystem in microcosm make the area interesting to both casual visitors and classes in environmental studies.

Tidal Montsweag Brook is narrow at the point it passes the preserve, but widens above and below. The granite shore is lined with tall beeches, pitch pines, spruces and hemlocks. A thick layer of mosses clings to the ledges. The pink-flowered sea milkwort *(Glaux maritima)* grows abundantly in the higher salt marsh, among the salt hay. Migrating waterfowl feed on the mudflats and in the salt marsh.

Above the salt marsh, alders grow in the swampy area at the head of the creek. In the drier uplands, sections of spruce and fir contrast with stands of birch, beech and maple, especially when the leaves turn in the fall. In spring, Canada mayflowers and moccasin flowers bloom throughout the woods.

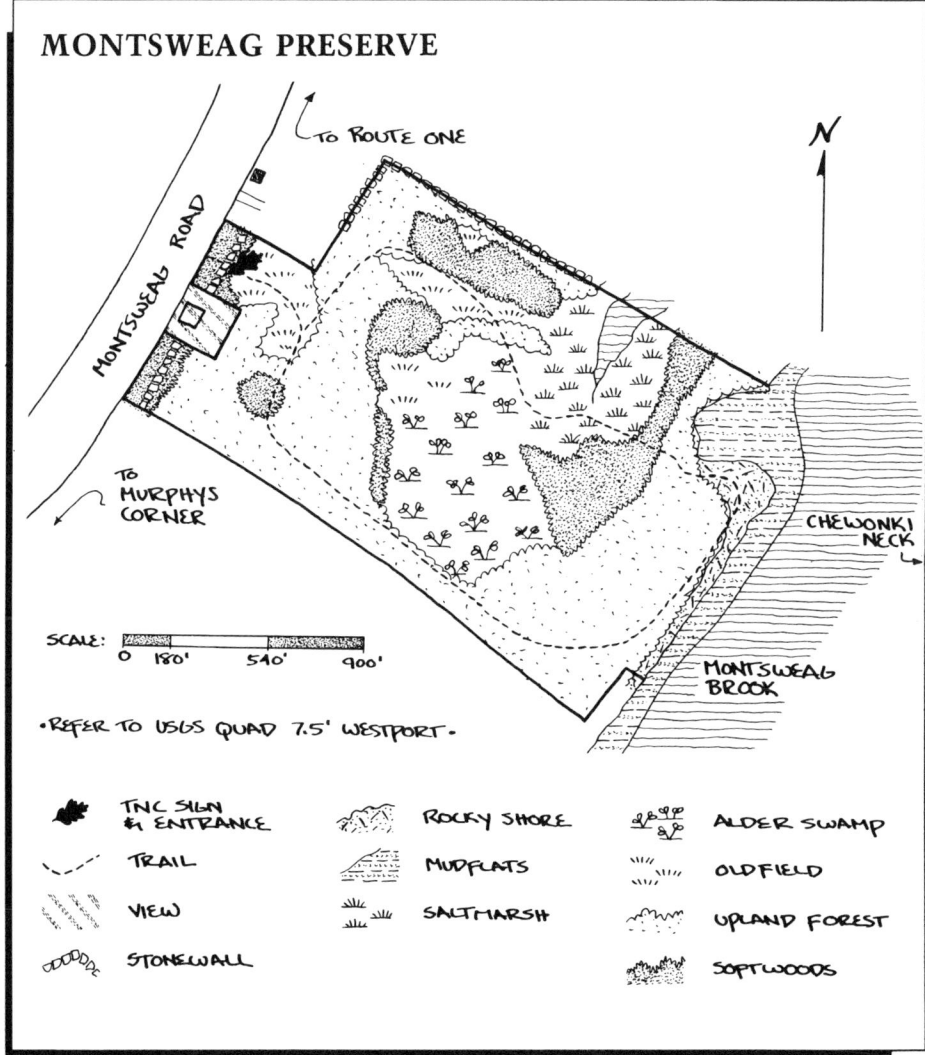

MONTSWEAG PRESERVE

TO ROUTE ONE

N

MONTSWEAG ROAD

TO MURPHYS CORNER

CHEWONKI NECK

MONTSWEAG BROOK

SCALE: 0 180' 540' 900'

•REFER TO USGS QUAD 7.5' WESTPORT•

TNC SIGN & ENTRANCE

TRAIL

VIEW

STONEWALL

ROCKY SHORE

MUDFLATS

SALTMARSH

ALDER SWAMP

OLDFIELD

UPLAND FOREST

SOFTWOODS

There is evidence of Indian presence in the area, but signs of more recent human use of the land are far more prevalent. Old apple trees and stonewalls outlining the fields of an earlier time are reminders that the land was once farmed, primarily in the 1800s by the Hunnewell family. The land was later logged, although never heavily. At one time, there were 10 to 15 brick yards located along Montsweag Creek. The bricks, made from the excellent local clay, were loaded onto scows a short distance downriver from the preserve.

The Chewonki Foundation, an environmentally oriented educational organization, resides on the opposite shore of Montsweag Brook. Participants in the foundation's programs and summer camp have been frequent visitors to Montsweag Preserve. Chewonki students prepared the preserve's initial natural resource inventory in 1974.

Montsweag Preserve was donated to the Conservancy by Mrs. Lois Thurston in 1966. She was deeply committed to the Conservancy, and served on the Maine Chapter board as officer and trustee for many years.

ESTUARIES Estuaries are incredibly productive ecological zones. Defined strictly by salinity, they occupy the fluctuating band between the salt water of the ocean and the fresh water of rivers.

On fall nights, every stroke of the oars or paddle will be rewarded with a brilliant luminous display by one of the estuary's microscopic denizens, the single-celled organism called *Noctiluca*, or "light of the night."

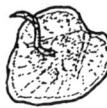  

Upon her death, her home near the preserve came to the Conservancy to be sold to provide income to acquire other natural areas.

  Visitors are welcome at any time of the year. A trail loops through various habitats on the preserve, beginning in the quiet woods, passing near the shore of Montsweag Brook, crossing the salt marsh and alder swamp, then returning through the old field and more woods. The loop is about a mile and half long and is marked with blue blazes. It may be rough and wet in spots.

DIRECTIONS: Heading from Bath to Wiscasset, take a right onto Montsweag Road (about a mile and half south of the Route 144 junction). Go 1.3 miles down the Montsweag Road. The preserve entrance is on the left, and should be marked with a small yellow boundary marker. A preserve welcome sign with a trail map is located just inside the woods. Please park as far as possible off the main road and do not block private drives.

It is possible to land a canoe on the preserve shore.

Damariscove Island Preserve

209 acres, Boothbay

For more than 300 years, Damariscove Island was a thriving fishing and farming community. Today, the island is wild and open, a place of great peace and beauty to be enjoyed by all. A large colony of common eiders and other seabirds nest in the sanctuary of the northern half of the island.

Damariscove's calm harbor is as welcome to 20th century fishermen and sailors in search of safe anchorage and a respite on solid ground as it was to 17th century mariners sighting their first land after months at sea.

Lying about seven miles south of the Boothbay Harbor, the low island is nearly two miles long, but a scant quarter-mile wide. An anomaly among Maine's larger islands, it is nearly treeless. The famous harbor opens on the southern shore, and is protected by knolls to the east and west.

For generations, the Abnakis came to the island, which they called Aquahega, to fish and collect eggs. By 1600, European explorers had discovered abundant cod in the waters near "Damerill's Cove." Every summer, men fished offshore and brought their catch back to the island to be salted and dried.

For the first few decades of the 1600s, Damariscove was one of the New World's major ports. Less than 20 years after the islanders' first boatload of cod went to Europe, the harbor was a bustling place filled with "thirty ships of sail." In 1622, the Plymouth colonists came in search of food and were freely given everything they needed.

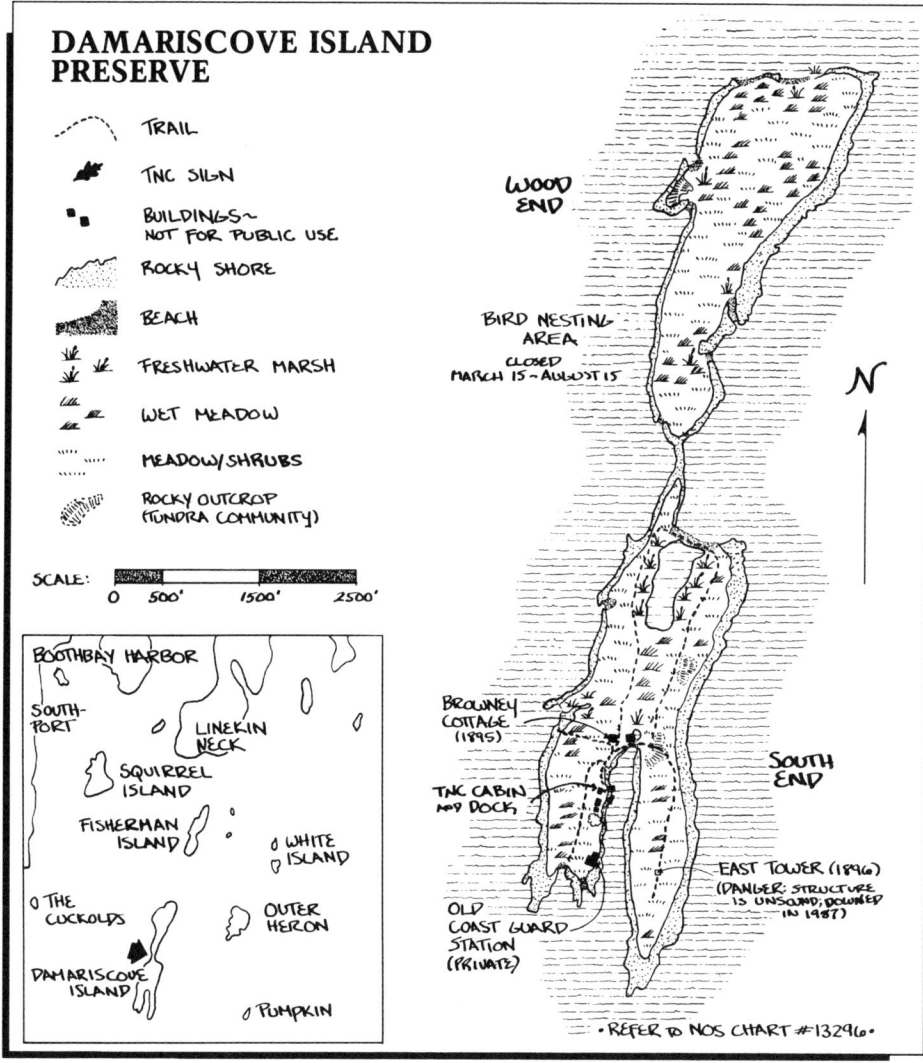

DAMARISCOVE ISLAND PRESERVE

- ˗˗˗ TRAIL
- TNC SIGN
- BUILDINGS~ NOT FOR PUBLIC USE
- ROCKY SHORE
- BEACH
- FRESHWATER MARSH
- WET MEADOW
- MEADOW/SHRUBS
- ROCKY OUTCROP (TUNDRA COMMUNITY)

SCALE: 0   500'   1500'   2500'

WOOD END

BIRD NESTING AREA
CLOSED MARCH 15~AUGUST 15

N

BOOTHBAY HARBOR
SOUTH-PORT
LINEKIN NECK
SQUIRREL ISLAND
FISHERMAN ISLAND
WHITE ISLAND
THE CUCKOLDS
OUTER HERON
DAMARISCOVE ISLAND
PUMPKIN

BROWNEY COTTAGE (1895)

TNC CABIN AND DOCK

SOUTH END

EAST TOWER (1896) (DANGER: STRUCTURE IS UNSOUND; DOWNED IN 1987)

OLD COAST GUARD STATION (PRIVATE)

• REFER TO NOS CHART #13296 •

For the next 300 years, with some interruptions during the King Phillip's War and the Revolutionary War, the islanders made a steady living fishing and farming. In 1896, the Coast Guard built a lifesaving station on the island's southwestern tip. In the early part of the 20th century, the island's farm supplied milk and fresh produce to the summer colonies nearby.

In 1939, the last family left the island; 20 years later the last year-round fisherman departed, and the Coast Guard decommissioned the lifesaving station. Left to the incessant ocean winds, the abandoned farm buildings disintegrated. The pastures and fields, once shorn to the ground by cattle and sheep, grew up into moors of fragrant wild rose, bayberry and grasses.

Damariscove can legitimately be considered Maine's earliest permanent settlement. The entire island was designated a National Historic Landmark in 1978.

Much to the surprise and interest of ecologists, Damariscove's vegetation has not reverted to forest since the pastures were abandoned. Although there is a clump of willows near the harbor, and a few dwarfed apple trees, the island shows no sign of becoming "covered with noble evergreens," as it was in the 17th century.

Bayberry and steeplebush are the most common plants, but botanists have found more than 300 species on the island. Wild roses grow profusely along the old stone walls; cranberries and rose pogonias inhabit the wetter spots. Typical coastal tundra vegetation, including fragile lichens and mosses, grows on the plentiful exposed granite and gneiss bedrock ledges.

Every spring, up to 1,000 pairs of common eiders return to nest on Wood End, the northern end of the island. They are joined by black guillemots, greater black-backed gulls, and herring gulls. Wood End was covered with spruce until it burned in the 1890s. It has become an ideal seabird nesting ground with grassy, shrubby slopes.

More than 150 bird species have been spotted on Damariscove. Ospreys frequently fish just offshore. The island's large pond, a rare resource on coastal islands, attracts a wide variety of seabirds in summer and migratory birds in spring and fall. Snowy owls regularly winter on the island.

Damariscove is also home to a large population of muskrats that have adapted successfully to life in a largely non-aquatic, upland habitat. The muskrats' runs crisscross the fields everywhere.

Today, Damariscove's only human inhabitants are a few fishermen who occasionally stay on the island, and the owners of the Coast Guard lifesaving station. They help the Conservancy look after the island.

In 1966, Mr. and Mrs. K.L. Parker donated Damariscove Island to the Conservancy.

 During the summer, Conservancy caretakers help protect the island and assist visitors. There is a well-marked trail system and a Conservancy dock. Trail brochures and other materials are available on the island.

In many places, especially on the open ledges, the vegetation cannot survive trampling. Please stay on the trails or on the rocky shore. The Coast Guard Lifesaving Station is privately owned; the stone wharf and other dilapidated structures on the island are unsound, unsafe and off limits.

Although camping on the island is not allowed, it is fine to stay in the harbor for the night. Please consider the neighbors when anchoring.

The northern end of the island is a nesting sanctuary and is closed to the public during the March 15 to August 15 nesting season.

DIRECTIONS: Damariscove is approximately seven miles from Boothbay Harbor. The harbor entrance is guarded by a set of notorious ledges called The Motions, and a submerged ledge. Consult the chart carefully. Plan to bring a dinghy for landing.

Musquash Pond Preserve

205 acres, Jefferson

The unspoiled ponds and wetlands of Musquash Pond Preserve attract many species of waterfowl and songbirds. The quiet woods and pond shores offer an interesting and pleasant walk.

Touching on three ponds and crisscrossed by their drainages, Musquash Pond Preserve contains a wide variety of habitats ranging from freshwater wetlands to forested uplands. The scenic, undeveloped pond shores offer excellent bird watching, especially for warblers and waterfowl.

The western and eastern sections of the preserve, Dyer Neck and Musquash Pond, are separated by a large swampy area that is passable only when frozen.

Dense swamp, dominated by shrubs such as winterberry, mountain holly and alder, lines the shores of Dyer, Long and Flood ponds. In a small section of the western shore of Musquash Pond, tamarack, leather leaf, Labrador tea and other bog species grow in a mat of sphagnum moss.

The forest is a patchwork, reflecting the varied topography and past land use. Ecologists have identified a dozen different forest types here, including red maple and black ash swamp; stands of hemlock and white pine; and rich hardwoods with white ash, hop hornbeam (ironwood) and yellow birch—as well as the familiar eastern deciduous forest of red oak, maple and beech.

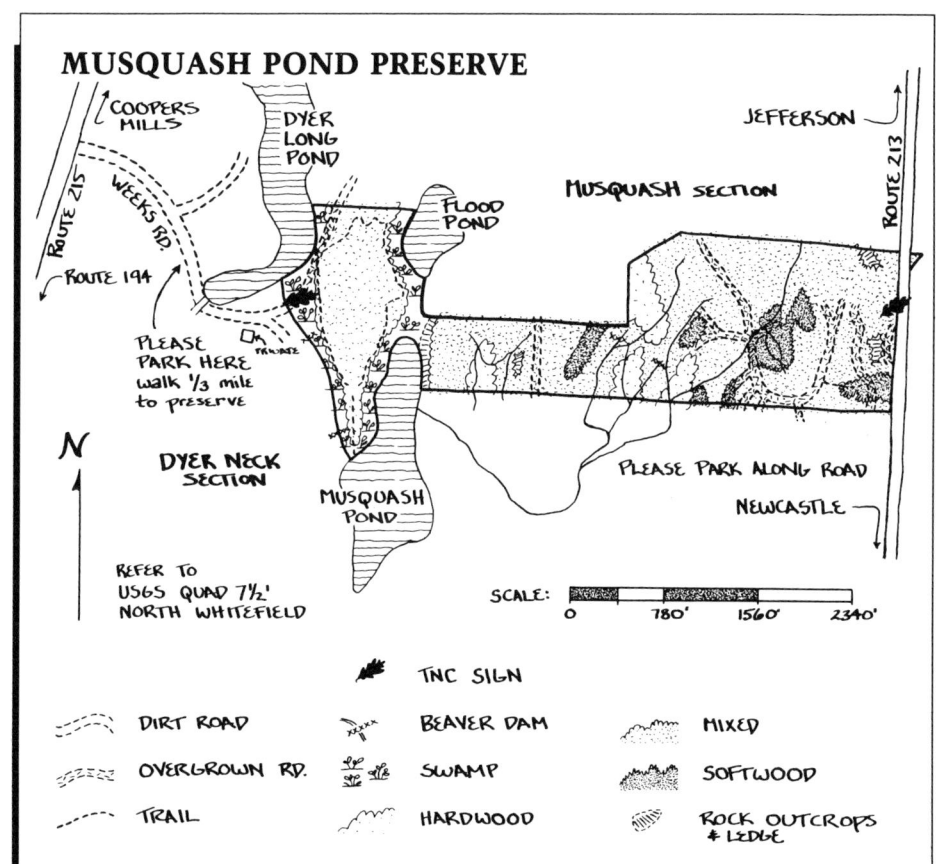

MUSQUASH POND PRESERVE

COOPERS MILLS
DYER LONG POND
JEFFERSON
ROUTE 215
WEEKS RD.
ROUTE 194
FLOOD POND
MUSQUASH SECTION
ROUTE 213
PLEASE PARK HERE walk 1/3 mile to preserve
N
DYER NECK SECTION
PLEASE PARK ALONG ROAD
NEWCASTLE
MUSQUASH POND
REFER TO USGS QUAD 7½' NORTH WHITEFIELD
SCALE: 0   780'   1560'   2340'

TNC SIGN
DIRT ROAD   BEAVER DAM   MIXED
OVERGROWN RD.   SWAMP   SOFTWOOD
TRAIL   HARDWOOD   ROCK OUTCROPS & LEDGE

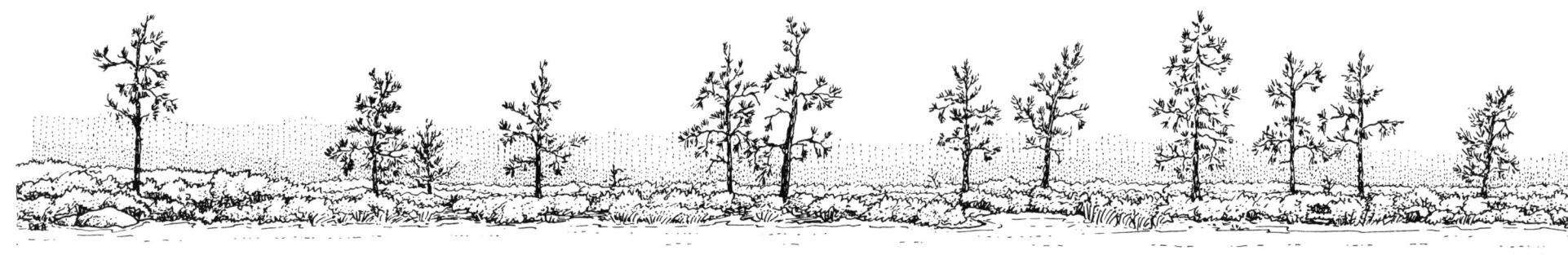

The land was farmed until the turn of the century. Stone walls and abandoned roads run throughout the property. Over the years, the area was also selectively logged. A mill was located on Dyer Neck near the old county road to Wiscasset.

Dyer Neck was donated to the Conservancy in 1975 by Mr. and Mrs. Richard Saltonstall, Jr. Two years later, their neighbors, Mr. and Mrs. Harry Edelson, added their land, expanding the preserve to its current size. A longtime Conservancy supporter, Richard Saltonstall served as Maine Chapter board vice-chairman for several years.

Dyer Neck, the western portion of the preserve, is the most easily accessible. At one time, a maintained trail looped around the height of land, passing through the different wetland and pond shore natural communities. The trail is no longer easy to find, but it is possible to explore the woods and pond shores without following it. The woods on the eastern side, of Musquash Pond are laced with overgrown logging roads, none of which are maintained. The preserve is ideal habitat for mosquitoes; bug dope is highly recommended. During hunting season, please take the necessary precautions.

DIRECTIONS: Dyer Neck section: Heading south on Route 215 in Jefferson, go three miles past the intersection with Route 126, turn left onto Weeks Road (dirt, unmarked). Take a sharp right back down the hill opposite the Trask Lawn Cemetery, and bear right at the fork. Park just before the bridge and walk into the preserve (about a third of a mile). A welcome sign is posted at the preserve entrance. Musquash Pond section: Heading south on Route 213 from the Jefferson Town House (Jct. Routes 126/213), go three miles. The preserve, marked by a small TNC sign, is on the right. Please park along Route 213.

ICE-OUT In early spring, skunk cabbages push their way up through the still-frozen swamp by melting the surrounding ice with their own heat. The plants smell like rotting meat, all the better to attract the first flies of the year to pollinate their flowers.

Rachel Carson Salt Pond Preserve and La Verna Preserve

La Verna, 119 acres, Bristol;
Salt Pond, 70 acres, New Harbor

The quarter-acre Rachel Carson Salt Pond, named for the renowned conservationist and author who helped found the Maine Chapter, is an ideal place to observe the life of the sea. La Verna's rugged shore offers a quiet spot to enjoy the view across Muscongus Bay.

Rachel Carson Salt Pond

The retreating tide exposes most of the quarter-acre Salt Pond, making it an excellent place to study intertidal and subtidal life. At the upper reaches of the tide, the gray rocks are covered with barnacles and flat, brownish-green rockweed. Below this, long, slippery fronds of knotted wrack blanket the shore. Hidden under the cool, moist weed and in the waters remaining in the pool are blue mussels, hermit and green crabs. Rough, common and smooth periwinkles graze on the rock algae and weeds. Common starfish and green sea urchins can be spotted at the lowest tides. Careful observation will reveal dozens of other inhabitants, from juvenile fish to predatory dogwinkles.

Rachel Carson gathered some of the material for her book, *The Edge of the Sea*, at the Salt Pond. The preserve was dedicated to her in 1970.

Inland from the Salt Pond, the preserve includes fields and forest that were originally part of Danforth Farm. For the past century the farmland has gradually reverted to woods.

The Salt Pond was donated to the Conservancy in 1966 by Helen Williams and her sisters, Elizabeth Gardner and Anne Hinners. The following year, Robert and Helen Search donated the upland portion.

A guide to the geology and beach features of the Salt Pond is available from the Maine Chapter office.

 The Salt Pond is a perfect place to explore. However, be careful on the slick seaweed. Please do not throw rocks or carry them away. The inhabitants of the tide pool will fare better if they are disturbed as little as possible. Please return all creatures, rocks and other elements to their original places.

A trail and old logging roads traverse the upland section of the preserve. The trail begins across Route 32 from the parking lot. A brochure is available at the preserve registration box.

DIRECTIONS: The Salt Pond parking area is on the bay side of Route 32, about a mile north of New Harbor. Please park in the lot and use the steps to the beach to prevent further erosion of the shoreline.

La Verna

The La Verna Preserve protects some 3,600 feet of rugged shore on Muscongus Bay, as well as coniferous forest, swamp, freshwater marsh and overgrown farmland.

Steeply sloping ledges near Brown's Head contrast with a gravel beach at Leighton's Cove. The variations in the texture and form of the rock are impressive: the layered, folded rocks are frequently intruded by granite dikes and sills. Sundews and mountain sandwort grow near small springs and freshwater seeps in the rocks.

The southern section is dominated by dense 60-to 100-year-old white and red spruce. Along the western edge, a tamarack swamp borders on Tibbitts Pond. In the center the forest is more open, with cellar holes and stone walls remaining from earlier settlements. In the northern section, red oaks and white birches mix with the spruces and white pines.

Many birds, including ospreys, nest at La Verna. Many more species pass through on migration. The woods are also excellent habitat for deer and small mammals.

Miss Elizabeth Hoyt and her sister, Mrs. Anna Mavor, donated two portions of preserve on the condition that the Conservancy raise the money to buy the rest. Chapter volunteers completed the acquisition in 1965.

A trail leads to the shore through the southern section. Dogs are absolutely not allowed on the preserve or the private road leading to it through the neighbors' sheep pastures.

DIRECTIONS: Heading north on Route 32, go three miles past New Harbor to Tibbitts Road, a gravel road on the right, opposite the "North Country" sheep barn. This road is private, so cars must be left along Route 32. Walk the half mile in to the preserve. Keep to the right at the turn-around. The trail begins just before the pond and is marked with a TNC welcome sign.

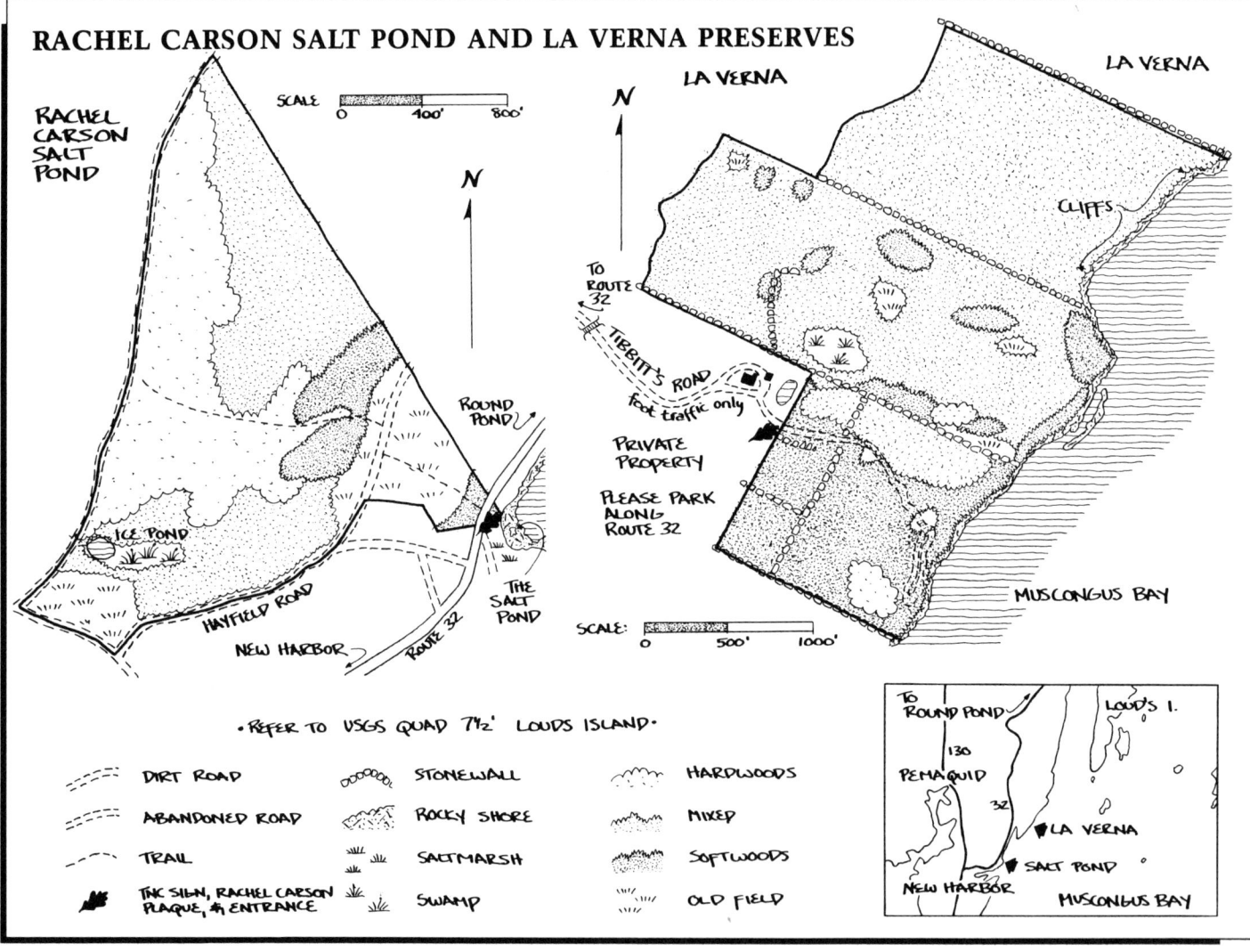

RACHEL CARSON SALT POND AND LA VERNA PRESERVES

The Brothers and Hay Ledge Preserve

12 acres, St. George

The dense, stunted vegetation on the Brothers and Hay Ledge offers ideal habitat for nesting sea birds such as black guillemots, common eiders, double-crested cormorants, and herring and greater black-backed gulls.

The Brothers and Hay Ledge, four small, treeless islands, lie a mile off Port Clyde. Exposed to the open waters of lower Penobscot Bay, the islands are battered by winter winds and storm tides. They are wild and isolated: just the kind of environment sought by nesting seabirds.

Laughing gulls, common terns and arctic terns, species in decline along the Maine coast, once nested here. In the past few decades, a dramatic increase in the numbers of very competitive herring and greater black-backed gulls has contributed to a steady reduction in the number of tern colonies.

Currently, black guillemots, double-crested cormorants, and common eiders, as well as herring and greater black-backed gulls, nest on the islands. The Brothers and Hay Ledge are listed on the state Register of Critical Areas for their nesting colonies.

The islands are not large. Together, the Brothers add up to only five acres. Big Brother and tiny "Baby" Brother are connected at low tide, but separated from Little Brother by a 10- to 12-foot wide channel. Six-acre Hay Ledge is about 400 feet southeast of the Brothers.

Constant exposure to wind and waves hinders the accumulation of soil and limits the vegetation to grasses, herbs and dense shrubs. The sole tree is one stunted white spruce that has managed to survive on Little Brother. The birds find ideal nest sites in the cover provided by the thick grasses and shrubs.

All four islands are gentle domes of coarse-grained, dark granite. The bedrock appears to be peeling off in layers like an onion, a process known as exfoliation. This phenomenon is clearly visible around the perimeters of Big and Little Brothers.

Aside from occasional recreational use, there seems to have been little human activity on the islands in the past. Only Little Brother shows signs of previous exploitation; drilling holes and cutting scars on its western shore indicate some quarrying.

The Brothers and Hay Ledge were donated to the Conservancy in 1979 by Mrs. Roscoe Hupper.

Nesting islands: closed to the public during the March 15 to August 15 nesting season. Please do not harass the nesting seabirds by landing on the islands or lingering offshore. Disturbances may result in serious nest losses.

At other times of the year, it is possible to land on the islands and walk around.

DIRECTIONS: In light seas, a small boat can be landed on the sheltered, shallow and rock-studded cove on the northern shore of Big Brother. Watch out for submerged and intertidal ledges, and keep an eye on the tide and shifting currents.

Harbor Seal (Alan Hutchinson)

Penobscot Bay Region

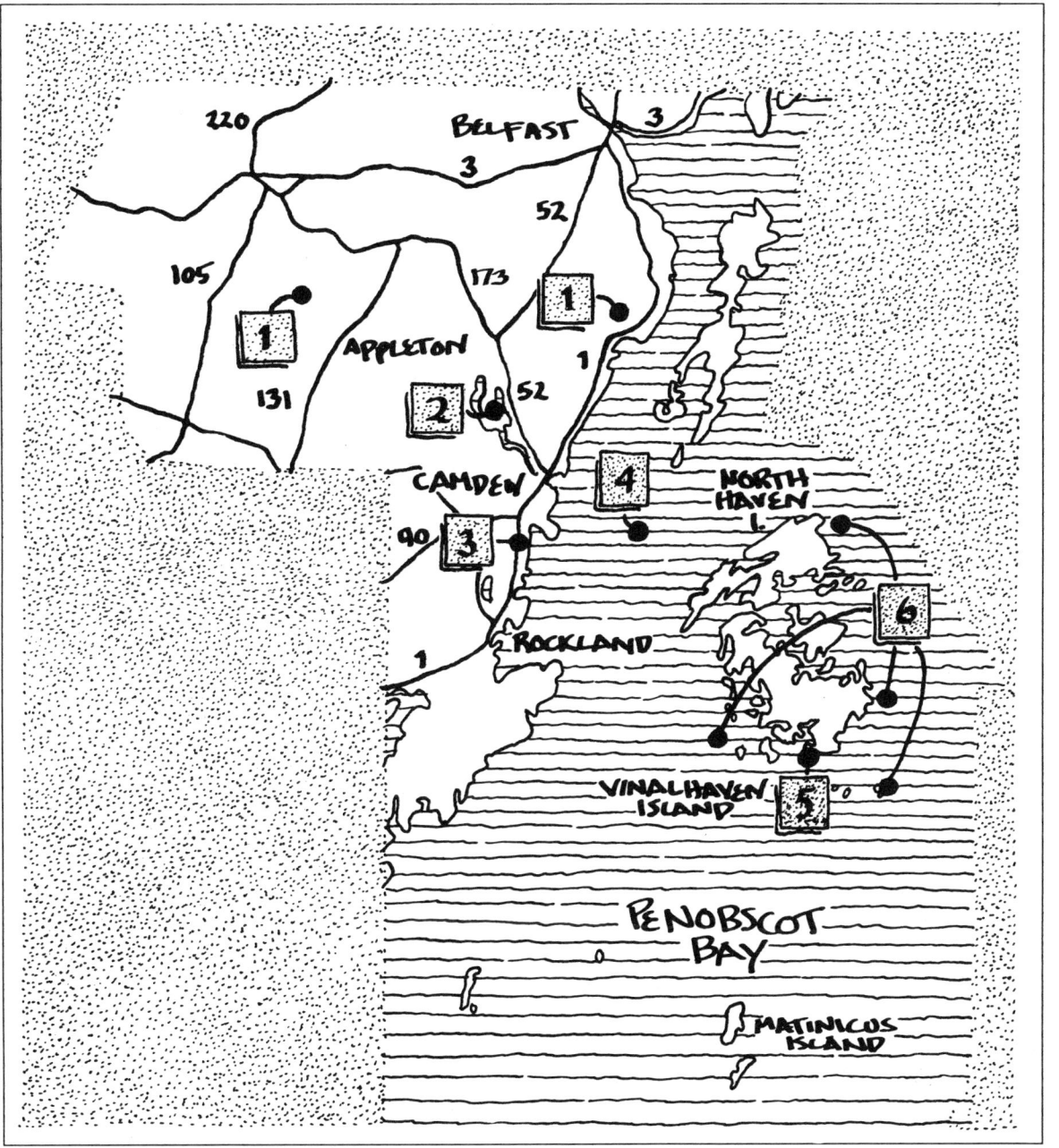

Penobscot Bay Region

slands big and small are scattered in clusters throughout the broad reach of Penobscot Bay. Nine are Conservancy preserves; three more are protected by easements held by the Conservancy. All of the Conservancy islands are near North Haven and Vinalhaven in the middle of the bay. Their landscapes vary from the open moors on Lane's Island Preserve (Vinalhaven) to spruce-fir forest on Big Garden Island Preserve (Vinalhaven). (*Please note*: the islands of East Penobscot Bay are included in the Deer Isle region.)

Many of the islands share a common history of sheep. Although they may have been covered with trees when the first settlers arrived, they were soon cleared and used for many years afterward as naturally fenced pastures.

The island preserves have not been grazed for decades. They are still largely open, but are now covered with a tangle of briers, shrubs and grasses that suit nesting seabirds like common eiders perfectly.

Along the coast of Maine, boats planked in cedar tie up next to wharves resting on cedar pilings, near houses sided with cedar shingles. Cedar fence posts line the fields; under the grass, cedar coffins contain the remains of the departed. The wood is legendary for its ability to withstand rot, and the demand for it has continued unabated over the centuries.

One of Maine's three cedar species, Atlantic white cedar, reaches its northern limit in the state. The species was once common throughout its range along the Atlantic coastal plain. Today, after years of logging and clearing, untouched stands of any significant size are rarely found.

Two of Maine's largest remaining stands of Atlantic white cedar grow near the western shore of Penobscot Bay, in Appleton Bog Preserve (Appleton) and bordering St. Clair Preserve on Knight's Pond. Appleton Bog and its cedars are difficult to see without a knowledgeable guide. The cedars on Knight's Pond are in an open bog near the northwestern shore and can be easily seen from the water.

A tree species far more threatened than the Atlantic white cedar, the American chestnut, survives in a grove protected by the Conservancy, at the Harkness Preserve in Rockport.

A century ago, the American chestnut was one of the largest and most common trees in the East, ranging from Maine to Ontario down to Kansas and Alabama. By 1915, large numbers of trees in New York City, Philadelphia and northern New Jersey had been destroyed by an introduced fungal parasite. Within decades, nearly all of the chestnuts were gone. Remarkably, most of the trees at the Harkness Preserve have escaped infection. Researchers are studying them to learn their secret and to develop new ways to treat the disease.

Most of the Conservancy preserves in the region are open for careful day use. The exceptions are: Appleton Bog (which is essentially impassable), the Harkness Preserve (whose chestnuts are very susceptible to damage), and two nesting islands that are closed from March 15 to August 15, Mark and Little Brimstone.

Fernald's Neck Preserve, a wooded peninsula on Lake Megunticook, was saved from development by a group of local people who bought it and transferred it to the Conservancy. Harkness, St. Clair and Simonton Corner Quarry preserves were donated, as were portions of Appleton Bog. Eight of the Conservancy's nine island preserves in the region were also gifts from their owners. Vinalhaven's residents acquired the remaining island, Lane's Island, to keep it from being developed, then transferred it to the Conservancy.

The Conservancy's partners in the Penobscot Bay Region include local land trusts and the Hurricane Island Outward Bound School. The Conservancy has also helped with projects like the state wildlife refuge at Hurd's Pond in Swanville.

The Nature Conservancy's preserves in the Penobscot Bay region are taken care of by several volunteer stewardship committees. For more information, please contact the Maine Chapter stewardship office in Topsham.

Appleton Bog Preserve and St. Clair Preserve

Appleton Bog, 85 acres, Appleton;
St. Clair, 304 acres, Northport

Atlantic white cedar, a species threatened throughout its range on the eastern seaboard, finds sanctuary on the Penobscot Bay coast in two very different landscapes: the deep woods of Appleton Bog and the open shore of Knight's Pond at St. Clair Preserve.

Appleton Bog

The Atlantic white cedar stand at Appleton Bog is one of the northernmost occurrences of this species in North America. It shares this honor with a stand at Knight's Pond in Northport, the site of the Conservancy's St. Clair Preserve. Extensive logging and land development have caused a severe decline in the abundance of Atlantic white cedar, and undisturbed stands are now rare throughout the species' range along the Atlantic coastal plain. Appleton Bog is one of just a handful of extensive stands remaining in Maine. It has been designated a National Natural Landmark and is on the state Register of Critical Areas.

Pure cedar stands, such as those on the Conservancy preserve, cover more than 200 acres at Appleton Bog. In some areas there are more than 4,350 trees per acre. The trees average six to 16 inches in diameter, and reach 60 feet in height.

The dense canopy of cedar prevents the growth of shrubs. However, a variety of shade-loving herbaceous plants resides on the hummocks at the base of the trees. Royal and cinnamon ferns as well as bog species such as insectivorous sundews and pitcher plants grow in a carpet of sphagnum moss.

The hollows between the hummocks are underwater much of the time. New hummocks form where trees have fallen. Seedlings become established on the drier hummocks and flourish in the sunlit openings, continuing the cycle of the forest.

The wet areas between the cedar swamp and uplands, known as laggs, are filled with black spruce, tamarack, and northern white cedar mixed with shrubs such as rhodora, winterberry and high-bush blueberry.

At the southern end of the cedar swamp lies The Pool, a small, open, quaking bog populated with orchids, Virginia chain fern and cottongrass. Newbert Pond, at the northern end, contains a pondweed, *Potamogeton confervoides*, officially listed as threatened by the state. It is found at only three other sites in Maine. The pool and pond are on private property, but the owners have agreed to work with the Conservancy to protect the areas and the plants found there.

In the mid-19th century, most of the bog was owned by the Stover family. Jacob Stover ran a sawmill nearby, but cut only enough for his immediate needs and took trees from outside the bog proper. Although there are stumps scattered throughout the bog and a few acres were cut in the 1950s, Appleton Bog's cedars have escaped heavy cutting.

Today the ownership of the bog is fragmented, but the cedar swamp remains largely intact. In 1973, one of the Maine Chapter's founders, Miss Dorothea Marston, acquired an 85-acre parcel for the Conservancy. She saw this narrow strip across the middle of the bog as the first step toward protection of the entire area, an effort that is still actively underway.

 Appleton Bog is not suited to casual visits. The cedar swamp is dense and wet. The few old paths that exist are indistinct and not always complete or logical, making it easy to become lost. There are no trails on the Conservancy preserve. The best way to see the bog is to go with a guide on one of the Chapter's periodic field trips.

St. Clair

The St. Clair Preserve protects nearly all of the shore of pristine Knight's Pond. Although located within earshot of the hum of traffic on Route One, the area is remarkably unspoiled. The pond borders on one of Maine's few substantial stands of Atlantic white cedar. The stand is listed on the state Register of Critical Areas. Except for the bogs, swamps and wettest lowlands, the area around Knight's Pond was farmed in the 19th century. The uplands have now grown up into woods. Spruce and fir tend to dominate the steeper slopes, while mixed woods of beech, red oak, paper birch and sugar maple cover the gentler slopes at lower elevations. The age of the woods varies from young "doghair" spruce and cedar to older stands with spruces up to two feet in diameter. Apple, black cherry and white pine grow along the old stone walls.

On the southwestern shore, Ducktrap Mountain rises up from the pond shore to more than 700 feet. The mountainside is steep and forested with mixed woods.

According to tradition, the Ducktrap area got its name because the Indians waited for ducks to settle in the narrows of the river that drains Knight's Pond, then flushed the birds into nets.

An open bog borders the pond's upper shore and the channel connecting Knight's with Pitcher Pond. Atlantic white cedars are scattered on the bog's hummocks of sphagnum moss, joined by sweet gale, leatherleaf, steeplebush, bog cranberry and rushes. Unlike the dense stands of cedars at Appleton Bog, the trees here are dwarfed and widely scattered.

Black bears, bobcats, fishers, foxes, deer and very possibly wolves and coyotes find open country in the preserve. Loons nest at the edge of the pond; hawks, ravens, ospreys and kingfishers regularly visit its shores.

The eastern portion of the preserve was part of the original Muscongus Grant made by King Charles in 1629. For a time, the land was owned by Revolutionary War General Knox. In the mid-1800s, there were three houses on the property, and most of the land had already been cleared for fields and pasture by the Knight family. The Knights farmed the land for more than a century. After they abandoned the farm, the land was divided up and left fallow.

Cary Bok acquired the eastern portion in the late 1940s with the idea of returning it to farmland. He later changed his plans, and donated the land to the Conservancy in 1962. The preserve is named in honor of his caretaker, Eugene St. Clair.

In 1988, a Swiss couple bought 52 acres on the western shore of Knight's Pond from a developer, then donated the land to the Conservancy as an addition to the St. Clair Preserve.

  Both shores of the preserve are easily reached by canoe, beginning at the town landing near the lower end of Knight's Pond.

The eastern portion of the preserve is bisected by Knight's Pond Road, which is passable by car as far as the town landing. A trail leading to the pond leaves the road on the right, slightly more than a half mile before the town landing. On the western shore, an unmaintained woods road follows along the pond shore at the base of Ducktrap Mountain.

DIRECTIONS: From Route One in Northport, turn left on Beech Hill Road. Go about two and half miles, then turn left on Knight's Pond Road and follow it until it ends at the town landing.

Fernald's Neck Preserve

315 acres, Camden and Lincolnville

The peaceful forest and shores of Fernald's Neck Preserve on Lake Megunticook offer a pleasant afternoon's walk. The preserve protects more than three miles of unspoiled shoreline, and an interesting array of woodland and wetland habitats.

Heavily wooded Fernald's Neck Preserve includes more than three miles of frontage on Lake Megunticook. Its uninterrupted forests and 60-foot shoreline cliffs are especially impressive when viewed from the water.

On the northwestern portion of the preserve, the forest is predominately white and red pines and hemlock. Toward the south, the forest becomes more open and varied, with red oak, white birch and beech mixed in with the conifers. In summer the 11-acre hayfield at the entrance of the preserve is dotted with cow vetch, clovers, hawkweed and blue-eyed grass.

A large wetland at the center of the preserve supports bog species such as pitcher plant, rose pogonia, blue flag iris, and a variety of sedges, grasses and rushes. Aquatic plants such as pipewort, arrowhead, bur-reed and bulrush grow along the highly indented lake shore.

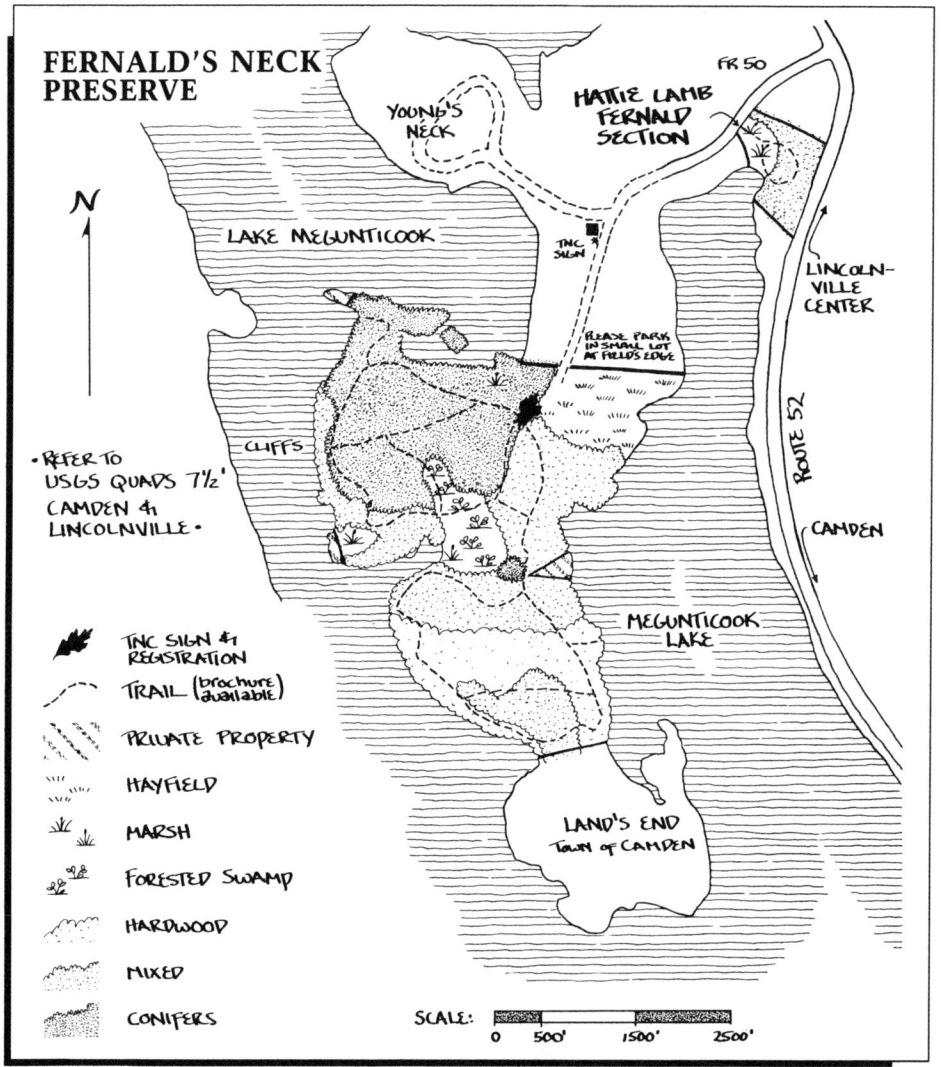

FERNALD'S NECK PRESERVE

N

YOUNG'S NECK

HATTIE LAMB FERNALD SECTION

FR 50

LAKE MEGUNTICOOK

TNC SIGN

LINCOLN-VILLE CENTER

PLEASE PARK IN SMALL LOT AT FIELD'S EDGE

ROUTE 52

CLIFFS

CAMDEN

• REFER TO USGS QUADS 7½' CAMDEN & LINCOLNVILLE •

MEGUNTICOOK LAKE

TNC SIGN & REGISTRATION

TRAIL (brochure available)

PRIVATE PROPERTY

HAYFIELD

MARSH

LAND'S END TOWN OF CAMDEN

FORESTED SWAMP

HARDWOOD

MIXED

CONIFERS

SCALE: 0 500' 1500' 2500'

Deer and moose occasionally find refuge in the dense interior, and a variety of small mammals live in the woods and fields. Bass, pickerel, trout, smelt, perch and land-locked salmon make Lake Megunticook popular with fishermen.

The property that is now Fernald's Neck Preserve was owned by the Fernald family from 1806 until 1969. They kept the land in woodlots, pastures and cultivated fields. In the past half century the open land has gradually returned to forest. Log loading ramps, abandoned farm implements, and stone walls are all that remain from the Fernald farm.

The natural beauty of Fernald's Neck has long been appreciated. When developers expressed an interest in the property in 1969, local residents quickly raised the money to buy the land, then transferred it to the Conservancy. Margaretta Thurlow donated a separate 30-acre section in memory of her mother, Hattie Lamb Fernald.

The Megunticook Lake Association works to preserve water quality in the lake, and has hired a warden who helps monitor Fernald's Neck. The town of Camden owns the tip of the neck and manages the land as a park accessible only by water.

A well-marked system of trails was laid out by students of the Chewonki Foundation in 1980. The trails meander through the preserve, offering striking views from the cliffs on the western shore and plenty of opportunity to enjoy the quiet woods. There are three privately owned inholdings in the preserve; please keep on the trails and on Conservancy property. A trail brochure is available at the preserve entrance.

DIRECTIONS: By land: Coming north from Camden on Route 52, turn left at FR 50, just past Youngtown Corner. The Hattie Lamb Fernald Section is on the left, about a third of a mile in from the road. To reach the main section, continue on this road (which changes to dirt), bearing left at the fork. Continue past the farmhouse at the end of the road to the small parking lot. Please do not drive any farther into the field. A small Conservancy sign at the edge of the woods marks the entrance; follow the path to a welcome sign and registration box. By water: There is a public landing on the southern shore of Lake Megunticook, just off Route 52.

QUIET Whenever she feels in need of a break, volunteer preserve steward Margaretta Thurlow likes to go for a walk in the preserve. "I like to listen to the silences," she says. "Silences include sounds...the wind in the pine trees...it's a very refreshing place to be."

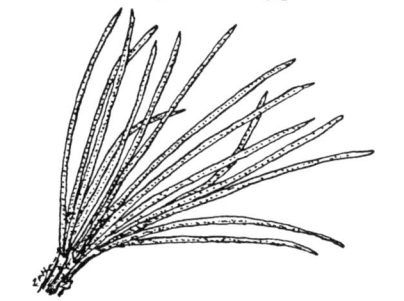

Harkness Preserve

5 acres, Rockport

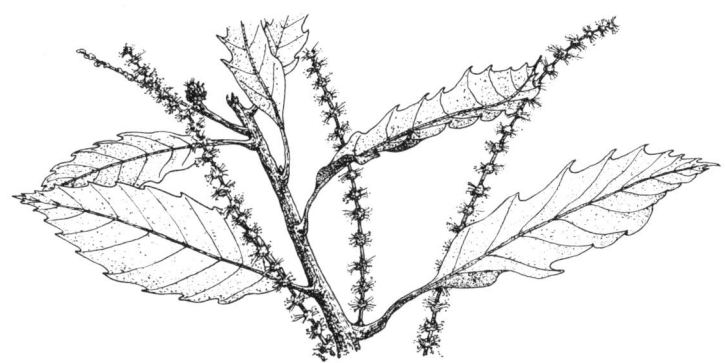

Biologists are studying the small stand of American chestnuts at the Harkness Preserve in order to find ways to help protect the species from the blight that decimated it earlier in this century and that continues to kill the majority of young chestnuts.

In the early part of this century, a fungal blight brought from China or Japan virtually eliminated the American chestnut throughout its natural range in North America. Once one of the most striking and valuable of American hardwoods, the stately chestnut disappeared in a few decades.

The blight enters the tree through wounds in the bark, then eventually kills the tree by interfering with its nutrient transport system. Chestnuts readily sprout from the stump, even those killed by the blight, but the sprouts rarely reach maturity.

The tiny Harkness Preserve protects a small stand of American chestnuts that are remarkably healthy. Most of the trees are yet unaffected by the blight and therefore are of great interest to scientists because they may have a special resistance to the blight. The few trees that have succumbed have become the subject of experiments designed to develop an effective treatment. A "vaccine" that would make it possible to inoculate healthy chestnuts against the blight appears promising.

The preserve is densely wooded, with few openings. The chestnuts grow in the northern portion, where the ground is gently sloping and marked with hummocks, wind-throws and intermittent streams. Much of the area is poorly drained and swampy. Striped maple, aspen, balsam fir and sugar maple make up the rest of the forest.

On the south side of Ott Brook, the land rises steeply and becomes rockier before gradually leveling off. The well-drained soils support mature oaks and maples, with a few white pines that emerge above the broad leaf canopy.

The ground cover is thick, with heart-leaved aster, bush honeysuckle and Canada mayflower. Wild sarsaparilla, clintonia, star flower, tall meadow rue and bunchberry occur frequently, along with sensitive, cinnamon, interrupted and bracken ferns.

Stone walls along the two property lines once bordered pastures, but it has been more than a century since the land was grazed.

The Harkness Preserve was donated to the Conservancy in 1966 by Mr. and Mrs. Ambrose Cramer.

 Because the chestnuts can be easily damaged and made more susceptible to the blight fungus, visitors are discouraged from entering the preserve. It is possible to see and enjoy the trees from Spruce Street.

DIRECTIONS: From Route One in Rockport, turn right on Pascal Street, right on School Street, then finally right on Spruce Street.

Mark Island Preserve

36 acres, West Penobscot Bay (unorganized)

Bald eagles nest on Mark Island, which lies by itself in the open waters of West Penobscot Bay. Unlike most of the bay's islands, Mark Island has a sizable hardwood forest in addition to spruce and fir.

In the fall it becomes clear that Mark Island is different. Its hardwood forest of giant sugar maple, yellow birch, American beech and red oak provides a brilliant contrast to the dark green spruce-fir forests that typically cover the rest of the islands in Penobscot Bay. For most of the year, Mark Island's hardwoods are screened by a band of spruce and fir, but when the weather turns chilly, the island's secret is revealed.

It is unusual to find such a vigorous and undisturbed hardwood forest on an island this far north. The island's reasonably sheltered location at the tip of the Islesboro chain may be one factor. Its geology provides another clue: the bedrock is apparently cleft along vertical planes, creating many crevices. Organic materials build up in the weathered cracks, creating soils that are more fertile, much deeper and better drained than those of most of Maine's offshore islands. Also, Mark Island's indented, rugged coast and paucity of level ground have discour-

aged human use. The island was never inhabited or used for grazing, and the hardwood forest has grown undisturbed for generations.

Until recently, Mark Island's hardwood forest was home to a thriving nesting colony of great blue herons. The heronry grew quickly from a dozen nests in 1975 to a high of approximately 80 nests four years later. In 1982, a pair of bald eagles took up residence on the island. By 1983, it appeared that most of the herons had moved to a new site, not uncharacteristic behavior for these birds. The return of eagles to the island may have precipitated the move, but the relationship of herons and eagles is still not well understood. Ospreys also nest on the island.

Mark Island was donated to the Conservancy in 1969 by Mr. and Mrs. Garrison Norton.

 Nesting island: closed to the public during the March 15 to August 15 nesting season. Please do not harass the bald eagles or great blue herons by landing on the island or lingering offshore.

During the rest of the year, it is possible to land at low tide on the small cobble beach on the northeastern tip, but beware of submerged rocks. The high, imposing shoreline is somewhat discouraging.

Mark Island figures prominently in panoramic views from Camden or the top of Mount Battie in Camden Hills State Park.

Lane's Island Preserve

45 acres, Vinalhaven

The people of Vinalhaven joined with the Conservancy to protect Lane's Island, keeping it open and unspoiled for everyone to enjoy. The preserve offers grand views of the open ocean and pounding surf.

As the Rockland ferry enters Carver's Harbor on the southern shore of Vinalhaven, the windswept moors of Lane's Island appear to starboard in front of the dark green bulk of the Vinalhaven mainland.

Shrubs, grasses and ferns cover nearly all of Lane's Island. The few clumps of spruce stand conspicuously exposed on the open land. Fire and generations of grazing sheep have kept the trees back. The fires were used primarily to keep the shrubs from taking over a small cranberry bog at the center of the island.

Bayberries, blackberries, raspberries, alders, junipers, and lowbush blueberries are common. At the northern corner of the preserve, near the entrance, a small cattail marsh provides ideal nesting habitat for red-winged blackbirds. Goldenrods, asters, evening primrose, blue flag iris, beach pea, jewelweed, and three-toothed cinquefoil rim the shore.

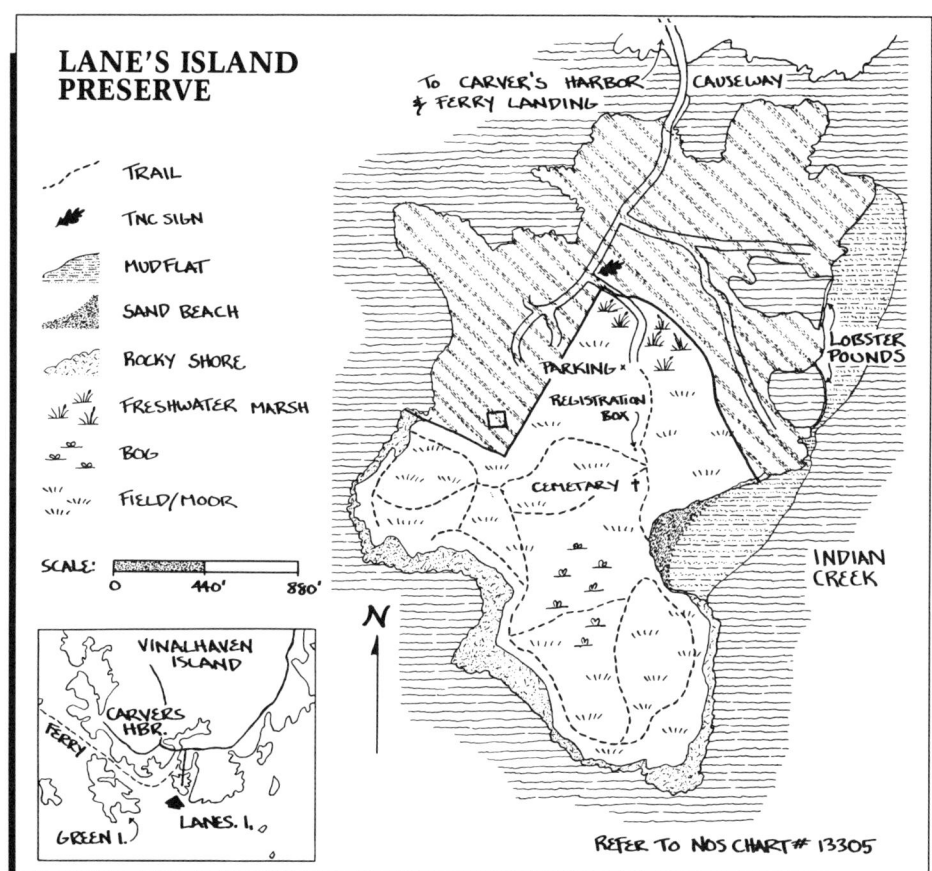

LANE'S ISLAND PRESERVE

- ∙∙∙∙∙ TRAIL
- TNC SIGN
- MUDFLAT
- SAND BEACH
- ROCKY SHORE
- FRESHWATER MARSH
- BOG
- FIELD/MOOR

SCALE: 0 440' 880'

TO CARVER'S HARBOR & FERRY LANDING • CAUSEWAY

LOBSTER POUNDS

PARKING

REGISTRATION BOX

CEMETARY

INDIAN CREEK

N

VINALHAVEN ISLAND

CARVERS HBR.

FERRY

GREEN I.

LANES. I.

REFER TO NOS CHART # 13305

The island attracts birds throughout the year. In spring and summer, spotted and least sandpipers as well as common terns, ospreys, great blue herons and little green herons visit the shore. Many songbirds breed here, including ovenbirds, savannah sparrows, black-and-white warblers and parula warblers. Merlins, kestrels, and marsh hawks patrol the island through the fall and winter. Flocks of snow buntings arrive in the fields near the shore in winter. Seabirds wintering offshore include common goldeneyes, old squaws, horned grebes, great cormorants and the occasional Bonaparte's gull.

The island's shoreline is not steep, but it is ragged and rocky, with only a few cobble and sand beaches. The surf on the exposed southern shore is often spectacular.

There are indications that Indian Creek on the eastern shore was inhabited from 4,000 B.C. to colonial times by the Susquehanna and Red Paint peoples. In the early 1800s, the tall white house on the hill was built by Captain Timothy Lane, whose monument stands in the family cemetery above the sand beach on the eastern shore. (The house and surrounding land are not part of the Conservancy preserve.)

SHEEP AND ISLANDS The number of islands named Sheep and Cow, not to mention Ram, Ewe and Hog, gives a good indication of the historic importance of Maine's offshore islands as convenient pastures. In a tradition that is continued today by a few farmers, the animals were ferried out for a summer of uninterrupted grazing. Sheep raised in the fogs and cool breezes of the islands are reputed to have especially fine wool.

For years, residents of and visitors to Vinalhaven have enjoyed Lane's Island. The annual Vinalhaven Fourth of July picnic is held in the field near the preserve entrance.

In 1968, Lane's Island was threatened with commercial development. Determined Vinalhaven residents quickly raised the money needed to buy the southern two-thirds of the island. They transferred the property to the Conservancy to ensure that it would remain undeveloped and open to the public for quiet recreational use.

Lane's Island Preserve is 15-minute walk from the ferry landing on Vinalhaven. Numerous rough trails crisscross the preserve. Several lead to the shore and prime surf- and birdwatching spots.

DIRECTIONS: Take the Maine State Ferry from Rockland (1 hour, 15 minutes). On the island, bear right and go straight through town to the last business block and turn right at the fountain. Go past Armbrust Hill, down and over the Indian Creek causeway and a quarter of a mile to a TNC sign. Turn left at the sign and follow the road through the cattail marsh to the trails. No cars are allowed beyond the parking lot. It is possible to visit Lane's Island between morning and afternoon ferries. A car is not necessary.

Vinalhaven-North Haven Archipelago

Big Garden Island, 25 acres, Vinalhaven;
Big White Island, 25 acres, Vinalhaven (partial ownership);
Sheep Island, 25 acres, North Haven;
Smith Island, 8 acres, Vinalhaven;
Brimstone Island, 37 acres, Vinalhaven;
Little Brimstone Island, 45 acres, Vinalhaven

These six islands are arranged like satellites around the major islands of Vinalhaven and North Haven in the middle of Penobscot Bay. While sharing many common features, such as similar vegetation, each is an individual gem in its own right.

Big Garden and Big White islands

Big White and Big Garden are the two largest islands in the White Island group, located some two miles southeast of Vinalhaven.

Like many of Maine's offshore islands, the interiors of these islands are nearly impenetrable spruce-fir forest. The central stand of red spruce and balsam fir is surrounded by white spruce, which is more tolerant of salt spray.

While Big White is almost all spruce-fir forest, on Big Garden there is an old field that is now a tangle of wild roses and raspberries. Blue flag irises and evening primroses grow wherever they can find space. Blueberries abound on the extensive open ledges. Oyster leaf, beach pea, yarrow, bayberry, orache, sea blite, mountain cranberry and rugosa rose grow along the shores of both islands.

The shore of Big Garden is particularly impressive, with long, smooth granite ledges that slope down to the water. A cobble beach connects Big Garden with South Big Garden at low tide. Both islands have broad intertidal zones; Big Garden is especially known for its clam flats.

The berries on Big Garden attract an impressive number of migrating warblers. Ospreys nest on Big White.

Along with many other Penobscot Bay islands, Big Garden was quarried extensively in the 19th century. Today, the only signs of the industry that remain are a cellar hole, a stone wall, and drill marks in the ledges.

Participants in the Outward Bound Program based on nearby Hurricane Island use the islands for solo experiences. In return, they help watch over and take care of them.

Big Garden, including South Big Garden, was donated to the Conservancy in 1967 by Charles and Anne Morrow Lindbergh. Big White is only partially owned by the Conservancy. Partial interests in the island were donated to the Conservancy by the estate of Charles Cunningham in 1967 and by Austin Lamont in 1968. The other two sizable islands in the White group are privately owned. The state owns the five nearby ledges and leases them to the Conservancy for management.

Day visitors are welcome on Big Garden and Big White. There are no real trails on either island, and the dense vegetation makes the interior somewhat uninviting. It is easy to walk along the shore.

DIRECTIONS: A small boat can be pulled up in the cove between Big Garden and South Big Garden, or on the northern end of Big White. There is a relatively deep channel between Big and Little White islands. Both islands can be seen easily from the Vinalhaven ferry.

Sheep Island

According to the scanty records that remain, the inhabitants of North Haven began grazing sheep on nearby Sheep Island in 1786. The pastures were abandoned early in this century, and are now overgrown with wild roses and cow parsnips. Thickets of staghorn sumacs and raspberries expand each year.

The rest of the island is a patchwork of typical coastal spruce-fir forest and mixed hardwood forest that is composed mainly of very old white birches and red oaks.

Boulders of North Haven volcanic greenstone, tossed and weathered for centuries, form the island's shore. There is one small cobble beach.

The island's thickly overgrown fields and forest are excellent cover for nesting songbirds. Bald eagles nesting on nearby islands use Sheep for roosting.

In 1974, Mr. and Mrs. Arnold Beveridge gave a conservation easement on the island to the Conservancy. A descendant of one of the farmers who grazed sheep on the island, Mr. Beveridge inherited Sheep Island from his sister Olive Beveridge, who bought it in 1937 to return it to the family. In 1983, Mr. and Mrs. Beveridge donated fee interest in the island to the Conservancy in memory of his sister.

 There are no trails on Sheep Island, but it is possible to walk on the shore. The fields are rough going, due to the briers.

DIRECTIONS: On good days, a small boat can be landed on the gravel beach on the western end. On days with an easterly wind, the surf pounds on the exposed shore, making access all but impossible.

Smith Island

Years of grazing by determined sheep have kept Smith Island open, although its open fields are now grown up with shoulder-high grasses and shrubs including blueberries, raspberries and rugosa roses.

Smith Island is rimmed by a wide band of rocky shore that is interrupted by two cobble beaches, and a section of 20- to 30-foot cliffs on the western shore. The island's exposed rocks show the region's geology well; the contact zone between much older sedimentary rocks and the intruding granite that also forms Vinalhaven is clearly visible.

Common eiders, black guillemots, and common and arctic terns frequent the nearby waters. Minks have discouraged any nesting, aside from a small group of herring gulls and double-crested cormorants on the southeastern tip.

Smith Island was donated to the Conservancy in 1967 by Dr. and Mrs. Austin Lamont, along with a conservation easement on Coombs Neck on nearby Vinalhaven.

 There are no trails on Smith Island, but it is easy to walk around.

DIRECTIONS: Two cobble beaches on the eastern and western sides of the island offer landings for small boats.

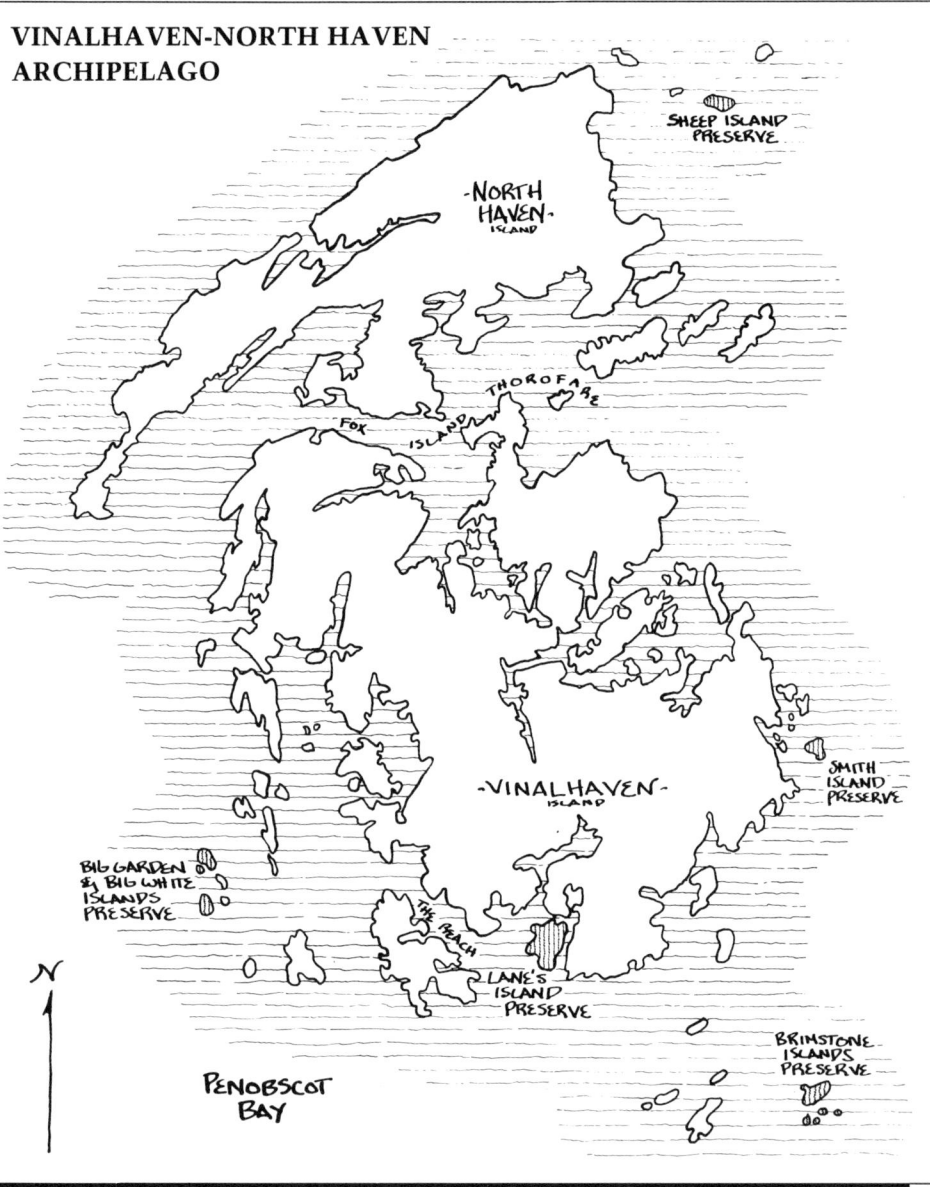

VINALHAVEN-NORTH HAVEN ARCHIPELAGO

Brimstone Islands

The Brimstone Islands lie three miles southeast of Vinalhaven, within an archipelago of five major islands and associated small islands and ledges.

The northern shore of the largest island, Brimstone, rises to a height of 112 feet and offers a tremendous view of the coast and the open ocean. This end of the island is steep; the rest of the island slopes gradually to shore ledges and two beaches of polished greenstone that gave the island its name.

Little Brimstone is directly south of Brimstone. Roughly circular in shape, it is much smaller and lower. Grasses, shrubs and wildflowers such as yarrow, blue flag iris and goldenrod cover both islands. Just a few stunted spruce cling to the shore of Brimstone Island.

Hundreds of common eiders, black guillemots and herring gulls nest on the Brimstones. A small colony of Leach's storm-petrels also nests on Brimstone. Seals haul out in large numbers on the offshore ledges.

Eiders, scoters, oldsquaws and cormorants winter offshore. An impressive variety of raptors, including sharp-shinned hawks, peregrine falcons, kestrels, merlins and ospreys stop by the islands during migration.

The Maine Department of Inland Fisheries and Wildlife considers the entire Brimstone archipelago to be one of the most important wildlife areas in Penobscot Bay. Both Brimstones are on the state Register of Critical Areas.

The name Brimstone was attached to the islands before the Revolutionary War. Sheep were pastured on the island from a very early time until the 1970s. There is no indication that there were ever any permanent residents, although a small cabin existed on the island at the turn of the century, probably for the use of lobstermen and duck hunters.

The Brimstone Islands were donated to the Conservancy in 1986 by three children of Alexander M. White: Alexander M. White, Jr., Sheila White English and Elinor White Montgomery in memory of their parents.

Brimstone Island has been a popular place for picnics for generations. A trail leads from the beach to the top of the island. Please leave the plants, animals and brimstones as you found them for all to enjoy.

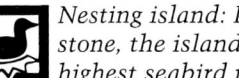 *Nesting island: Little Brimstone, the island with the highest seabird nesting density, is closed to the public during the March 15 to August 15 nesting season. Please do not harass the nesting seabirds by landing on the island or lingering offshore.*

DIRECTIONS: The best anchorage is on the northwest side of Brimstone Island, off the north beach. Those unfamiliar with the area may find the anchorage difficult; during rough weather it may be impossible to land at all.

Crockett Cove Wood Preserve (David Muench)

Deer Isle Region

1. Sheep Island and Bradbury
   Island Preserves/71
2. Crockett Cove Woods Preserve
   and Barred Island Preserve/72
3. Wreck Island and Round
   Island Preserves/74

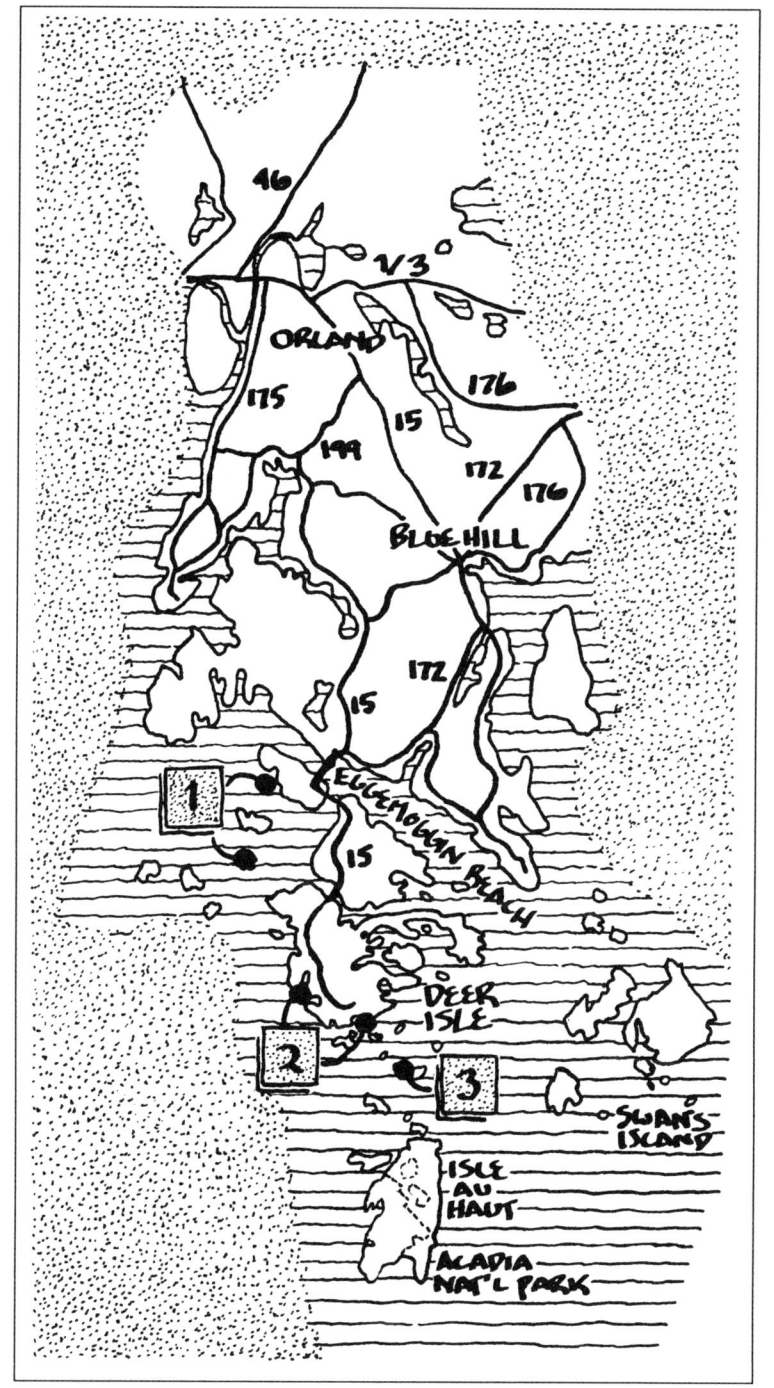

Deer Isle Region

The islands of the Deer Isle archipelago form the eastern border of Penobscot Bay. They vary from tiny, barren ledges to substantial islands with forests and fields. Some of the islands have human communities, at least in summer; many others were inhabited or served as pasture land for nearby communities in the past.

The Conservancy has responsibility for 15 islands in the Deer Isle region, five that it owns and manages as preserves and 10 that are protected by conservation easements it holds.

West of Deer Isle, Conservancy preserves include Bradbury, Sheep and Barred islands. Conservation easements safeguard Great Spruce Head Island; the southern four of the Barred Islands; Pickering Island; and Outer Scott Island. The old fields of Outer Scott are used by a sizable nesting colony of common eiders, while the island's spruce-fir forest provides suitable nesting sites for ospreys. Heavily forested Bradbury Island Preserve is home to a pair of bald eagles that also nest at times on nearby Crow Island, a small island owned by the state Bureau of Public Lands. The remaining islands are known for their scenic splendors, including the dramatic, 250-foot headland of Great Spruce Head and Pickering's 13 sand and cobble beaches.

The islands of East Penobscot Bay are the focal point of the famous and breathtaking view from Caterpillar Hill on Route 175/15 in Sedgwick.

South of Deer Isle, Wreck Island and Round Island preserves are a study in contrasts: the former still with a working sheep pasture, the latter covered with a thick spruce-fir forest that seems never to have been touched by man. The islands of Merchant's Row protected by conservation easements (Second, Big Coombs and Shingle) are all classic Maine islands ranging from exposed granite ledge to dense spruce-fir forest. Conservation easements also protect two sites on Kimball Island, to the west of Isle au Haut.

Crockett Cove Woods, the only preserve in the region that can be reached by car, provides an opportunity for the landbound to see what the vegetation of the Deer Isle region's offshore islands is like. The preserve's quiet "fog forest," complete with a luxuriant growth of mosses, lichens and other moisture-loving plants, is typical of the forests found in the many of islands' interiors.

The Conservancy works with several other organizations in protecting the islands of the Deer Isle region. The Maine Department of Inland Fisheries and Wildlife, which ranked the East Penobscot Bay/Little Deer Isle region as a Class A wildlife area in its 1986 Penobscot Bay Conservation Plan, owns and manages 10 seabird nesting islands and ledges in the area. Acadia National Park has land on Isle au Haut and holds conservation easements on nine other islands. The state Bureau of Public Lands owns several islands and ledges in the archipelago. Private organizations, including the Friends of Nature, Island Institute and local land trusts care for still more.

The Conservancy's Deer Isle region preserves are watched over by a local volunteer stewardship committee. For more information about the preserves, please contact the Maine Chapter stewardship office in Topsham.

Please note: Although the islands with conservation easements are an integral part of the Conservancy's protection efforts in the Deer Isle region, like all properties with conservation easements they are still privately owned. Please respect the owners' wishes and do not land on these islands.

Sheep Island and Bradbury Island Preserves

Sheep Island, 5 acres, East Penobscot Bay; Bradbury Island, 180 acres, Deer Isle

Sheep and Bradbury islands are part of an archipelago of nearly two dozen islands in East Penobscot Bay that have been protected by The Nature Conservancy and other conservation interests.

Sheep Island

Sheep Island was used for grazing for many years. Since the grazing stopped, a small spruce forest has grown up and the openings have filled in with juniper, bayberry, raspberry, blueberry, and specked alder. The varied yellows of goldenrods, cinquefoils and evening primrose mix in the old field with the brilliant magenta of fireweed.

Ospreys nest on the tip of the island. Common eiders nest on the ledges just off the steep, rugged shore.

Acquired by the Conservancy in 1974, Sheep Island is also protected by a conservation easement given to Acadia National Park by a former owner.

 Sheep Island's steep shore makes landing difficult. There is an excellent view of the island from Blastow Cove on Little Deer Isle.

DIRECTIONS: With care, a small boat can be landed at several points along the shore.

Bradbury Island

The cliffs on Bradbury Island soar nearly a hundred feet above the surf. A pair of bald eagles and several pairs of ospreys nest in the island's secluded forest.

Bradbury is almost entirely covered with forest, much of which is a mixture of maple, birch and beech. The island's red spruce and balsam fir were cut in the 1940s. Spruce and fir remain only on the steeper slopes and in a few stands of old trees scattered among the hardwoods.

Several streams flow down toward the island's eastern shore from the height of land, 164 feet above the sea. Readily accessible water and the extensive hardwood forest create ideal habitat for an unusually large population of deer.

The island appears to have been inhabited from 1850 to 1880. Aside from 100 or so sheep that were pastured here in the 1940s, there have been no regular inhabitants in this century.

Bradbury Island was acquired in 1969 by David P. Becker, who donated it to the Conservancy with the exception of an unlocated small inholding. The Conservancy also holds conservation easements on several nearby islands.

 Nesting island: closed to the public during the March 15 to August 15 nesting season. Please do not harass the eagles and ospreys by landing on the island or lingering offshore.

At other times of the year, walking around is not easy; the shore is steep and there are no trails.

DIRECTIONS: Small boats can be landed on the cobble beaches on the northern and southwestern shores. Strong currents around the island make it generally unsafe to swim or moor a boat for any length of time.

Crockett Cove Woods Preserve and Barred Island Preserve

Barred Island, 2 acres, Deer Isle;
Crockett Cove, 100 acres, Stonington

The dark, cool spruce-fir forest of Crockett Cove Woods is a lush habitat for mosses, lichens and other moisture-loving plants. At the head of Crockett Cove, tiny Barred Island is connected to the Deer Isle shore by a sand bar.

Crockett Cove Woods

On drizzly, overcast days the Crockett Cove Woods Preserve is a rich jewel of vibrant greens and grays. The quiet woods come alive with the songs of warblers, kinglets and chickadees.

Unlike the forests of the northern part of Deer Isle, which are mostly hardwoods, Crockett Cove Woods is spruce and fir. The preserve's southwest exposure and consistently moist climate have created a coastal "fog forest" of red spruce, where mosses and lichens blanket large granite boulders left by the retreating glaciers. Old man's beard lichen hangs delicately from the trees.

Tamaracks and northern white cedars grow in the wetter areas. In a small bog near the middle of the preserve, round-leaved sundews and pitcher plants are scattered throughout a spongy mat of sphagnum moss. A wet woodland adjoining the boggy area is thick with shrubs such as sheep laurel, mountain holly, winterberry and witherod.

Crockett Cove Woods is a place to explore on hands and knees while peering through a hand lens. Dozens of species of mosses, lichens and liverworts await close inspection; oddities such as black, white, pink and yellow slime molds, which are primitive organisms combining the characteristics of fungi and protozoa, positively demand it.

Architect and artist Emily Muir donated Crockett Cove Woods to the Conservancy in 1975. She designed several of the houses near the preserve.

 A short nature trail winds through the fog forest in the southern section of the preserve. Several other trails traverse the length of the preserve, offering a good walk. A brochure describing the nature trail and a simple key to the most common lichens and mosses are available at the preserve's south entrance.

DIRECTIONS: Heading south on Deer Isle on Route 15, turn right at the Deer Isle Post Office and follow the road to Sunset. A little more than three miles past the Sunset Post Office, turn right on Whitman Road. Go a short distance, turn right onto another dirt road, which leads to the preserve entrance, marked by a small TNC sign and registration box. There is room to park several cars.

Barred Island

Tiny Barred Island sits at the mouth of Crockett Cove, connected to the mainland by a sand bar.

The island is largely covered with spruce and fir, although an old burn in the interior is now filled with an impenetrable raspberry thicket. Red-berried elder, skunk currant and hay-scented fern also grow in the burn, along with winterberry, a species not commonly found on islands.

In the spruce forest, thick mats of mountain cranberry, snowberry and black crowberry make up the ground cover.

The large, smooth ledges of the island's shore are broken only by the sand bar at the northern end. The bar is home to razor clams, which are not common in Penobscot Bay due to the general lack of sand. Limpets, dog whelks, periwinkles and sea urchins also inhabit the waters near the bar.

Barred Island was donated to the Conservancy in 1969 by Miss Carolyn Olmsted, a great-niece of Frederick Law Olmsted, the well-known landscape architect.

 No trails exist, although there are animal paths on the western shore. Walking along the broad granite shore ledges is the preferred activity.

DIRECTIONS: Since the Conservancy's ownership extends only to the bar, public access is by boat. Small boats can be easily pulled up on the bar, but watch the tide. To approach by land, please get permission from the owners of Goose Cove Lodge, whose property must be crossed on the way to the bar.

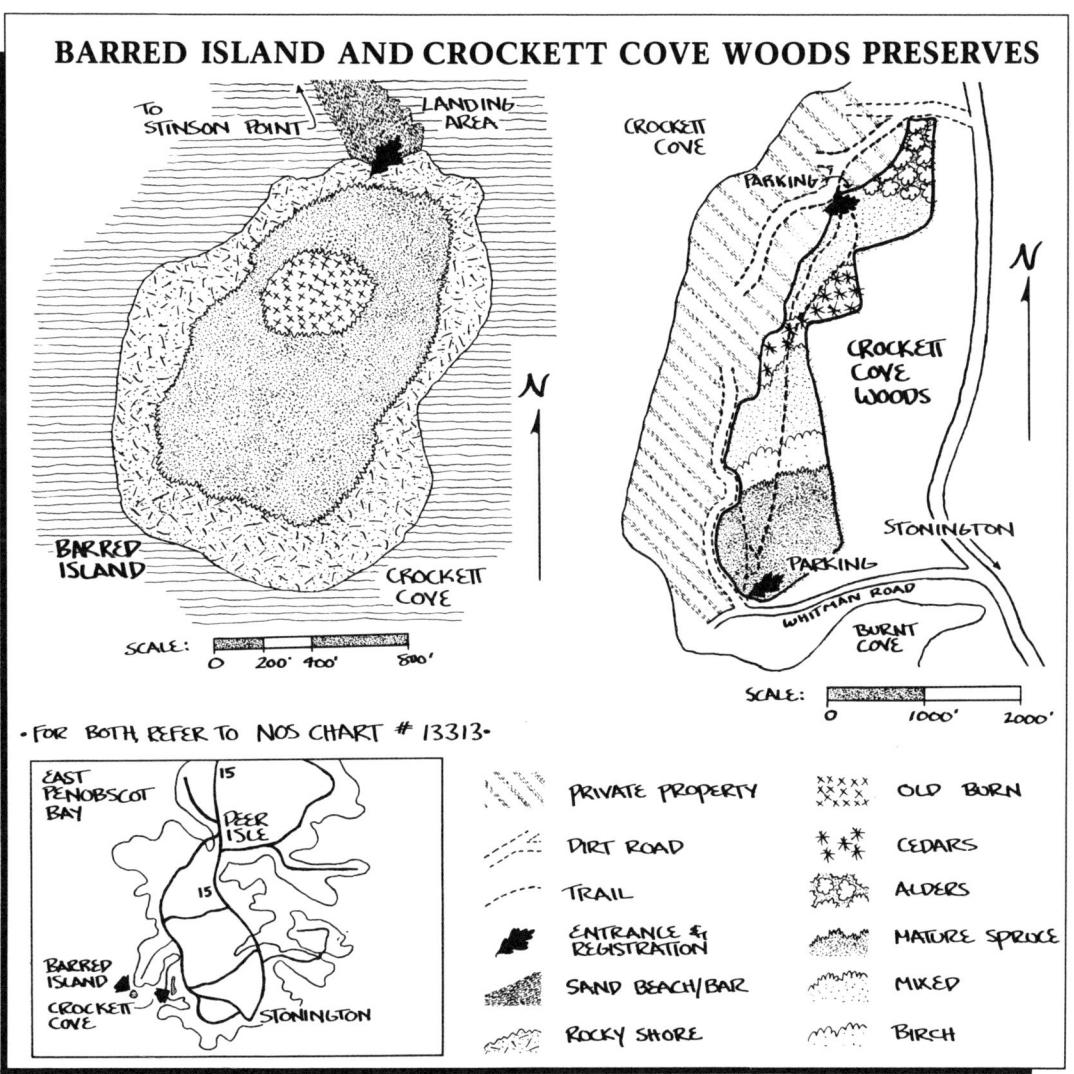

BARRED ISLAND AND CROCKETT COVE WOODS PRESERVES

TO STINSON POINT

LANDING AREA

CROCKETT COVE

BARRED ISLAND

CROCKETT COVE

PARKING

CROCKETT COVE WOODS

STONINGTON

PARKING

WHITMAN ROAD

BURNT COVE

SCALE: 0 200' 400' 800'

SCALE: 0 1000' 2000'

• FOR BOTH, REFER TO NOS CHART # 13313 •

EAST PENOBSCOT BAY

DEER ISLE

15

15

BARRED ISLAND

CROCKETT COVE

STONINGTON

PRIVATE PROPERTY

DIRT ROAD

TRAIL

ENTRANCE & REGISTRATION

SAND BEACH/BAR

ROCKY SHORE

OLD BURN

CEDARS

ALDERS

MATURE SPRUCE

MIXED

BIRCH

Wreck Island and Round Island Preserves

Wreck Island, 80 acres;
Round Island, 46 acres.
Both in Stonington

In Merchant Row off Stonington, Wreck Island's meandering stone walls, old cellar holes, open fields and a flock of sheep offer a pastoral contrast to neighboring Round Island's impenetrable spruce-fir forest.

Wreck Island

A flock of sheep keeps the spruce and fir on Wreck Island at bay. Sheep have been pastured on the island for years; this most recent flock was introduced in an effort to keep the island open. The effect the sheep have on the vegetation is being monitored by the College of the Atlantic and the Island Institute.

The western half of the island and part of the eastern half are covered with a mature forest of salt-tolerant white spruce, also known as cat or skunk spruce for reasons that are clear to the nose as soon as the needles are crushed. The ground cover is composed of familiar woodland flowers, including abundant Canada mayflowers and bunchberries. Within the forest, there are openings with large granite outcrops that are very wet and covered with sphagnum moss.

Grassy fields with raspberry patches make up most of the interior. A few alder saplings and young spruce have escaped the sheep, especially along the southern shore. Meadow voles have runs everywhere in the fields.

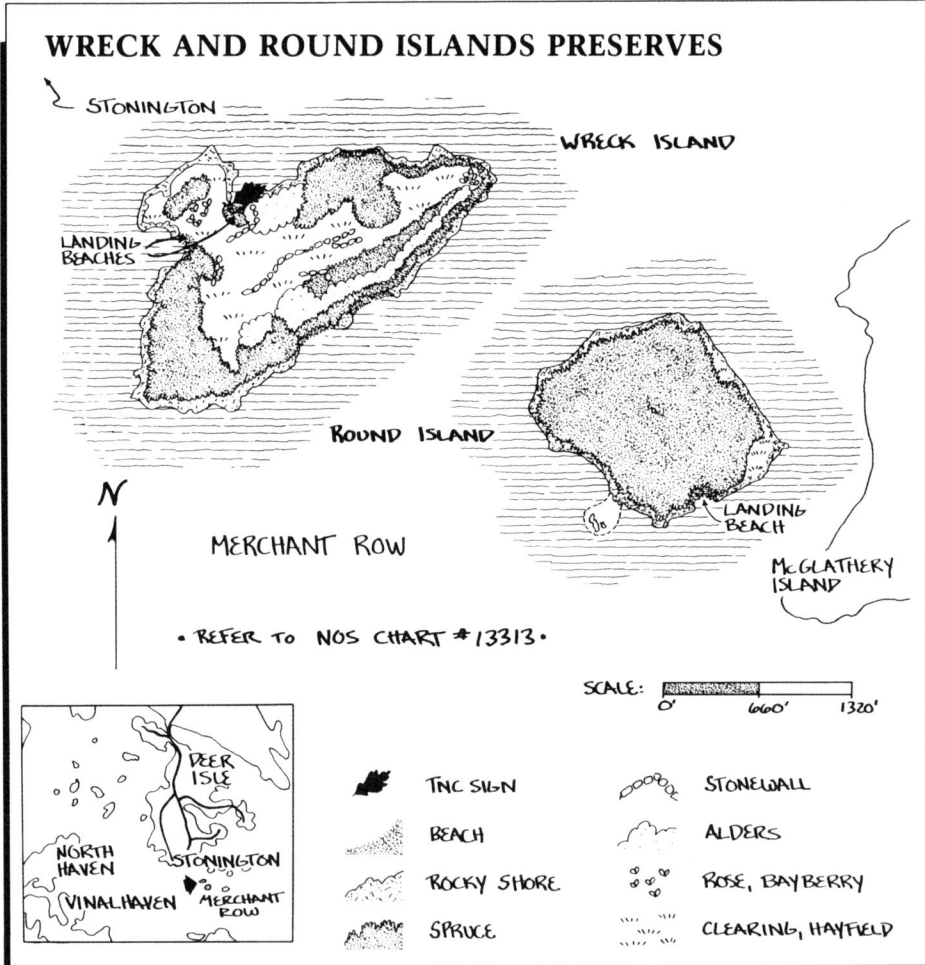

WRECK AND ROUND ISLANDS PRESERVES

STONINGTON

WRECK ISLAND

LANDING BEACHES

ROUND ISLAND

N

MERCHANT ROW

LANDING BEACH

McGLATHERY ISLAND

• REFER TO NOS CHART #13313•

SCALE:
0'   660'   1320'

DEER ISLE

NORTH HAVEN   STONINGTON

VINALHAVEN   MERCHANT ROW

TNC SIGN   STONEWALL

BEACH   ALDERS

ROCKY SHORE   ROSE, BAYBERRY

SPRUCE   CLEARING, HAYFIELD

There are four gravel beaches: two on the eastern shore, and two on either side of the "thumb" on the northwestern shore. Blocky, angular granite cliffs form the remainder of the shoreline.

First settled in the 1700s, Wreck Island was apparently never inhabited by more than three families at any one time. The families farmed the land and raised sheep and cows. The island has not been inhabited for more than 50 years. Old foundations, cellar holes and stone walls are all that remain. A natural granite pier, which the settlers must have used, juts out from the southern shore.

A part-owner of Wreck Island, Emily Muir, offered her share of the island to the Conservancy if it could acquire the rest. The all-volunteer Chapter raised the funds and acquired the entire island in 1967.

 Although there are no trails, it is possible to explore most of the island. The height of land offers excellent views of Stonington to the north and Isle au Haut to the west. Please refrain from bothering the sheep and be careful of the fences and old foundations. Dogs are absolutely not allowed on the island.

DIRECTIONS: Wreck Island is in Merchant Row, two and a half miles from Stonington. The two beaches on either side of the "thumb" are best for landing.

Round Island

Set alongside Wreck Island in Merchant Row, Round Island looks like a prickly green hedgehog.

The domed island is covered with a century-old forest that is predominantly mature red and white spruces with a few oaks, alders and poplars mixed in. The dense forest opens up where there are exposed ledges, but is nearly impenetrable otherwise. The only real clearing, a small old field on the southeastern shore, is being taken over by blueberries and raspberries as well as young spruces.

Steep granite cliffs rounded by the glaciers make up most of the shoreline. The bulk of the island rises steeply from the cliffs to an elevation of just over 100 feet. On the southern shore, a small sand and mud beach nestles in the cliffs.

Round Island appears on maps made in the 1700s. It was inhabited for a time and sheep were kept on the island until a century ago. In recent years, the only regular visitors were fishermen who stayed in the now tumbled-down cabin near the shore.

In 1969, the Conservancy bought Round Island at a bargain price from an owner interested in seeing the island protected. Neighboring McGlathery Island is also protected; it is owned and managed by the Friends of Nature. The Conservancy also holds conservation easements on several nearby islands: Second, Big Coombs and Shingle.

 Round Island's steep cliffs and dense spruce forest are a little discouraging, but it is possible to walk along the shore. There are no trails.

DIRECTIONS: Round Island is two and a half miles from Stonington on Merchant Row. The only possible landing is the small beach on the southern shore.

Black Guillemonts (Alan Hutchinson)

Mount Desert Island Region

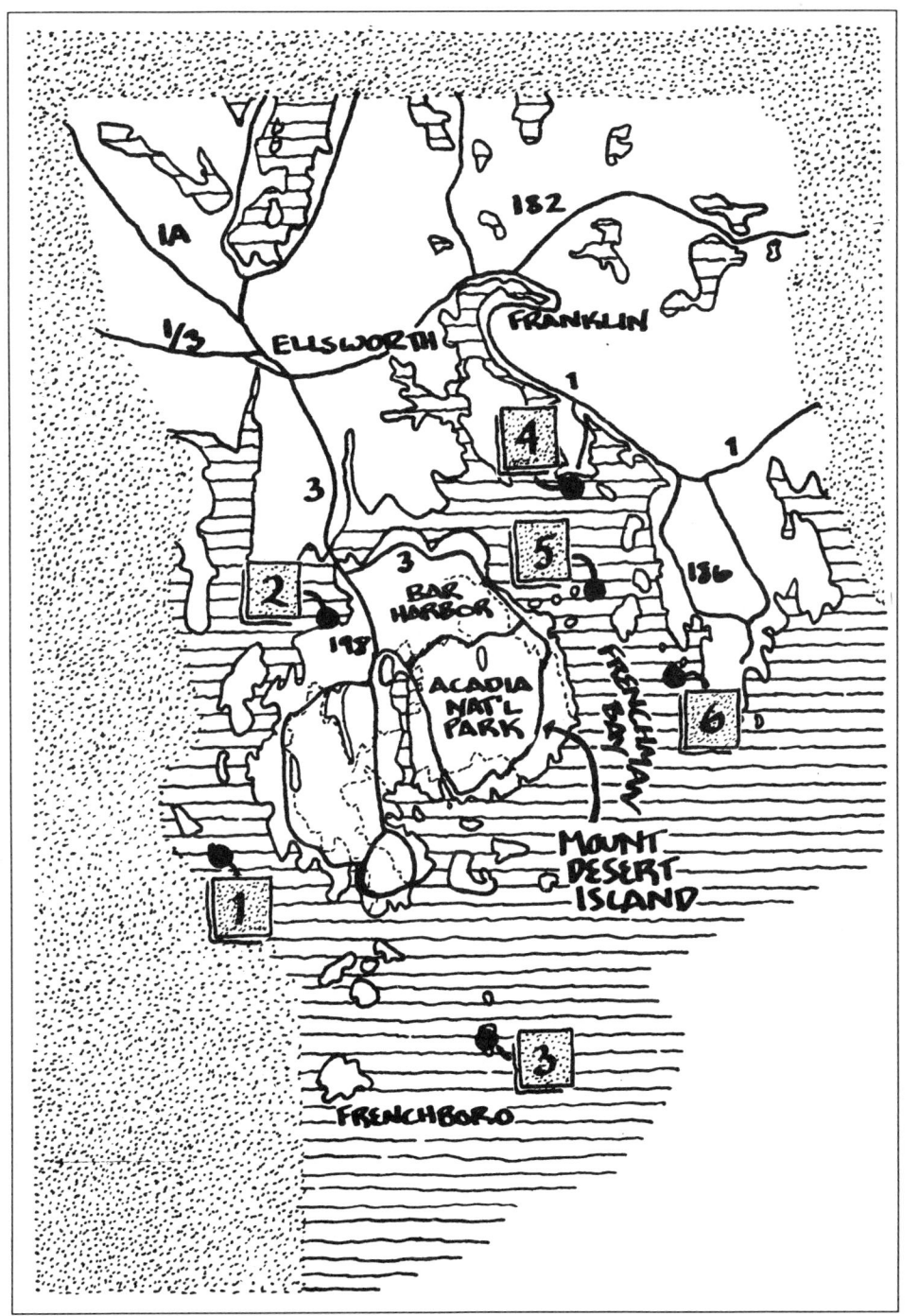

Mount Desert Island Region

Every summer, thousands of people migrate to the Mount Desert Island region to flock along Ocean Drive, perch on Cadillac Mountain and forage in the shops of Bar Harbor. Every summer, thousands of seabirds also migrate to the area, to raise their young on the outer islands. Colonially nesting birds like Leach's storm-petrels, black guillemots, great blue herons, black-crowned night herons, common eiders, and gulls, as well as loners like bald eagles and ospreys, nest in the sanctuary of the Conservancy's island preserves: Ship, Bar and Trumpet (Tremont); Placentia and Great Duck (Frenchboro); Long Porcupine (Gouldsboro); and Turtle (Winter Harbor).

Nesting island preserves are closed during the March 15 to August 15 breeding season. With the exception of Placentia, which is not open to the public due to a life estate retained by the donor, it is possible to visit these islands during the remainder of the year, but be prepared for rough seas, sudden fogs and difficult landings.

The other preserves in the region offer year-round opportunities to enjoy a day by the water. The Maine Chapter's most popular preserve, Indian Point-Blagden in Bar Harbor, is an ideal spot to walk quietly through the woods and along the shore while looking for woodpeckers, deer, harbor seals and other wildlife. The Ketterlinus Preserve (Tremont) protects the shores of Seal Cove Brook. Away from Mount Desert Island, on the eastern side of Frenchman Bay, Preble and Dram islands form a scenic backdrop to Sorrento's harbor.

The Maine Chapter works with many partners in protecting the Mount Desert Island region. It has helped Acadia National Park with several additions, including the western half of Baker's Island (Cranberry Isles). The Maine Department of Inland Fisheries and Wildlife (IF&W) is a partial owner and co-steward of Great Duck Island, and also monitors the seabird nesting islands. The state's Donnell Pond/Black Mountain/Tunk Lake Public Reserved Land (Sullivan, T9SD, T10SD) was acquired as result of the Conservancy's actions as intermediary and lead negotiator. The Conservancy also stepped in and saved a bald eagle nesting site on Taunton Bay (Hancock) from a controversial development.

The Nature Conservancy's preserves in the Mount Desert Island region are taken care of by several stewardship committees and one pair of permanent caretakers. For more information, please contact the Maine Chapter stewardship office in Topsham.

Ship Island Group Preserve

Bar Island, 13 acres;
Trumpet, 5 acres;
Ship Island, 11 acres.
West Barge Island, 1/2 acre;
East Barge Island, 1/2 acre.
All in Tremont

Before a 1980 epidemic of avian cholera, these islands supported the third largest nesting colony of common eiders in Maine. The islands remain important nesting habitat for the recovering population.

A landmark well-known to everyone familiar with the entrance to Blue Hill Bay, the Ship Island group is a long chain running down the middle of the bay between the Brooklin peninsula and Mount Desert Island. Bar, Trumpet and Ship islands are part of a submerged ridge that begins with Tinker Island to the north. East and West Barge are small satellites located off the southern tip of the ridge.

Until 1980, this island chain hosted the third largest nesting colony of common eiders in Maine. More than 1,000 pairs, five percent of the state's nesting population, nested here then. Bar and Ship are on the Register of State Critical Areas.

During the height of the 1980 nesting season, infectious avian cholera struck. The epidemic was centered in Blue Hill Bay. More than 1,700 birds—eiders, gulls and cormorants—died on Ship, Bar and Trumpet alone.

Eiders continue to nest on the islands, along with double-crested cormorants and greater black-backed and herring gulls, but it will be years before they regain their former numbers. The islands are also an important stop for brant and other migrating species.

The three larger islands are covered with a dense layer of shrubs, including red-berried elder, black cherry, rugosa rose and raspberry. A few mountain ashes, speckled alders and white spruces survive on Bar. The shoreline is rimmed with familiar sea-strand plants like beach pea and orache.

The three major islands are part of a large deposit of sand and gravel till. They are surrounded by cobble and sand beaches that widen considerably with the ebbing tide. Trumpet Island almost doubles in size and connects to Ship with a bar; Bar also joins Tinker Island (not part of the preserve). At high tide, the two Barges are barely above water. The ledges around the islands are haul-outs for harbor seals.

In the past, the islands were used for grazing sheep from time to time. At the turn of the century, there was a year-round community on Bar, and seasonal fishing camps on Ship and Trumpet.

The southern third of Bar Island, and a one-half interest in Ship Island and the two Barges were donated to the Conservancy in 1979 by Mr. and Mrs. Sohier Welch. The Conservancy purchased Trumpet Island, and the remaining interest in Ship and the Barges, completing the acquisition in 1984. The nouthern two-thirds of Bar Island is privately owned.

 Nesting islands: closed to the public during the March 15 to August 15 nesting season. Please do not harass the birds by landing on the islands or lingering offshore. Disturbance can cause serious nest losses.

At other times of the year, it is possible to beach a small boat. The camp on Bar Island is not part of the preserve.

DIRECTIONS: The Ship Island group is approximately five miles from Bass Harbor. The waters around the islands are quite shallow.

Indian Point-Blagden Preserve

110 acres, Bar Harbor

Untouched by the devastating fire of 1947, the forest of Indian Point-Blagden Preserve is an inviting glimpse into the past. The preserve fronts on Western Bay, where seals haul out on nearby ledges.

The cool dense coniferous forest of the Indian Point-Blagden Preserve stands in contrast to the thin open woods of most of Mount Desert Island, which was severely burned in 1947. The fire began less than five miles northeast of Indian Point, but the winds blew it away from the preserve land.

Most of the forest is tall red spruce, white cedar and balsam fir. Although some of the trees were cut over the years, the forest has been left largely undisturbed. There are several blowdowns, the largest of which is over 10 acres. Yellow and white birch, red oak and red maple are more common in the blowdowns and near the edge of the coniferous forest. At the center of the preserve, where it is wetter, young tamaracks occupy more than eight acres. There is a small pond and wetland near the preserve entrance.

Birders have spotted black-backed three-toed woodpeckers, ruby-crowned kinglets, boreal chickadees and more than 130 other bird species on the preserve. Two pairs of ospreys nesting on the preserve are remarkably habituated to discreet observers of their domestic activities. Varying hares and white-tailed deer are seen regularly; in winter, their tracks run throughout the snowy woods.

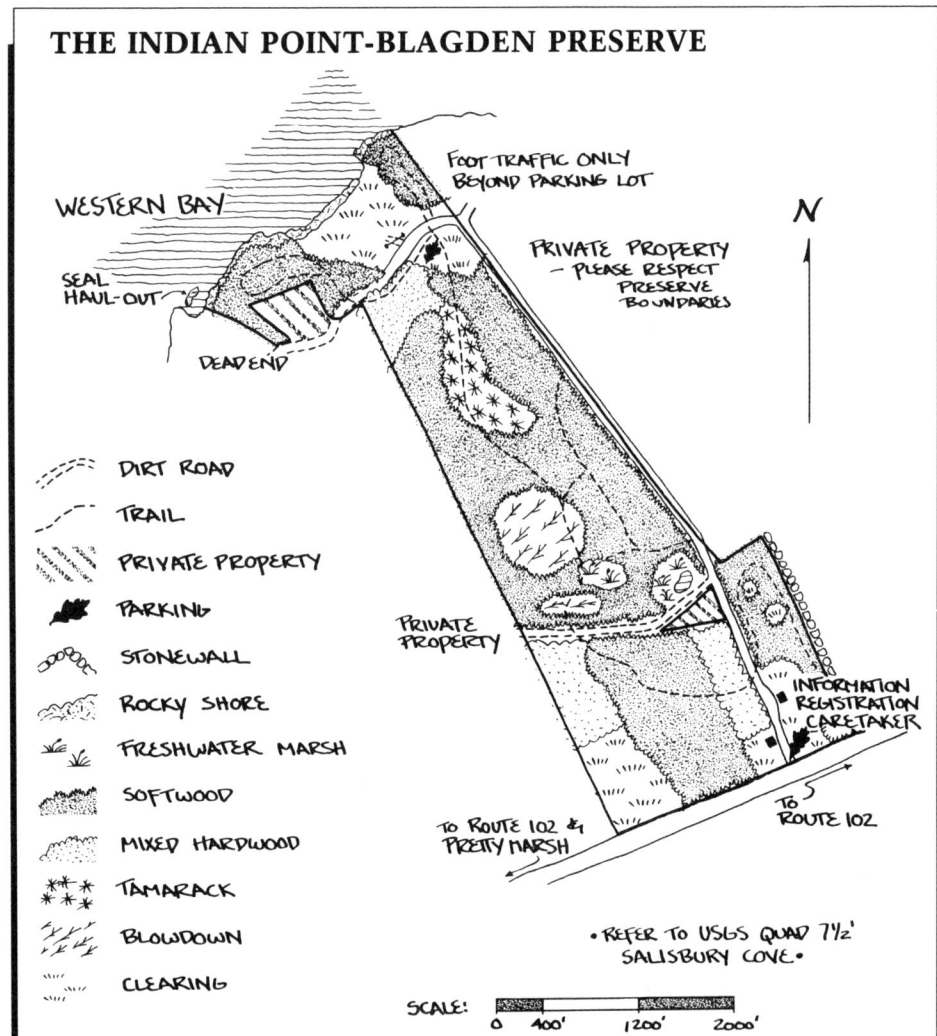

THE INDIAN POINT-BLAGDEN PRESERVE

WESTERN BAY

FOOT TRAFFIC ONLY BEYOND PARKING LOT

N

PRIVATE PROPERTY – PLEASE RESPECT PRESERVE BOUNDARIES

SEAL HAUL-OUT

DEAD END

PRIVATE PROPERTY

INFORMATION REGISTRATION CARETAKER

TO ROUTE 102 & PRETTY MARSH

TO ROUTE 102

- - - - DIRT ROAD
— — — TRAIL
PRIVATE PROPERTY
PARKING
STONEWALL
ROCKY SHORE
FRESHWATER MARSH
SOFTWOOD
MIXED HARDWOOD
TAMARACK
BLOWDOWN
CLEARING

• REFER TO USGS QUAD 7½' SALISBURY COVE •

SCALE: 0   400'   1200'   2000'

The preserve includes more than 1,000 feet of shoreline on Western Bay. The shore is rocky, with several small gravel beaches. Seals haul out and bask on the intertidal ledges located just offshore near the northwestern corner of the preserve.

The seaward side of Indian Point is composed of folded, tortured layers of Ellsworth schist, a metamorphic rock that began as sediments laid down about 450 million years ago. Approximately 75 million years later, the Mount Desert Island area experienced the first in a series of invasions of molten rock that formed the mountainous bulk of the island. Near Indian Point, there is a massive band of the rock formed by this first influx, a dark, fine-grained, banded rock known as diorite. On the preserve, the diorite is in direct contact with the Ellsworth schist. At the point of contact, the schist was transformed by the extremely hot magma into hornfels, a recrystallized, dense, brittle material.

Early records show that Indian Point was settled in the 1700s. Old fields and apple orchards remain near an old home site near the shore.

Indian Point-Blagden Preserve was donated to the Conservancy in 1968 by Donald and Zelina Blagden, who kept it as a summer retreat for many years. At their request, their home was dismantled in 1984, returning the site to nature.

Carefully laid-out and marked trails wind through the woods and fields to the shore. The preserve is open year-round, but closes every night at 6 p.m. Please stop and register at the caretakers' house. Trail brochures and checklists of the preserve's birds and plants are available, and the caretakers will be happy to answer questions. The preserve is nestled between privately owned properties; please be careful to stay on the Conservancy's land and away from areas marked private.

DIRECTIONS: Take Route 102/198 south toward Somesville. After 1.8 miles, turn right onto Indian Point Road toward Pretty Marsh. After 1.7 miles, bear right at the first fork and go about 200 yards to the preserve entrance road on the right. The entrance is marked with a sign. Cars may be parked near the caretakers' house or in the parking area near the shore.

SEAL WATCHING Boaters love to try to get good close looks at seals hauled out on the rocks. But no matter how carefully and quietly they approach, the apparently somnolent seals warily watch for awhile, then suddenly flee their warm ledges for the safety of the water. This can happen dozens of times a day, totally disrupting the animals' lives, especially those of mothers and nursing young.

Kayakers are a particular problem. Their boats draw little water and are highly maneuverable, making them ideal for getting close to the ledges. Researchers also hypothesize that a person in a kayak who is silently and stealthily approaching looks and behaves like a killer whale, one of the seals' main predators.

To watch seals without disturbing them, invest in a good pair of binoculars. Sneaking up on seals will not work; try staying well off the ledges and practicing the art of indirection: look at them while heading somewhere else. Pretending to haul traps can be effective, but a thorough acting job is guaranteed to capture the full attention of the nearest lobsterman.

Great Duck Island Preserve

245 acres, Frenchboro

For more than a century, ornithologists and conservationists have studied the birds of Great Duck Island and sought ways to protect them. Today, the island is a sanctuary for the largest colony of Leach's storm-petrels in Maine.

Every spring, an estimated 20,000 Leach's storm-petrels come home to Great Duck Island. Great Duck, at the edge of the open Atlantic eight miles south of Mount Desert Island, is one of Maine's most important seabird nesting sites. Seventy-five percent of Maine's storm-petrel population shares the island with black guillemots, common eiders, and herring gulls.

Storm-petrels never set foot on land except at nesting time. They range over the Atlantic Ocean, spending the summers in the north and the winters in the south off the shores of South America. The dark gray, robin-sized birds flutter over the waves, sometimes pattering on the surface, snatching small fish, crustaceans and tiny squid.

Each summer, the Leach's storm-petrels cease their wandering and come ashore on a few islands like Great Duck to nest in burrows dug in the soft duff of the islands' spruce forest. Each pair produces one chick that stays secure in its burrow, never seeing the light of day until it is fledged. At night, the parents fly back from the open ocean to feed the chick, running the gantlet of gulls waiting on the shore. In the wee hours of the morning, the island's stillness is broken by the chatter of the adult storm-petrels as they return.

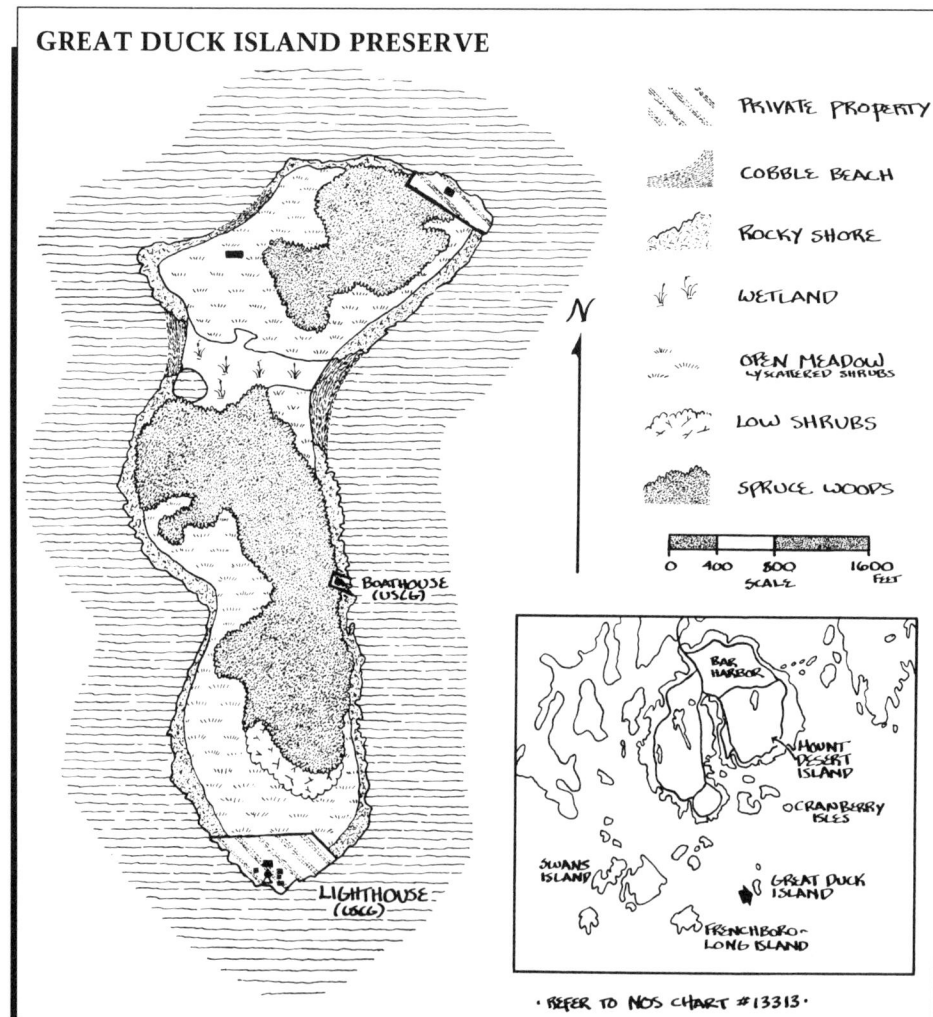

GREAT DUCK ISLAND PRESERVE

PRIVATE PROPERTY

COBBLE BEACH

ROCKY SHORE

WETLAND

OPEN MEADOW & SCATTERED SHRUBS

LOW SHRUBS

SPRUCE WOODS

N

0 400 800 1600 FEET

SCALE

BOATHOUSE (USCG)

LIGHTHOUSE (USCG)

BASS HARBOR

MOUNT DESERT ISLAND

CRANBERRY ISLES

SWANS ISLAND

GREAT DUCK ISLAND

FRENCHBORO-LONG ISLAND

· REFER TO NOS CHART #13313 ·

After the storm-petrels grow quiet in the early morning, the black guillemots fly from their nests in crevices along the broken rocky shore, filling the air with their tinkling, crystalline songs.

Black guillemots are members of the auk family. They "fly" under water on their short stubby wings, feeding on rock eels and small crustaceans inhabiting the rocky bottom. In summer, black guillemots are absolutely unmistakable, compact little black birds with white wing patches and bright red feet. They fly fast and low over the water, like hyperactive bumblebees. For those who long to see another auk family member, the common puffin, at sea, practice watching black guillemots is invaluable; puffins fly the same way at about twice the speed.

Spruce forest covers more than half of Great Duck. Where gales have leveled patches of forest, rich new growth has sprung up from seeds long dormant in island soils or brought to the island by countless migrating birds.

Fields of grasses, wildflowers and shrubs along the northern and western shore offer good cover for the nesting eiders and gulls. A marsh divides the northern third of the island from the southern two-thirds.

A diminutive member of the purslane family, blinks (*Montia fontana*) inhabits wet, brackish spots. Rediscovered on the island in 1986 after a gap of more than a century, blinks is an ephemeral, spring-flowering, sub-arctic plant that disappears by mid-summer. Its seeds go wherever winds, waves and birds take them.

The island's shore is steep granite ledges interrupted by several boulder beaches and cobble beaches.

Great Duck was first settled in the early 1800s. The islanders fished, farmed and ran a fish oil factory. The island was also a prime supplier of fine plumage for ladies' hats; in the summer of 1881 alone, 800 ducks were shot and their feathers sold to the trade.

Many lives and cargoes were lost when ships failed to clear the island in heavy weather. In 1890, the Coast Guard built a lighthouse on the island's southern tip. The light was one of the last to be manned by keepers; it was automated in 1986.

In 1929, renowned ornithologist Olin Sewall Pettingill came to Great Duck to do his first ornithological research project. The following year, the National Audubon Society acquired a management lease on the island and hired the lighthouse keeper as warden to protect the nesting colony of endangered herring gulls.

Most recently, Great Duck was used as a retreat by a Gestalt psychiatrist who ran a clinic on the island for almost a decade.

The Conservancy acquired Great Duck Island Preserve in 1985, raising the money through hundreds of individual donations. The Department of Inland Fisheries and Wildlife, which had listed Great Duck as its top priority for acquisition since 1978, purchased a 10 percent undivided interest in the island and now shares responsibility for the island and its nesting birds.

The Conservancy preserve includes all of the island except two inholdings: a private lot on the northern shore and the property surrounding the lighthouse.

 Nesting island: with thousands of nesting birds hidden all over the island from the depths of the spruce forest to the edge of the rocky shore, it is almost impossible to visit Great Duck without disturbing them. Visits to the island during the March 15 to August 15 nesting season are discouraged.

At any time of the year, it is difficult to land on the island. There are no good anchorages, and the only landing spots are the cobble or boulder beaches, which frequently experience heavy surf. Please avoid wandering through the spruce forest and compacting the soil where the petrels burrow.

The Maine Chapter offers periodic field trips to study the wildlife of Great Duck and surrounding waters. On a clear day, the island is also visible from the southern peaks of Mount Desert Island.

DIRECTIONS: Great Duck is seaward of Little Duck, eight miles south of Northeast Harbor.

Dram Island and Preble Island Preserves

Dram Island, 6 acres; Preble Island, 75 acres. Both in Sorrento

Well-loved landmarks of the town of Sorrento, Dram and Preble islands were saved from development by the generosity of a local family and some creative trading involving a church organ.

Dram and Preble islands lie just off the town of Sorrento, sheltering the mainland from the open waters of Frenchman Bay and forming the town's harbor. The two islands are separated by a deep channel only 100 yards wide.

Like sisters, the two islands are from the same family: steep, spruce-fir forested islands with 20- to 30-foot cliffs along much of their shores. On Preble, the big sister, the cliffs are punctuated by shingle and cobble beaches. On Dram, the cliffs are limited to the northern shore; the remainder of the shore is rough ledges.

The islands are capped with a layer of extremely resistant, dark, granite-like rock called diorite. Under this is a layer of softer sedimentary rock that is easily worn away. The diorite is continually undercut by the waves and eventually gives way along vertical fracture lines, creating and perpetuating the exceptionally steep shoreline cliffs. The different beaches are derived from the two kinds of rock: the hard diorite resists the pounding of the sea and forms blocky cobbles; the sedimentary rock peels off in layers and ends up as smaller, well-polished, flattened stones.

Preble towers over its little sister, rising to an elevation of 171 feet. Its interior is mature spruce-fir forest. On the northern tip, cooler, moister conditions have created a coastal "fog forest," where the trees, rocks and ground are decorated with an especially lush growth of lichens, mosses and ferns.

On Dram, every year the storm winds blow down a few trees at random, creating a forest with trees of many different ages. In one large clearing, the ground is densely covered with American yew (*Taxus canadensis*), a species not commonly found on islands. Northern white cedars grow among the spruces and firs on the western end.

The islands' forests attract few human visitors, but ospreys find them ideal for roosting and nesting. Eagles have nested on Preble in the past; although none are currently in residence, there is every reason to hope that a pair will move in as the Frenchman Bay population continues to recover.

In the mid-1960s, the residents of Sorrento learned that Dram Island might be sold for its pulpwood. Its owner, a minister living in Wyoming, badly wanted an organ for his church. To save Dram, Sorrento summer resident and former Conservancy Board of Governors member Bayard Ewing bought an organ and swapped it for the island. He then donated the island to the Conservancy.

Preble Island had been in the Ewing family since the First World War. More than a decade ago, Bayard Ewing and his family donated a conservation easement on the island to Acadia National Park. In 1988, they donated title to Preble Island to the Conservancy.

 It is possible to land a small boat on either Dram or Preble and explore a bit along the shore and into the woods. There are trails on Preble. Please do not linger near the ospreys' nests. If you must have a fire, please build it below the high tide mark. The islands and ospreys can be seen clearly from the Sorrento shore.

DIRECTIONS: Dram and Preble islands are about a quarter-mile from the Sorrento town dock.

Long Porcupine Island Preserve

125 acres, Gouldsboro

Bald eagles have nested on the Porcupine Islands in Frenchman Bay on and off since the 1920s. Located out in the bay, away from the madding crowds of Bar Harbor, Long Porcupine offers bald eagles and other birds the peace they need to breed successfully.

The easternmost of the four Porcupine Islands, Long Porcupine is sheltered from the busy waters off Bar Harbor. The quiet wooded island is a sanctuary for nesting birds.

Even though they have had problems with fallen nests, the island's eagles have produced at least four chicks since 1981. Ospreys nest in trees along the shore; black guillemots find safe nesting niches in the cliffs on the southwestern shore.

Until 1938, Long Porcupine had a mature spruce-fir forest. That year loggers took off about 4,000 cords of wood, transporting it by coastal schooner to the paper mill in Bucksport. Fifty years later, the island is almost completely covered with a dense growth of young spruce and fir. The tightly packed trees are accompanied by slash and blowdowns, making the forest impenetrable as only a clearcut spruce-fir forest can be. The only large trees remaining on the island are a few hardwoods that were of no use for pulp. The forest does supply ample browse for a small deer herd.

At the northeastern end of Long Porcupine, a gravel beach known as a tombolo connects the island to a smaller, rounded island called The Hop. (The Hop is not part of the Conservancy preserve.)

Like its neighboring islands, Long Porcupine has a southern face that looks as though a large hand reached down and scooped up the shore, leaving behind steep cliffs instead of gentle slopes to match the rest of the island. Essentially, the glaciers did just that, easing over the northern ends of the islands, then freezing onto and pulling off chunks of bedrock as they moved on. The characteristic form left behind is aptly known as a plucked face.

Hidden among the 100-foot cliffs is a sea arch which spans a 10-foot-wide space and sits 40 feet above the waves. The arch is one of many bits of evidence scattered through the Mount Desert area showing that sea level was much higher here in the past. Released from the weight of the ice sheets, the islands rebounded, slowly but steadily, rising above the level of the surrounding sea.

On the calmest of days, the low spring tides reveal a sea cave. The cavern's ceiling curves some 70 feet above the anemones carpeting the tidepool on its floor.

In the late 1800s, Long Porcupine sustained a small fishing and farming community. It has not been inhabited for many years.

Long Porcupine was donated to the Conservancy in 1977 by Atwater Kent, Jr.

 Nesting island: closed to the public during the March 15 to August 15 nesting season. Please do not harass the birds by landing on the island or lingering offshore. Disturbance can cause serious nest losses.

At other times of the year, landing on the island is possible, but walking in the interior is extremely rough going.

Turtle Island Preserve

136 acres, Winter Harbor

A 150-year-old spruce-fir forest covers two-thirds of Turtle Island, providing a haven for a small nesting colony of great blue herons. The outgoing tide exposes broad ledges, creating extensive tidepools and an ideal basking beach claimed by harbor seals.

At the entrance to Frenchman Bay, Turtle Island emerges from the sea like a great green reptile heading upstream.

A small colony of great blue herons inhabits the densely forested interior. Harbor seals regularly sun themselves on the ledges off the southern tip of the island. Up to 75 seals have been seen at one time, a sizable number for a single haul-out.

Two-thirds of Turtle is covered with spruce-fir forest. The trees are tall, straight and closely spaced. It appears entirely possible that this forest may never have been cut. Core samples reveal that some of the trees are more than 150 years old. With so many of the trees on nearby islands having gone to feed the lime kilns in Rockport during the last half of the 19th century, it is surprising to find the old forest still intact.

The forest on the northern end of the island did go to the local mills; it was clearcut in the 1960s. Thickets of raspberries and blackberries now compete with cherries and grey birches in the cut area.

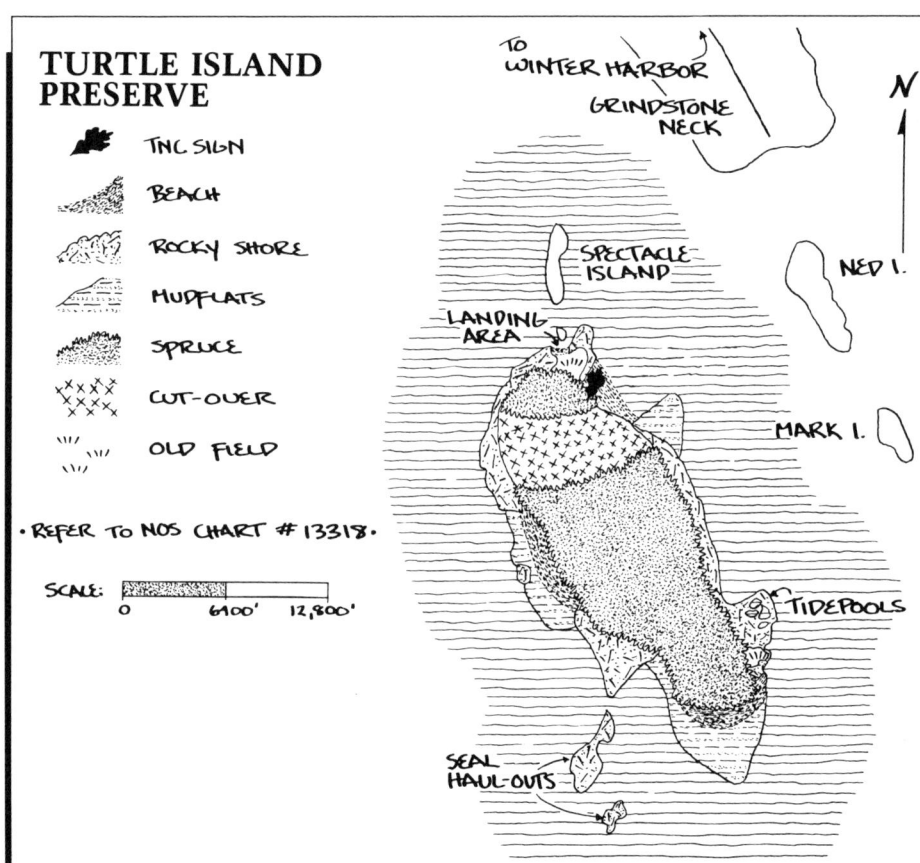

TURTLE ISLAND PRESERVE

TNC SIGN
BEACH
ROCKY SHORE
MUDFLATS
SPRUCE
CUT-OVER
OLD FIELD

· REFER TO NOS CHART # 13318·

SCALE: 0   6100'   12,800'

TO WINTER HARBOR
GRINDSTONE NECK
N
SPECTACLE ISLAND
NED I.
LANDING AREA
MARK I.
TIDEPOOLS
SEAL HAUL-OUTS

The island's shore is primarily cobbles and steep ledges. On the eastern shore, large depressions have been worn into the rock, creating extensive tide pools. The shallow pools left by the retreating tide are fascinating to explore.

Unlike most of the Schoodic peninsula and the offshore islands, the bedrock of Turtle Island is not fine-grained granite but volcanic rocks with small bits of sedimentary rock imbedded in them.

Roused by a letter in the local paper lamenting the logging operation on Turtle, Mrs. Elizabeth Crenshaw set out on a campaign to stop the cutting. After trying many approaches without success, she encouraged the Conservancy's board of trustees to come out to the island. In the spring of 1963, the trustees reached an agreement with the company that owned the cutting rights. By July the Conservancy owned Turtle Island, and the board volunteers set out to raise the money to repay the Conservancy's internal land acquisition loan fund.

MUSSELS AND RED TIDE Blue mussels fasten themselves on rocky shores from the lower intertidal zone to deep water. Considered a delicacy by common eiders and many people, mussels are a tempting addition to a summer picnic. Unfortunately, mussels are also an indicator species for paralytic shellfish poisoning, commonly called red tide. Mussels feed by filtering the water for plankton, including the single-

celled organisms that make up the "red tide." A mussel that has ingested these organisms is extremely poisonous to humans. The toxins are not destroyed by cooking.

As needed, the state closes parts of the coast to the taking of mussels, and other shellfish, during the warm months. Be careful; even the evidence of clammers at work is not enough, since mussels are more severely affected than clams. When in doubt, don't.

 The interior of Turtle Island is closed to the public during the March 15 to August 15 great blue heron nesting season. Please leave the herons in peace and walk only along the shore.

With the increasing number of visitors to Turtle, it is especially important that everyone treat the preserve with respect. Please remember to take litter off the island. Camping is not allowed.

DIRECTIONS: The most reliable landing is either of the small beaches on the northern end of the island, depending on the wind. The wind often comes up quickly, making it rough going for small boats.

Great Wass Island Preserve (David Muench)

Downeast Region

1. Upper Birch Island Preserve and
   East Plummer Island Preserve/91
2. Shipstern and Flint Islands Preserve/92
3. Great Wass Archipelago/94
4. Larrabee Heath Preserve/98
5. Salt Island Preserve and Stone
   Island Preserve/99
6. Cobscook Bay/100

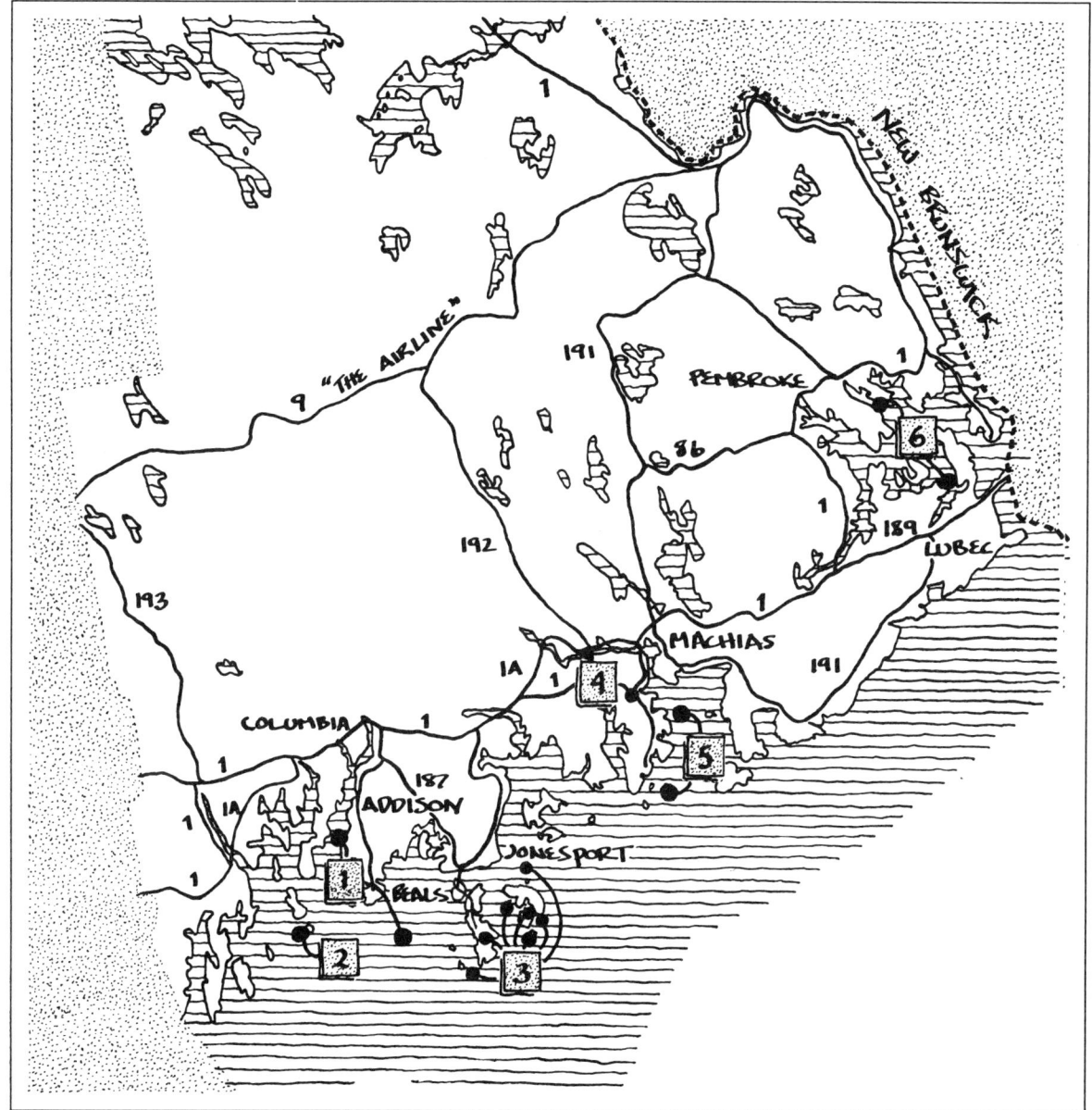

Downeast Region

East of Frenchman Bay, the country opens up. Barrens alternate with woods that are increasingly dominated by conifers: spruce, fir and tamarack. The trees lose the well-fed appearance of their siblings farther south, taking on instead the tough, compact look of enduring survivors. The ocean shore is rough and rocky. The region's 15- to 20-foot tides reveal extensive mudflats.

The relatively remote Downeast region is one of the nation's strongholds for bald eagles. The area is vital to the continued recovery of the eagle population. Many of Maine's more than 90 eagle nests are scattered on islands and remote shores up the coast, with 15 in Cobscook Bay alone. The Conservancy has protected eight bald eagle nesting sites in preserves, and several more on lands that it has helped others protect. A number of preserves without nests, but within the nesting territories of eagles, are regularly used for roosting and feeding.

Along the shore, the climate is strongly influenced by the Gulf of Maine. In summer, the prevailing winds blow over the ocean, bringing fog and much cooler temperatures. The region often shares weather with the Canadian Maritimes, rather than the rest of Maine. The islands of Great Wass archipelago in Jonesport-Beals are known for their distinctive habitats created by direct exposure to the ocean. Heaths cover the lowlands and continue right on up the slopes. Wildflowers, trees and shrubs normally found in the sub-arctic make up a large percentage of the flora. Scores of bird species, including many seabirds, nest on the islands.

The Conservancy protects more than a dozen islands in the Great Wass island ecosystem, both in preserves and through conservation easements. A half dozen more islands, five of which are in Pleasant Bay, are also kept natural and unspoiled by easements held by the Conservancy.

Bogs are a regular part of the Downeast landscape. The Conservancy's Larrabee Heath Preserve (Machiasport) is a fine, unspoiled example of a coastal raised peatland, a type of bog restricted in North America to a narrow band within influence of the sea from Maine through the Maritimes. The Conservancy also

helps the town of Columbia and the state protect Maine's largest bog, the Great Heath, through a management agreement with the town of Columbia.

Cobscook Bay is one of the nation's most vital and healthy coastal ecosystems. The bay is exceptionally important to breeding and migrating waterfowl, as well as bald eagles.

The Conservancy, state wildlife officials, local organizations and other conservation groups have joined forces to protect important habitats within the bay.

The Conservancy has preserved additional wildlife habitat by helping the U.S. Fish and Wildlife Service acquire Petit Manan Point and Bois Bubert Island, and the Cross Island archipelago.

Except for the nesting islands, which are closed during the March 15 to August 15 nesting season, the region's preserves are open to the public. Great Wass and Mistake islands are the only ones with maintained trails; the others offer opportunities to enjoy the peace and quiet of the land and water without human intrusions.

The Downeast preserves are watched over by several volunteer stewardship committees and one seasonal caretaker. For more information, please contact the Maine Chapter stewardship office in Topsham.

Upper Birch Island and East Plummer Island Preserves

Upper Birch Island, 27 acres;
East Plummer Island, 10 acres,
Both in Addison

A colony of great blue herons and a pair of bald eagles nest on Upper Birch Island, sheltered in the lower reaches of the Pleasant River. Bald eagles have nested for 25 years out on East Plummer Island in the open waters of Pleasant Bay.

Upper Birch Island

The largest island in the Pleasant River, Upper Birch is sheltered between Ripley Neck and the Addison peninsula. The oval island rises swiftly to a broad central plateau elevated some 60 feet above the water.

For more than 30 years, great blue herons have nested in the spruce forest on the southern side of Upper Birch. In 1983, the colony included 80 nests lodged in 60 trees. Since the arrival of a pair of nesting bald eagles, the number of herons has decreased, but the colony remains active.

The island's steep, ledgy shore drops off abruptly into deep water, creating a very narrow intertidal zone, except on the southeastern shore, where the land slopes gradually down to a gravel beach. The shore ledges are used regularly by harbor seals for haul-outs.

The island was used to graze sheep at one time, but may have been otherwise left alone. Fishermen once set weirs near the northern end; lobstermen still occasionally use the island as a stop-over.

The Conservancy purchased Upper Birch Island in 1983 to protect the nesting great blue herons and bald eagles.

 Nesting island: closed to the public during the March 15 to August 15 nesting season. Please do not harass the great blue herons and bald eagles by landing on the island or lingering offshore. Disturbance can cause serious nest losses.

At other times of the year, it is possible to land on the island and explore a bit. There are no trails.

East Plummer Island

East Plummer Island has been used by breeding bald eagles for most of the last 25 years. Located in the open waters of Pleasant Bay, the remote island is too difficult to reach, and its terrain too rough, to attract much human use.

A forest of mature red and white spruce covers most of the island, with yellow birch and mountain ash interspersed. The cool winds and plentiful fog of the bay have created ideal conditions for the growth of moisture-loving plants. Ferns, mosses and lichens, including old man's beard, grow luxuriantly in the forest.

Heavy storms have caused blowdowns where raspberry bushes intertwine with fallen trees in a prickly, impenetrable mass.

Over the centuries, the island's pink granite shoreline has weathered to smooth, almost billowy, shapes. There are no real beaches, but tidal flats extend out around the island for a considerable distance, especially on the eastern shore, where East Plummer is connected to West Plummer by a gravel and mud bar exposed at low tide.

East Plummer Island was donated to the Conservancy in 1979 by Mr. and Mrs. John Daigle. They also donated a conservation easement to the Maine Department of Island Fisheries and Wildlife, setting up a framework for cooperative management by the Conservancy and IF&W.

 Nesting island: closed to the public during the March 15 to August 15 nesting season. Please do not harass the eagles by landing on the island or lingering offshore. Disturbance can cause serious nest losses.

During the rest of the year, it is possible to land on the island and walk along the shore. There are no trails.

Shipstern Island and Flint Island Preserves

Shipstern Island, 8 acres (partial ownership);
Flint Island, 170 acres.
Both in Harrington

Steep, sculpted shore cliffs define these two Pleasant Bay islands. A pair of bald eagles claims both islands as part of their nesting territory.

Shipstern Island

Shipstern Island looms out of the fog looking uncannily like the stern of a Spanish galleon that chose Pleasant Bay for its final resting place. The sea has cut deeply into the island's ochre-colored cliffs, sculpting them into fascinating shapes.

A pair of bald eagles thrives on the isolated island, and has successfully fledged at least seven chicks in the past four years. The eagles also claim nearby Flint Island, which is currently used for roosting.

The forest on Shipstern is a mixture of old spruces and hardwoods, and includes a stand of mature yellow birches. Blowdowns are scattered throughout the island.

In 1980, Mr. and Mrs. Nathaniel French donated a one-half undivided interest in Shipstern Island to the Conservancy.

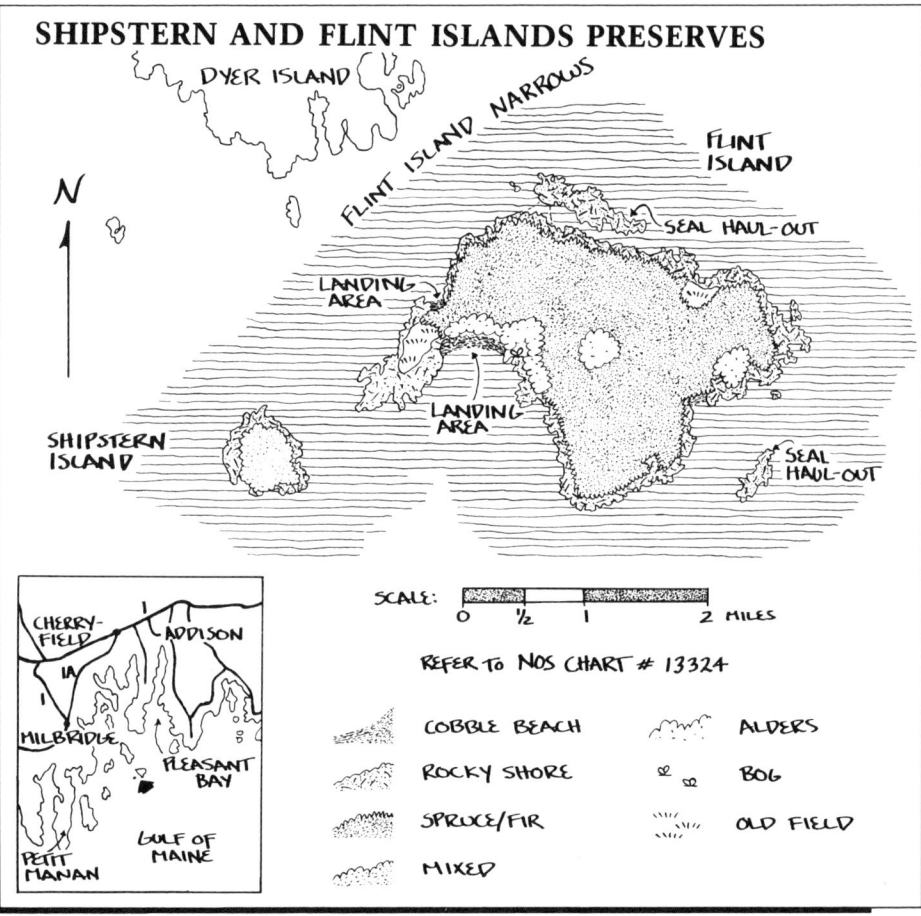

SHIPSTERN AND FLINT ISLANDS PRESERVES

DYER ISLAND

FLINT ISLAND NARROWS

FLINT ISLAND

SEAL HAUL-OUT

LANDING AREA

LANDING AREA

SEAL HAUL-OUT

N

SHIPSTERN ISLAND

SCALE: 0 ½ 1 2 MILES

REFER TO NOS CHART # 13324

— COBBLE BEACH   ALDERS
— ROCKY SHORE   BOG
— SPRUCE/FIR   OLD FIELD
— MIXED

CHERRY-FIELD
ADDISON
1A
1
MILBRIDGE
PLEASANT BAY
PETIT MANAN
GULF OF MAINE

Flint Island

The cool pale lavender-gray cliffs of Flint Island contrast nicely with the warm reds and yellows of Shipstern Island's shore.

Spruce-fir forest covers most of the island, broken only by two old fields and several alder swamps. Flint was once heavily grazed by sheep. Huge, gnarled, 100-year-old spruces, veterans of the former pastures, are scattered throughout the spruce-fir forest. Since they grew up standing alone in the open, these trees developed thick lower branches all around.

Two sub-arctic plant species, beach-head iris (*Iris Hookeri*) and oysterleaf (*Mertensia maritima*) grow in the rocks along the upper edge of the shore.

At least one pair of ospreys shares Flint with its pair of bald eagles. The rocks on the northern and southeastern shores are used as haul-outs by harbor seals and, occasionally, gray seals. Gray seals are larger than harbor seals and have distinct "horsey" heads. They prefer haul-outs in exposed and isolated locations where rough seas ensure privacy.

Flint Island's cliffs are not truly flint, but an exceptionally fine-grained siltstone that looks like chert or flint. At several points along the shore, there are sections of dark, fine-grained rock bearing fossils of crinoids, a marine echinoderm related to today's sea urchins and starfishes. The fossils, from the Paleozoic era, are estimated to be at least 420 million years old. Other sections along the shore are made up of shattered blocks surrounded by granite, evidence of violent volcanic activity.

The Conservancy acquired Flint Island at a bargain price in 1968, thanks to the generosity of Mr. and Mrs. George Milmine, whose family had owned the island since 1930. They dedicated the island to the memory of Joseph and Rose Parsons, Mr. Milmine's aunt and uncle.

 Nesting islands: Shipstern, the currently active nesting island, is closed to the public during the March 15 to August 15 nesting season. Please do not harass the eagles by landing on the island or lingering offshore. Disturbance can result in serious nest losses.

In any case, Shipstern's steep cliffs make landing almost impossible. It is possible to land on Flint at the shingle beach on the northwestern shore. There are no trails.

DIRECTIONS: Shipstern and Flint islands are across the narrows from Dyer Island in Pleasant Bay.

FOSSILS More than 500 million years ago, the area that now includes Flint Island was part of a warm, shallow sea that stretched across the continent. Lilylike animals called crinoids up to 50 feet long anchored on the sea bed in huge areas. Their remains were preserved in the bottom sediments, now turned to stone.

A few small crinoid species still exist, but most of the world's waters are too cold for them.

Great Wass Archipelago

Preserves: Great Wass Island, 1,579 acres, Beals; Crumple Island, 27 acres (partial ownership), Beals; Mistake Island, 21 acres, Jonesport; The Man Islands, 15 acres, Jonesport; Black Island, 10 acres, Jonesport; Little Hardwood Island, 10 acres, Jonesport; Mark Island, 41 acres, Jonesport. *Easements:* Great Wass Island, 150 acres, Beals; Seguin Island, 22 acres, Jonesport; Head Harbor Island, 700 acres, Jonesport; The Cow Yard Group (Devil, Marsh, Little Peabody, Big Peabody islands), 13 acres, Jonesport; Steele Harbor Island, 500 acres, Jonesport.

Beautiful in all seasons and all weathers, the wild, windswept islands of the Great Wass archipelago are especially memorable on a still, foggy morning. At the top of the ridge of Great Wass Island, the fog eddies over bare ledges through the twisted, dark forms of jack pines, touching their needles with crystal drops. Down on the shore, the mists ebb and flow, softening the pink of the granite ledges and turning the sea a platinum blue.

The Conservancy has protected nearly a third of the islands in the Great Wass archipelago. Eight of the islands, including much of Great Wass Island itself, are owned by the Conservancy; seven more are protected by conservation easements held by the Conservancy. Great Wass Island Preserve is also protected on its inland boundaries by three conservation easements.

The archipelago lies at the edge of the Gulf of Maine, just off the Jonesport peninsula. The islands exist in an oceanic micro-climate; they are always cool, wet and windy, but are buffered from the temperature extremes of the interior.

Although the islands in the group have much in common, they offer a fascinating diversity of landscapes. The largest, Great Wass, is fairly high, with a rough, rolling topography that closely echoes the form of its granite bedrock. Most of the island is forested with spruce and fir, but there are large open bogs in the lowlands and scattered stands of jack pine along the ridges. Southwest of Great Wass is Crumple Island, a small, barren island of fissured granite with a distinctive domed profile.

Moving east of Great Wass to the Head Harbor group of the archipelago, the island nearest the open ocean is Mistake Island. It is almost completely open heath land, with only a small area of alders and spruce on the northern end. Neighboring Steele Harbor Island is low and covered with spruce. North of Steele Harbor is the largest island in the group, Head Harbor Island, with densely forested slopes that rise nearly 200 feet above the water. Between Steele Harbor and Head Harbor lie the four forested little islands of the Cow's Yard, and their neighbor Black Island, a rounded dome also crowned with dense spruce-fir forest. East of these, off the tip of Head Harbor, are the two Man Islands. Both of these are treeless and are very exposed to the ocean.

To the west of Head Harbor is another forested island, Little Hardwood Island, which is home to a pair of nesting bald eagles. The last two islands are north of Head Harbor Island; Seguin, low and open and shrubby, and Mark, steeply sloping and covered with spruce, fir and some hardwoods.

The archipelago's climate encourages a specialized flora composed to a great extent of plants that are normally found much farther north in sub-arctic regions. The islands are a kind of southern outpost for these plant species and natural communities, several of which are rarely seen elsewhere in the United States. Jack pine is one of those species that reaches the southern edge of its range in Maine. The second largest stand in Maine, 550 acres, is on Great Wass. The trees are short, stunted and gnarled—expressions of the harsh conditions in which they survive.

Jack pine resembles pitch pine, which grows in many similarly exposed locations farther south. Jack pine has short needles in pairs; pitch pine's are much longer and in threes. Both species normally depend upon the heat of wild fires to open their cones, releasing the seeds. The jack pine cones on Great Wass open without fire, a trait that is of considerable interest to ecologists.

The islands' continually damp and cool climate is ideal for the formation of bogs. The conditions are so favorable that the bogs not only fill in the lowest spots, but form on land that slopes uphill significantly. The best examples of these shrub-slope peatlands are on Mistake Island, where more than 60 percent of the island is covered with low ericaceous (heath) shrubs such as leatherleaf, lambskill, Labrador tea, black crowberry and lowbush blueberry. Several feet of peat blankets the bedrock. Shrub-slope peatlands are found in the United

States on just a few islands and headlands in Washington County.

Another type of maritime peatland, the coastal raised peatland, occurs over large areas of Great Wass Island and in smaller patches on several other islands in the archipelago. The Great Wass peatlands are especially noteworthy, and are the easiest to see. Unlike inland bogs that evolve from ponds or wetlands, these bogs have only a faint trace of a bordering lagg, or moat; are quite firm; and develop a distinctly domed surface profile.

The bogs, or heaths as they are locally known, are essentially treeless, and are covered with a variety of ericaceous shrubs like the shrub-slope peatlands. On Great Wass, jack pine and black spruce are scattered in small clumps on some of the higher spots in the heaths. This the only place in the United States known to have jack pine growing in such a bog.

The surface of the heath is primarily sphagnum moss dotted with cranberry, black crowberry, pitcher plant, sundew and baked-apple berry. The baked-apple berry (*Rubus chamaemorus*) a small relative of the raspberry, produces a single golden berry that is a popular and important source of fresh fruit throughout the sub-arctic.

Down on the shore, several other sub-arctic species find conditions that approximate their more northerly habitats. Beach head iris (*Iris Hookeri*), a smaller version of the common blue flag iris, grows in crevices in the ledges at the upper edge of the shore. Bird's eye primrose (*Primula farinosa*) and roseroot sedum (*Sedum rosea*) also lodge among the rocks. Oysterleaf (*Mertensia maritima*) and more common plants such as beach pea (*Lathyrus japonicus*), harebells (*Campanula rotundifolia*), seabeach orach (*Atriplex arenaria*), and seabeach sandwort (*Arenaria peploides*) grow near the storm-tide line on the beaches and along the ledges. On Great Wass, Mistake and Crumple, star gentian (*Lomatagonium rotatum*) and blinks (*Montia fontana*), two species that are officially listed as threatened in the state, grow in spots that are still moist, but that are slightly more sheltered than the shoreline.

At the very edge of the open ocean, on Red Head at the southern tip of Great Wass, the invertebrate species living in the intertidal zone include a fair sampling of ones that are usually found offshore in deeper water.

The significant natural features of Great Wass, including the Red Head intertidal zone, the jack pine stand and the heaths, are listed on the state Register of Critical Areas.

The bedrock of the archipelago is of

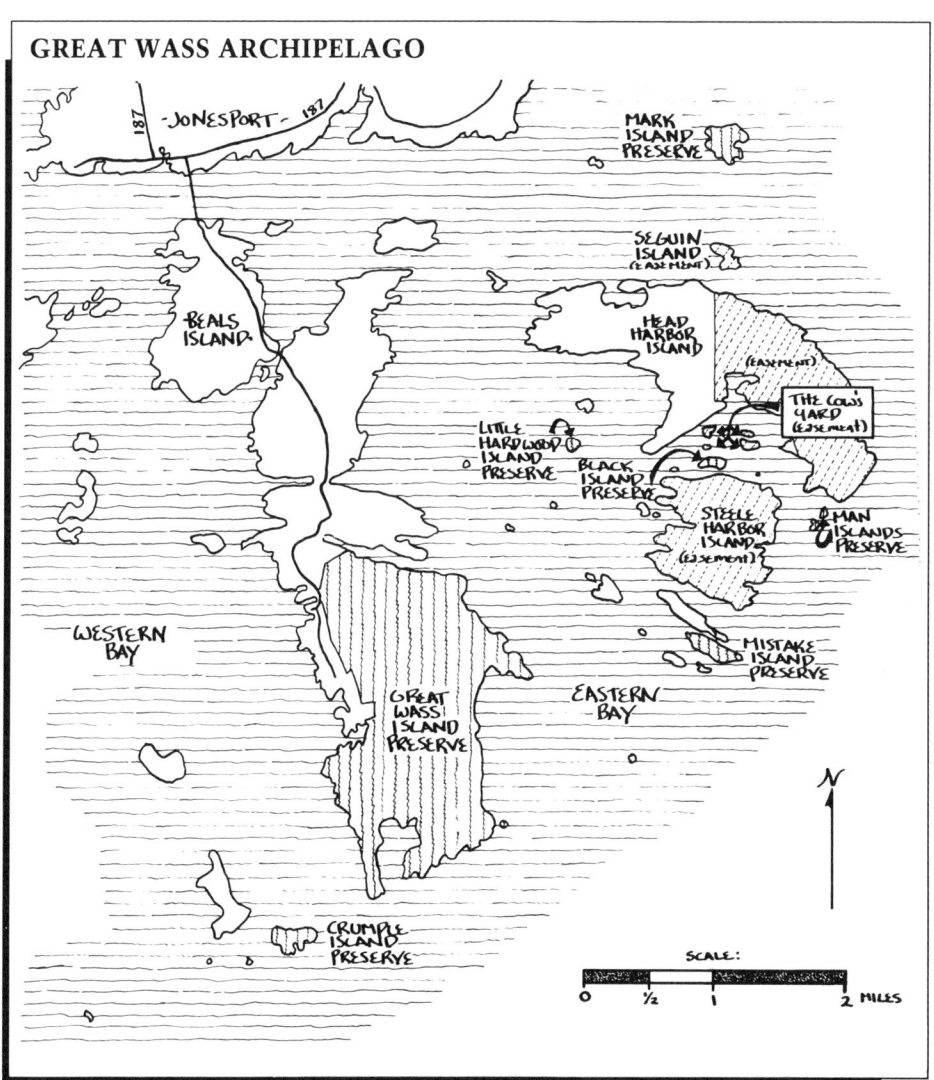

GREAT WASS ARCHIPELAGO

GREAT WASS ISLAND

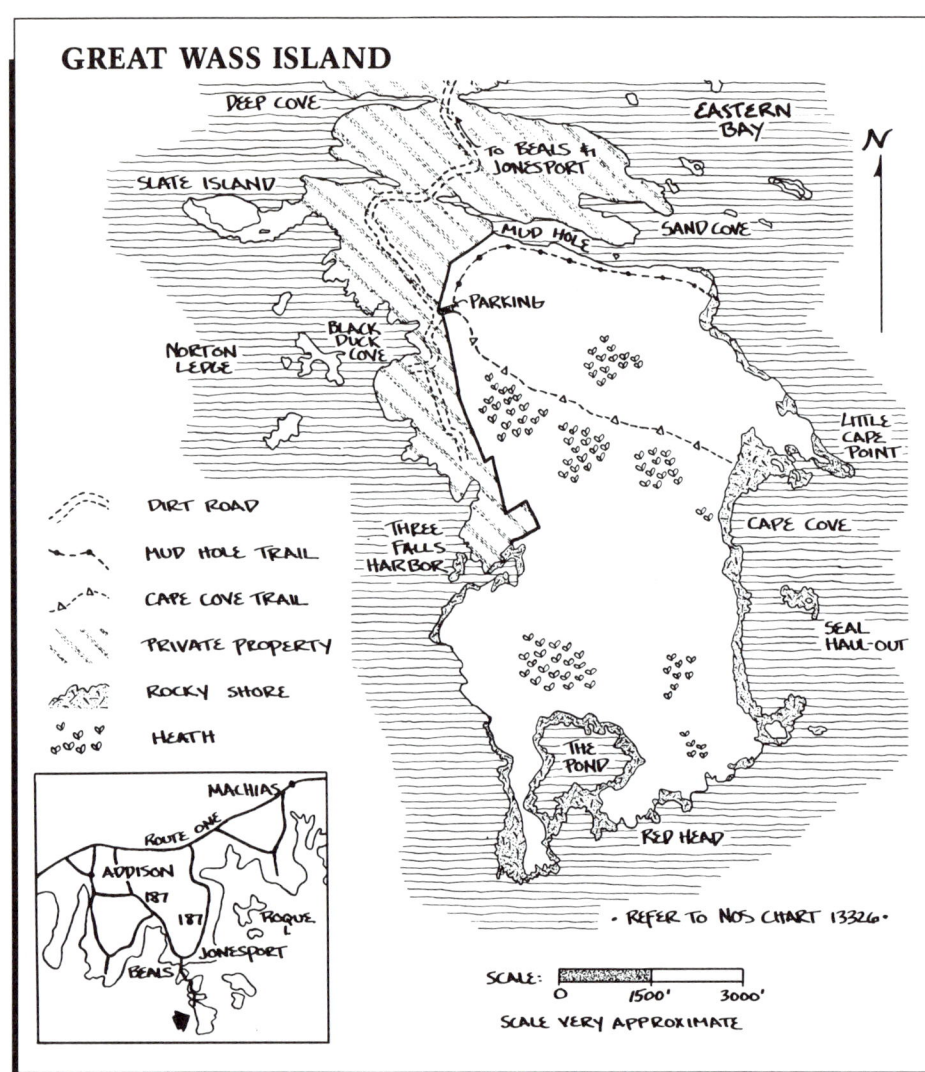

DEEP COVE
EASTERN BAY
SLATE ISLAND
TO BEALS & JONESPORT
MUD HOLE
SAND COVE
PARKING
NORTON LEDGE
BLACK DUCK COVE
LITTLE CAPE POINT
THREE FALLS HARBOR
CAPE COVE
SEAL HAUL-OUT
THE POND
RED HEAD

N

- - - - DIRT ROAD
- - - - MUD HOLE TRAIL
- - - - CAPE COVE TRAIL
PRIVATE PROPERTY
ROCKY SHORE
HEATH

MACHIAS
ROUTE ONE
ADDISON
187
187
ROQUE I.
JONESPORT
BEALS

· REFER TO NOS CHART 13326 ·

SCALE:
0   1500'   3000'

SCALE VERY APPROXIMATE

two distinct types. Great Wass, Crumple, Mistake and Steele Harbor islands all share the same rock: a fine pink granite that has weathered to form broad sloping shore ledges. The other 11 islands, which make up most of the Head Harbor group, have a dark metavolcanic and metasedimentary bedrock that tends to form steep slopes, rugged shores and cliffs.

Great Wass Island Preserve was acquired by the Conservancy in 1978 after a two-year fund-raising campaign. The Conservancy has purchased one three-acre parcel and one common undivided ownership on Crumple Island; the remainder are privately owned. In 1983, the Conservancy bought Mistake Island from the grandson of the man who served as keeper of the Moose Peak light from 1890 to 1910. The other islands of the Head Harbor group, five preserves (Mark, Little Hardwood, Black, Inner Man and Outer Man) and seven easements (Seguin, Head Harbor, Devils, Marsh, Little Peabody and Big Peabody) were transferred to the Conservancy by the National Audubon Society and Maine Coast Heritage Trust so that all of the islands in the archipelago could be managed as a group. Eleven of these islands were protected originally by Priscilla Williams, who donated title to or conservation easements on them.

Great Wass Island

Great Wass Island is accessible by bridge and causeway. There are two trails that begin together at the preserve parking lot, then diverge and go to different parts of the eastern shore. The Cape Point Trail climbs and traverses the jack pine ridges overlooking the heaths, then passes through a small wetland with sundews, pitcher plants and sedges and a dwarfed spruce forest before ending on the shore between two beaches fronted by an extensive intertidal zone. It is possible to make a loop by heading north along the shore to the eastern end of the second trail, the Mud Hole Trail. This trail follows along the shore of the Mud Hole (a cove far more attractive than its name) for a good distance, passing through a small area of birch and hardwoods that shelter an osprey nest (listening quietly is the best way to find it), then into a cool spruce forest blanketed with mosses and lichens. After a fair stretch along the shore the trail turns inland, climbs to the height of land and descends, and eventually rejoins the main access trail. The loop is approximately five miles long.

Be prepared for a reasonably strenuous and very likely damp hike. The walk along the shore over cobbles and ledges can be surprisingly tiring.

There are boardwalks over the regularly flooded spots, but the trails (and shore) are often wet going.

The southern end of the island, Red Head, can be reached only by walking along the shore. It is a stiff nine-mile round trip from the shore end of the Cape Point Trail.

A trail brochure and checklist of the island's birds are available at the registration box in the preserve parking lot.

DIRECTIONS: Take Route 187 from Jonesport to Beals Island. Go through Beals, over the causeway, and turn right on the road (which changes to dirt) to Black Duck Cove. The parking lot is on the left, just after the lobster pound and duck pond.

Mistake Island

A boardwalk built by the Coast Guard for access to the Moose Peak light is ideal for exploring the island without damaging the fragile vegetation. It is also possible to walk along the shore. Please do not go over to Knight Island; it is privately owned.

DIRECTIONS: There is an anchorage in the narrow cove between Mistake and Knight islands. A small boat can be pulled up on the intertidal bar between the two islands, but watch the tide.

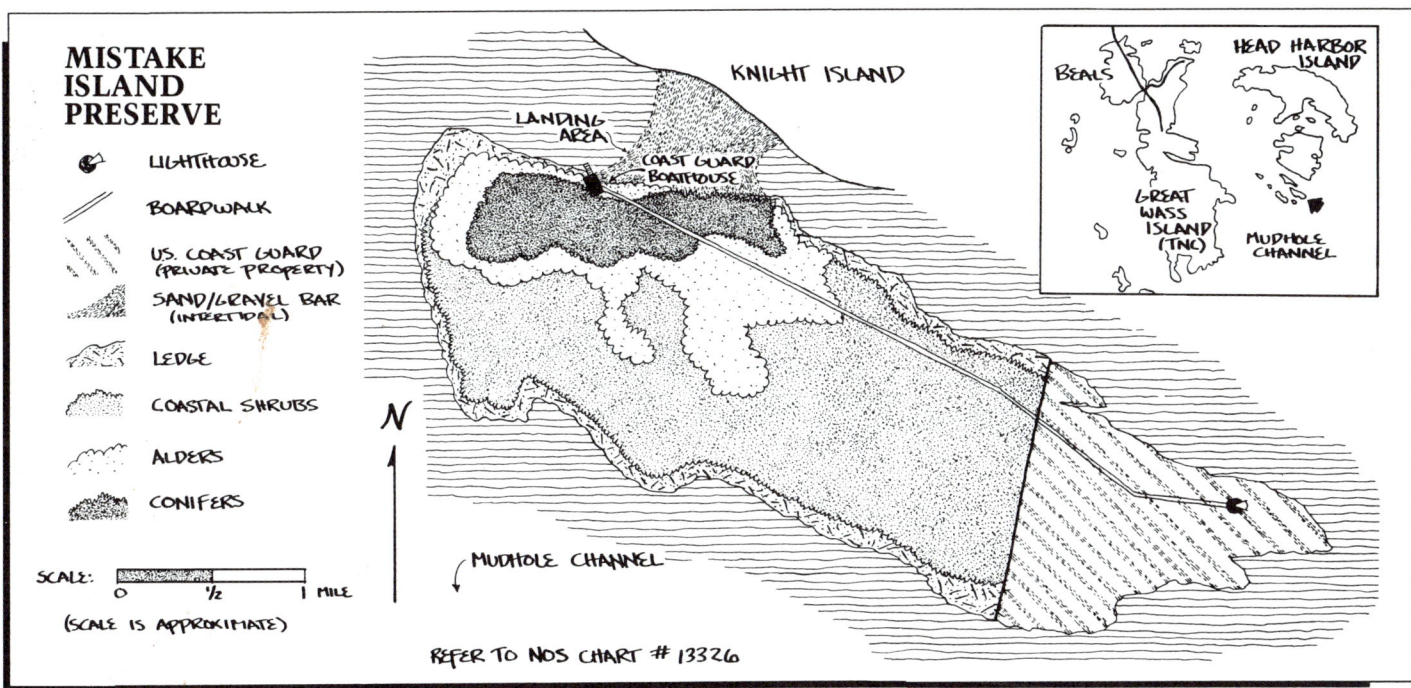

MISTAKE ISLAND PRESERVE

LIGHTHOUSE
BOARDWALK
U.S. COAST GUARD (PRIVATE PROPERTY)
SAND/GRAVEL BAR (INTERTIDAL)
LEDGE
COASTAL SHRUBS
ALDERS
CONIFERS

SCALE: 0   ½   1 MILE
(SCALE IS APPROXIMATE)

N

MUDHOLE CHANNEL

KNIGHT ISLAND
LANDING AREA
COAST GUARD BOATHOUSE

BEALS   HEAD HARBOR ISLAND
GREAT WASS ISLAND (TNC)
MUDHOLE CHANNEL

REFER TO NOS CHART # 13326

Visiting the other islands in the archipelago

With the exception of Little Hardwood Island, which is a bald eagle nesting site and is therefore closed during the March 15 to August 15 nesting season, the other Conservancy island preserves in the archipelago (Crumple, Black, Mark and the Mans) are open for careful day use. Landings can be difficult due to rough ledges, stiff winds and strong currents. Watch the tide. There are no marked trails; please walk along the rocky shore. If a fire is absolutely necessary, please build it well below the high tide mark.

The remaining islands in the archipelago Seguin, Head Harbor, Steele Harbor and the Cows Yard) are protected by conservation easements held by the Conservancy, but they are privately owned and therefore are not open to the public. Please respect the landowners' wishes and avoid landing on these islands.

Larrabee Heath Preserve

427 acres, Machiasport

Larrabee Heath is an excellent example of a coastal raised peatland, a type of peatland found only in the cool, damp coastal zone of North America. Although its thousands of tons of peat were of considerable commercial interest, the heath was left untouched.

Larrabee Heath sits in a valley in the middle of the Machiasport peninsula, within a mile of Little Kennebec Bay on the east and Machias Bay on the west. The climate in this area is consistently moist and cool; weeks of fog are a regular occurrence.

The heath is an excellent example of a coastal raised peatland, a type of peatland that occurs in North America only in a narrow band along the coast from Mount Desert to the Canadian Maritimes. It is an elevated plateau bordered by a short steep slope that drops down to a clearly defined moat or lagg.

The only trees on the heath, tamarack and black spruce, grow on scattered islands. Ericaceous shrubs such as sheep laurel, Labrador tea and rhodora dominate the plateau. Its surface is covered with a carpet of sphagnum mosses and black crowberry (*Empetrum nigrum*).

Below the plateau, the land drops down into wet meadows. Blue-joint grass (*Calamagrostis canadensis*) and tussock sedge (*Carex stricta*) make up most of the meadows.

Northern white cedar grows in the wet zone next to the lagg on the upland side. The land rises to a series of ridges wooded with mixed hardwoods and stands of spruce and fir. Near the eastern edge of the plateau, alder and meadowsweet thickets mark the transition between the heath and the old fields that remain from former farms.

Two streams flow east along the northern and southern sides of the heath, then join to form Meadow Brook, which empties into Machias Bay. Although Meadow Brook is occasionally dammed by beavers, flooding the wet meadows, this has little effect on the heath plateau.

Larrabee Heath is at least 9,000 years old. Its five- to 10-foot-deep layer of peat, composed of the remnants of old swamps and tidal marshes, rest on top of layers of silt, clay and sand left by the glaciers. The whole area is underlain with shales and siltstones formed up to 400 million years ago.

The Downeast heaths are a valuable source of peat. Several have been mined, including the nearby Jonesport Heath. Fortunately, Larrabee Heath has been spared, although it contains an estimated 125,000 short tons of air-dried peat. Except for haying of the wet meadow and some logging in the uplands, the heath and its adjacent lands have been left untouched.

In the 1800s, several people jointly owned Larrabee Heath. Over the years, the number of common undivided ownerships grew with the number of descendants, creating a very complex ownership pattern. In 1983, the Conservancy acquired two major portions of the heath with the support of John Mead Howells of Bucks Harbor and the assistance of the Maine Audubon Society. Since then, the Conservancy has steadily acquired the remaining interests. Today, the preserve protects essentially all of the peatland ecosystem.

 Please use discretion and care when exploring the heath; trampling compacts the spongy peat, destroying the habitat needed by the heath's indigenous plants. Winter is one of the best times to visit the heath. The peatland's distinctive landforms and varied habitats are clearly visible, and skiing or snowshoeing on the frozen heath causes much less damage to it. An abandoned woods road runs along the southern edge of the heath. Although there are no maintained hiking trails, there are plenty of game trails.

DIRECTIONS: Heading south from Machiasport on the Machias Road toward Bucks Harbor, go past Sanborn Cove on the left, cross the heath's outlet stream, and take the first road to the right. Park at the end of the road (look for Conservancy signs). Access to the heath is across private property; please stay on the old woods road. There is a sign dedicating the heath to John Mead Howells near the old woods road.

Salt Island and Stone Island Preserves

Salt Island, 40 acres (partial ownership);
Stone Island, 20 acres.
Both in Machiasport

These two small islands in Machias Bay are secure homes for nesting bald eagles, and in the case of Stone Island, great blue herons and ospreys.

Salt Island

Salt Island lies in Machias Bay, just off the Machiasport shore. The island is guarded by 20- to 30-foot cliffs on all but its northern shore, which has extensive mudflats. Bald eagles nest in the island's quiet woods.

An almost impenetrable mature spruce-fir forest covers most of the island, extending right to the edge of the cliffs.

A major fault line splits Salt across the middle.

In the early 1800s, salt makers cut the island's forest to fuel their fires, but little evidence of their logging or their factory remains. Today, clams and wrinkles (periwinkles) are harvested from the island's flats and intertidal zone.

In 1983, the Conservancy purchased the western half of Salt Island. The eastern half is privately owned.

 Nesting island: closed to the public during the March 15 to August 15 nesting season. Please do not harass the eagles by landing on the island or lingering offshore. Disturbance can cause serious nest losses.

During the rest of the year, it is possible to land on the flats and explore the Conservancy preserve on the western half of the island. Watch the tide on the flats.

Stone Island

On the seaward shore of Stone Island, 90-foot cliffs drop straight into water over 100 feet deep. The island is easily reached from the open ocean and is just off the Machiasport peninsula.

In the 1960s, Stone seemed like an ideal place to offload supertankers in Machias Bay. However, after a decade of public debate, the oil interests abandoned their plans. The Landguard Trust, a private group that had campaigned against the oil facility, quickly bought the island and resold it to the Conservancy at cost.

Stone's forbidding shoreline of cliffs and boulders discourages human visitors, allowing large numbers of great blue herons and ospreys to nest in peaceful isolation. In 1988, a pair of bald eagles began to nest, an event that apparently has been accepted by the other birds.

With more than 100 nests, Stone is one of the largest great blue heron nesting colonies in Maine. It also has one of the densest concentrations of nesting ospreys in the state.

The island is covered with spruce-fir forest, except on the northern end, where the nesting herons have killed many of the spruces with their droppings. The dead trees have blown down, leaving openings now filled with raspberry thickets and young trees.

 Nesting island: closed to the public during the March 15 to August 15 nesting season. Please do not harass the great blue herons or ospreys by landing on the island or lingering offshore. Disturbance can cause serious nest losses.

During the rest of the year, it is nearly impossible to land on the rugged shore of Stone Island and explore. There are no trails.

Cobscook Bay

Coggins Head, 53 acres, Pembroke;
Long Island, 120 acres, Lubec

Wild, remote, sparsely populated Cobscook Bay is a vital stronghold for breeding bald eagles. Dozens of species of waterfowl breed, migrate through or winter here, finding abundant food on the bay's extensive flats and open waters.

Cobscook Bay has one of Maine's densest eagle populations as well as one of the most consistently productive. It is also one of the state's four major bald eagle wintering areas. The state's relatively pristine marine and estuarine ecosystems are of major importance to feeding, breeding, migrating and wintering shorebirds and waterfowl, including black ducks. Atlantic sea-run salmon and brook trout pass through the bay each year.

The North American Waterfowl Management Plan, an agreement to protect waterfowl and wildlife habitat signed by Canada, the United States and Mexico, lists the bay as a top priority in North America for the acquisition and protection of key waterfowl habitats. For more than a decade, the Conservancy has been involved in efforts to protect significant natural areas in the bay, especially bald eagle nesting and roosting sites such as Coggins Head and Long Island. Joined with other public and private conservation organization in the Maine Wetlands Protection Coalition, the Conservancy has given special attention to preservation of areas identified in the waterfowl management plan.

In 1989, the Conservancy purchased more than 200 acres on Wilbur Neck in Pembroke on Denny Bay. The property includes thousands of feet of shorefront and many acres of intertidal flats that are prime waterfowl habitat. There is an active bald eagle nest on the wooded neck. According to current plans, the state Department of Inland Fisheries and Wildlife will eventually assume ownership and management of this area.

Coggins Head

Thickly wooded Coggins Head Preserve has been a productive bald eagle nesting site for many years. Located in the northern reaches of the bay on Hersey Neck, the preserve extends for nearly 4,000 feet along the Pennamaquan River. The headland rises more than 100 feet above the water.

The forest is mostly softwoods: red spruce and northern white cedar interspersed with white spruce, balsam fir and white pine. White pine dominates on the western shore; a few hardwoods, primarily red maple and white birch, mix in with the softwoods on the northern shore. The trees tower over thick understory vegetation, making ideal nesting and roosting perches.

The forest was logged periodically until early in this century. It has been left essentially undisturbed since then. There is a small clearing on the southeastern side of the preserve, and a few apple trees and field junipers remain from an old farm.

The preserve's balsam firs have been heavily attacked by spruce budworm. Although named spruce budworm, the insect definitely prefers balsam fir, and will consume the tender tips of all available firs before moving on to spruce buds. However, since the damage it caused was first

noticed on spruce, a species of much greater commercial interest, it was named the spruce budworm. Periodic population explosions of budworm have caused serious damage to Maine's forests.

Coggins Head is composed of rhyolite, a red, gray or black fine-grained, very dense granite that is common from Cobscook Bay to Penobscot Bay. A thin layer of glacial till covers most of the preserve. The 20-foot tides reveal extensive flats that are important waterfowl feeding areas.

There are few records of the history of Coggins Head, but tradition says that the founders of Pembroke are buried somewhere on the preserve property.

The Conservancy purchased Coggins Head Preserve in 1982 to protect the bald eagle nesting site.

 Nesting area: closed to the public during the March 15 to August 15 nesting season. Please do not harass the eagles by walking in the preserve or lingering offshore. During the rest of the year, the area is used by the eagles for roosting. The birds prefer quiet and isolated habitats, and are much more likely to remain and breed success-fully if they are left undisturbed at all times.

Long Island

Rugged Long Island in South Bay is also densely wooded. The island is a historic bald eagle nesting site, and is used currently for roosting and feeding.

The island's forest has been disturbed in two major ways: the hardwoods were taken off when the demand for them was high during the second World War; and the northern half of the island burned when fire jumped from the mainland in 1958. Only a narrow band of softwoods along the shore was left untouched by both loggers and fire.

In the burn, pin cherry and paper birch mix with bush honeysuckle and blueberry. On the rest of the island, paper birch is accompanied by red cedar, balsam fir, maple and spruce. There are a few open meadows.

Since the island is so close to the mainland, it serves as habitat for many mammals. White-tailed deer, snow-shoe hares, porcupines and wood-chucks come across in search of food and shelter. The ledges on the northern end of the island are used as a haul out by harbor seals.

EAGLES NEST Bald eagles mate for life, returning to the same nest year after year. The largest of all nests built by a single pair of birds, a bald eagle's nest of sticks is repaired and enlarged until it may reach the size of a small car. The nests are usually lodged in tall, sturdy trees, but they can outgrow their support and collapse. Unlike ospreys, bald eagles usually are not tolerant of human activities and will abandon their nests if sufficiently bothered.

Each eagle pair normally produces two eggs in early April. Two chicks is a kind of insurance policy; often one sibling completely dominates the other and is the sole survivor. It takes nearly four months, from early spring to mid-summer, before the young are ready to fly.

Aside from the logging and the fire, the island's past is not well known. There may well have been farms or orchards here in the past century.

Robert Rimoldi donated Long Island to the Conservancy in a series of gifts beginning in 1980.

 Long Island is an important sanctuary for bald eagles, including a pair currently nesting on nearby Hog Island. Please use discretion and consider the eagles' privacy when contemplating a visit.

DIRECTIONS: Long Island is just off the western shore of South Bay. It is possible to land on the shore, but watch the tide.

Big Reed Forest Reserve (Lee Carbonneau)

Northern Region

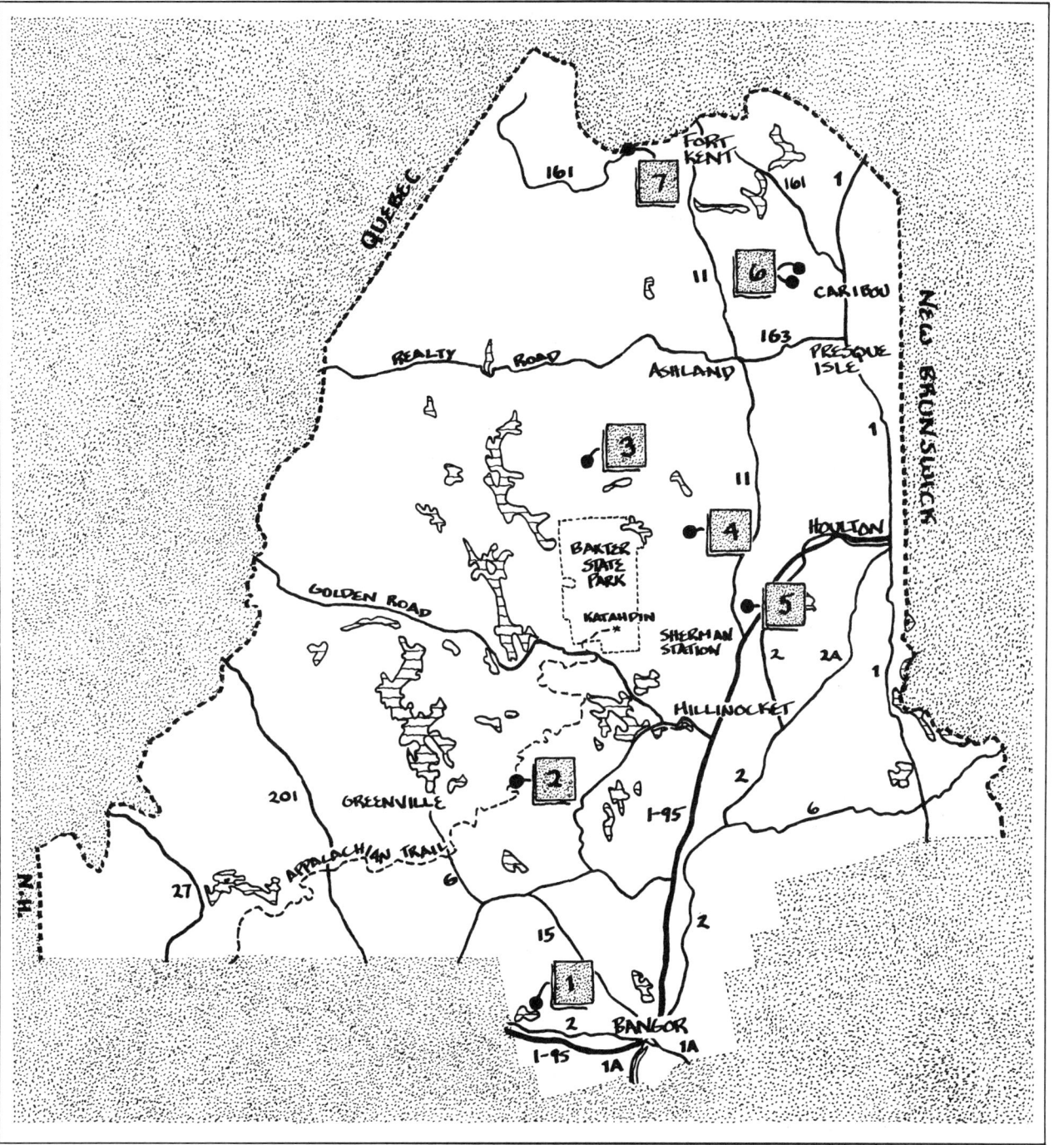

Northern Maine Region

The northern Maine section of this book includes several major physiographic regions, each of which has its own characteristic topography, habitats and special natural features.

A line of mountains crosses over the border from New Hampshire at Maine's western corner, then trends northeasterly up through Rumford and Skowhegan, ending in the vicinity of Mount Katahdin. A clearly visible change in grade separates the mountains from the lower, gradually sloping hills of the central uplands. The central uplands region covers a wide band that begins west of the Kennebec River and heads northeast through Dover-Foxcroft, and on to Houlton, Fort Kent and the New Brunswick border. Below the central uplands, to the southeast, a zone of scattered mountains and lakes divides the uplands from the Downeast coast.

In the northwestern corner of the state, in a roughly rectangular area bounded by the central uplands region to the east and the mountains to the south, the land is hilly and densely forested. This is the area that most accurately fits the image that comes to mind when northern Maine, or "The Great North Woods," is mentioned.

Although people tend to think of northern Maine as a vast primeval forest wilderness, in fact there is very little area that has not been managed as timberland for years and cut over several times. The largest unaltered, old-growth forest left in Maine (as well as New England) is the Conservancy's Big Reed Forest Reserve (T8R10, T8R11 WELS). The Reserve includes two ponds and several forest community types that provide habitat for seekers of quiet and solitude like loons, pine martens and moose.

Big Reed is special precisely because it is an old-growth forest ecosystem that has existed for centuries without human intervention. To allow the forest to evolve in its own way, access to the preserve is limited and aspiring visitors are encouraged to join one of the guided field trips periodically offered by the Conservancy.

In the mountains south of Baxter State Park, The Hermitage Preserve (Bowdoin College Grant East) contains a fine stand of majestic white pines. Farther south, Mullen Woods Preserve offers an opportunity to see different stages in a central upland farm's return to forest during the past 150 years.

Bogs, fens, swamps and other wetlands are common throughout northern Maine. Conservancy preserves protect several of the most ecologically important. They range from Crystal Bog, a large open bog and neighboring fen, to Woodland Bog, a cedar swamp surrounding a hidden fen. All of the northern wetland preserves are fragile places that are sanctuaries for plants that are adapted and restricted to their special conditions. Permission is required for visits, but the Conservancy does offer guided field trips to study the areas and their threatened flora.

The St. John River is the longest free-flowing river in the East. The vegetation of Rocky Island Preserve (St. Francis) is composed of rare plants that are limited to such rocky, periodically flooded river shores.

Hiking and canoeing are important avocations in northern Maine. The Seboeis River Gorge Preserve (T6R7, T5R7 WELS) protects a long corridor along one popular canoe route. The A.H. Dayton Natural Area (T40 MD) includes an island in Nicatous Lake. (Permission for access is required, due to a life tenancy.) The Conservancy has also helped federal and state governments, as well as other conservation organizations protect wilderness recreation areas, including lands along the Allagash River and Appalachian Trail. The state's newest National Wildlife Refuge was created when the Conservancy transferred Sunkhaze Meadows (Milford) to the U.S. Fish and Wildlife Service.

The Nature Conservancy's preserves in the northern Maine region are overseen by several volunteer stewardship committees. For more information, please contact the Maine Chapter stewardship office in Topsham.

Mullen Woods Preserve 117 acres, Newport

At Mullen Woods in the heart of north-central Maine, one of Maine's relatively few stands of old-growth white pine grows alongside land that was farmed for generations.

When Lincoln delivered the Gettysburg address, the white pines at Mullen Woods were already sizable young trees. The trees grew well in their undisturbed grove and are now more than 100 feet tall with diameters ranging from 14 to 42 inches. The stand is on the state Register of Critical Areas.

The area around Mullen Woods was settled in the 1820s. The preserve property was cleared for crops and pastures shortly thereafter. Although part of the land was farmed to some extent well into this century, the back 50 acres was abandoned soon after it was cleared. Here the forest is dominated by old white pines and hemlocks, joined by younger, shade-tolerant hardwoods.

A small tributary of Stetson Stream flows through the woods. It is bordered by thickets of northern white cedar that provide browse for a large deer population.

The former fields on the northern and southern edges of the western half of the preserve have filled in with hardwoods. Ashes and birches are most common, with a few bur oaks scattered throughout. Bur oak, a species characteristic of rich bottomlands in the Midwest, is restricted

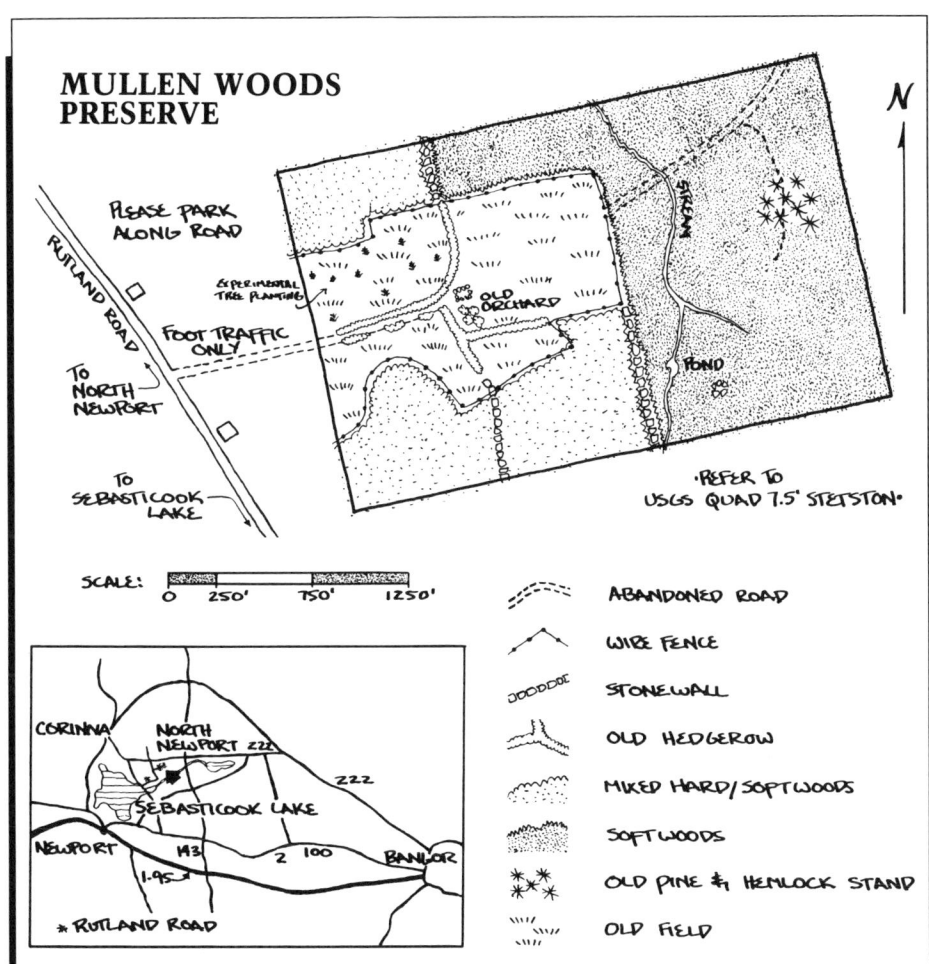

in Maine to the bottomlands along the Sebasticook River and the lower Penobscot River. Maine's bur oaks are an isolated population; the species' primary range is the upper Mississippi Valley, where individuals grow much larger, reaching diameters of more than six feet.

The preserve's most recently kept fields are now filled with masses of bushy young white pine. The old orchard and hedgerows are steadily being overtaken by the vigorous young trees.

In 1980, the University of Maine's School of Forest Resources began a long-term study of how potentially valuable commercial tree species, such as walnuts, would adapt to the northern Maine environment. Tree seedlings were planted in the north field just beyond the preserve entrance. Most of the seedlings have not fared well; undoubtedly some served as additional browse for the preserve's deer.

The Conservancy bought Mullen Woods from Mr. and Mrs. Arthur Hartwell in 1967, after a long search for a healthy, undisturbed stand of old-growth white pine. The preserve is named for Guy Mullen, Mrs. Hartwell's grandfather.

ABANDONED FARM   In the early 1800s, the major occupations of Maine people were fishing, farming and lumbering—frequently a combination of all three. Throughout central and southern Maine, the land was cleared for crops and pasture. Unfortunately for the farmers, much of Maine's land is composed of thin organic soils barely concealing layers of clay, sand, gravel and rocks. It is not an especially fertile combination. Mainers abandoned their farms, taking up more lucrative pursuits or migrating to the greener, less stony, pastures of the western frontier.

Years passed. The farm buildings were stripped of anything useful and left to decay. White pine, hemlock and hardwoods reclaimed the land. The old cellarholes, decaying stonewalls, rusting graniteware pots, and forlorn, light-starved lilacs remained, lost in deep woods, mute memorials to broken dreams.

Although there are no maintained trails, it is possible to explore the old fields—and the woods that have claimed them. To see the old pines, begin at the northern corner of the stone wall that separates the recent fields from the middle-aged conifer and hardwood forest, follow the abandoned road for less than 1,000 feet, then turn right onto a rough trail which ends in the pine grove. It is easy to get turned around; a topographic map and compass are suggested equipment for wandering around Mullen Woods.

DIRECTIONS: From Etna Center, head north on Route 143 and turn left onto Route 222. Go about three miles and turn left onto Rutland Road. Go about one mile to the preserve entrance, a grassy, two-track old road on the left. There is no sign. Please park well off Rutland Road and do not block the nearby woods roads. The track to the preserve passes through private property; only pedestrians are allowed.

The Hermitage Preserve

35 acres, T7R10 NWP
(Bowdoin College Grant East)

Along the northern shore of the West Branch of the Pleasant River, the majestic white pines of The Hermitage give today's travelers a glimpse of the forests that towered over those passing this same stretch during the first days of exploration.

More than 150 years ago, when the white pines now at the Hermitage were seedlings, lumbermen were boasting about the huge pines they were hauling out of the woods. The trees they took were truly giants: heights of nearly 200 feet and diameters exceeding five feet were not uncommon.

Interest in Maine's tall, straight white pines—trees that were perfect for masts and timber—began when the first European explorers found them growing near its southern rivers. After two centuries of very selective cutting, the best pines in the south were gone. The lumbermen kept moving north and east. By the early 1860s, the pine timber in the Penobscot valley had been thoroughly thinned as far north as Medway, some 30 miles northeast of The Hermitage. It is likely that the area now called The Hermitage lost its largest white pines to the loggers before then.

The Hermitage's white pines are well on their way to attaining the magnificence of the primeval pines. The trees are more than 120 feet tall, with diameters of up to three feet. Even though these pines were too young to have attracted much attention from the first wave of loggers, the fact that they were left unmolested until today is due to the good fortune that gave them custodians with no desire to convert them into boards. The stand is a National Natural Landmark and is listed on the state Register of Critical Areas.

The grove of white pines is destined to be naturally replaced, however. The forest understory is almost completely beech, sugar maple and hemlock. As the pines die these young trees will take over.

The preserve slopes back from the north bank of the West Branch of the Pleasant River in a glacially formed topography known as kame and kettle. The retreating glaciers left behind a 20- to 40-foot deep layer of clay, silt, gravel, boulders and huge chunks of ice. The ice melted, leaving large holes (kettles) between ridges of till (kames). There are five small kettles separated by kames running in an east-west line across the preserve. Moose often feed in the largest kettle, Pugwash Pond, which is the only one to hold water year-round.

Before reaching The Hermitage, the river descends over five major falls and three miles of continuous rapids in Gulf Hagas, one of the most spectacular gorges in the state. First protected voluntarily by the timber companies, the land around Gulf Hagas is now owned by the National Park Service and is a National Natural Landmark.

Just downriver from The Hermitage, the mountain southwest of Silver Lake contains a vein of high sulfur iron ore. Nearly 6,000 years ago, people collected red ochre from the mountain for their ceremonial graves. In the 1830s, settlers began mining and smelting the iron. In the ironwork's heyday between 1870 and 1885, there were 15 charcoal kilns operating. With the coming of steel and falling prices for refined iron, the company shifted to pig iron, then to wooden spools, in an attempt to stay solvent, but finally shut down in 1911. The townspeople opened their hotel to sportsmen, and built more camps for the lumbermen and tourists.

The township containing The Hermitage was granted to Bowdoin College in 1813, and was later sold to a series of timberland owners. In 1892, Campbell Young built a cabin under the pines and lived in splendid isolation for a few years, giving the area its name. The Pleasant River Pulp Company used The Hermitage as an executive sporting camp until the company failed in the Wall Street Crash of 1929.

In 1941, Mrs. Sara Green bought The Hermitage. A local legend honored with the title "The Mayor of Katahdin Iron Works," Mrs. Green did everything from running a lumber camp to acting as mail carrier, fire patroller and bus driver. She kept the camps at The Hermitage for her family and friends, and would not let the pines be cut. In 1967, she sold The Hermitage to the Conservancy to protect the trees.

The Appalachian Trail passes through The Hermitage on its way from Georgia to Mount Katahdin, 81 miles to the northeast. The trail fords the swift West Branch of the Pleasant River at The Hermitage, a chilling prospect most times of the year.

Old logging roads and trails approach The Hermitage on the northern side of the river, requiring a walk in of approximately a mile and half. The preserve entrance and the Appalachian Trail are well-marked. A brochure is available at the northern entrance. A loop through The Hermitage and Gulf Hagas makes an ideal day trip.

Although camping and fires are not allowed in the preserve, there are several campsites nearby. An area map is available at the Katahdin Iron Works.

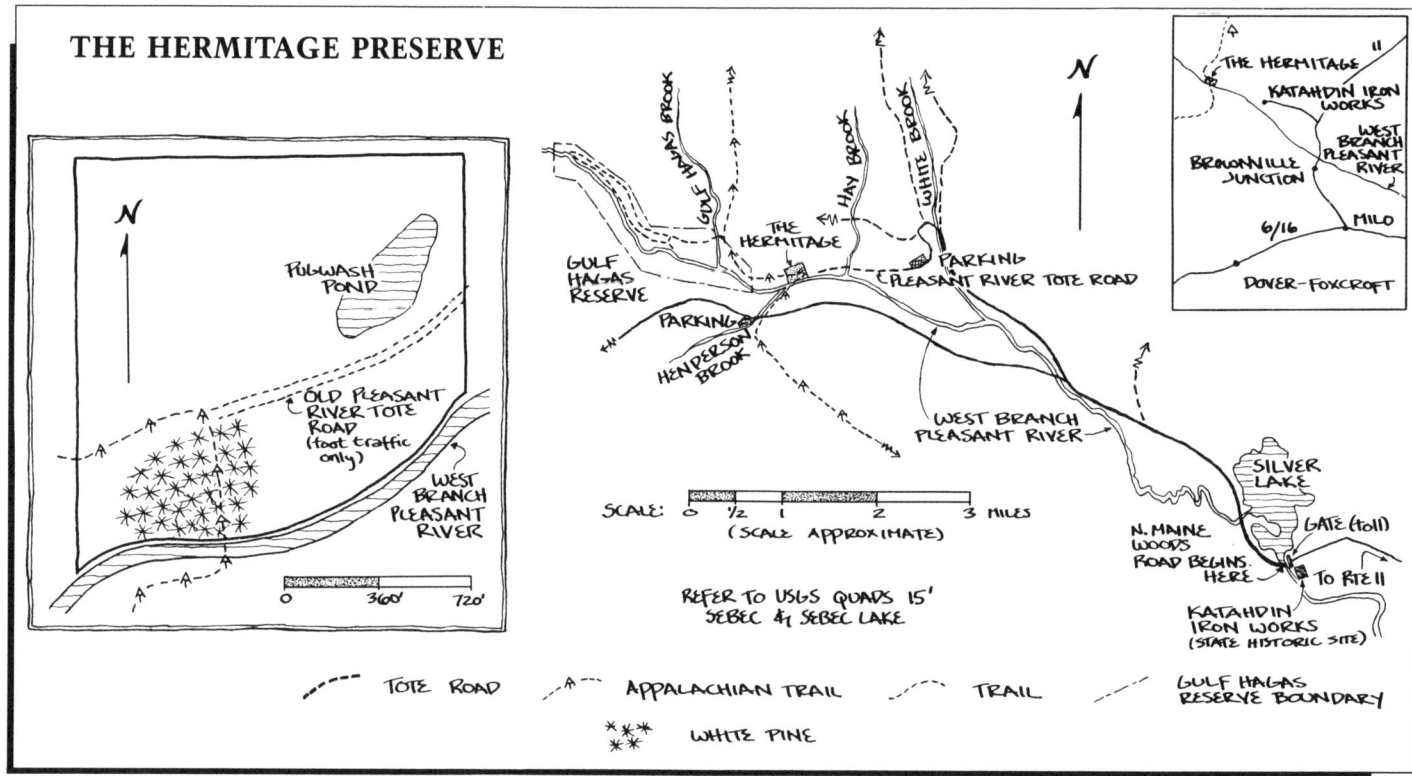

THE HERMITAGE PRESERVE

DIRECTIONS: Heading north from Brownville Junction on Route 11, go five miles and turn left at the Katahdin Iron Works sign. Go seven miles to the iron works and gate. Check in and pay the fee (if any). Go another eight miles on private logging roads to the parking area at Hay Brook.

Warning: logging trucks have the right of way on private logging roads. Stay alert and give them plenty of room.

Big Reed Forest Reserve

3,800 acres,
T8R10, T8R11 WELS

The last remnant of Thoreau's "wildest country," the Big Reed forest wilderness is the largest remaining example of what Maine's forests were like when the first European settlers arrived.

The 3,800-acre virgin forest wilderness around Big Reed Pond is the largest old-growth forest in Maine—and all of New England. The Big Reed forest represents more than two-thirds of the old-growth left in Maine's 17 million acres of forest lands.

The Big Reed old-growth forest has developed over thousands of years into a forest wilderness that is distinctly different from the managed timberland that surrounds it. Within the old-growth area, there is an impressive diversity of undisturbed forest ecosystems and plant communities. The varied topography of the preserve covers elevations from the 1,895-foot summit of Big Reed Mountain to the ponds some 700 feet below, creating several levels of exposure, from sheltered coves and valleys to wind-swept northern slopes. Moisture regimes range from ponds and cedar swamps to dry, well-drained ridges. Soils cover a spectrum from deep rich loam to gravel and rock.

All of these variables, together with general influences such as climate, combine to form a variety of habitats. Each habitat supports an association of plants and animals adapted to its specific set of the environmental conditions.

Contrary to what is commonly expected of a classic north woods forest, the most widespread forest type at Big Reed and much of this part of northern Maine is not a deep, dark stand of spruce and fir, but mixed woods dominated by sugar maple, American beech and red spruce. The mixed woods forest is found on sheltered southerly slopes at middle elevations. Soils are fairly deep and the ground is littered with fallen trees in various stages of decay.

Forests of balsam fir and red spruce do occur on the exposed bedrock ridges, steep rocky slopes (especially those which face north) and well-drained upper valleys.

Unlike the hardwoods, which are firmly rooted and tend to lose only branches in a gale, the shallow-rooted spruces and firs are easily toppled. An entire stand may be felled by just a few storms. The openings created, called blowdowns, provide cover and food for many animals. Bears enjoy the raspberries, and moose and snowshoe hares seek out the tender young shoots of the poplars, aspens and birches that quickly claim the sunlit openings.

The Big Reed spruce-fir forest is a mosaic of mature forest, blowdowns and regenerating forest. The mature stands are dominated by red spruce, many of which are of great size; one of the oldest trees found so far is estimated to be 280 years old and measures two feet in diameter.

Pine martens (*Martes americana*), the most arboreal members of the weasel family, prefer mature spruce-fir forest with plenty of openings. They find ideal habitat at Big Reed.

Hardwood forests of sugar maple, American beech and hop hornbeam are found on the well-drained soils of the flattened ridgetops. Wildflowers and ferns grow abundantly on the banks of intermittent streams that flow down through the woods.

Nearly pure stands of northern white cedar grow in seepage swamps that occupy low areas along the pond shores. In the swamps, the forest floor is almost covered with mosses and other moisture-loving plants, including the tiny calypso or fairy slipper orchid (*Calypso bulbosa*). The standing deadwood attracts two boreal species of woodpecker, the black-backed three-toed and the northern three-toed, which nest in cavities in the trees.

Below Big Reed Pond is the Reed Deadwater, a level bog that has

characteristic bog plants such as sedges, wool-grass and sweet gale growing on a mat of sphagnum peat. Tamaracks, cedars and black spruces grow on the higher, more well-drained hummocks. The deadwater area is a heavily used winter deer yard.

The preserve's two ponds, 90-acre Big Reed and 25-acre Little Reed, are a magnet for wildlife, including mink, river otter, muskrat, moose, osprey and loon. The clear, cold waters of Big Reed are home to one of the world's few populations of the state endangered blueback char (*Salvelinus alpinus oquassa*). Ten thousand years ago, the retreating glaciers landlocked arctic char in isolated ponds. The char evolved into a new sub-species that is now found in only ten ponds in the world, all of which are in Maine.

The Big Reed old-growth forest was passed over by generations of Maine loggers, at first because it was not worth harvesting. There was relatively little white pine and the land was more than two miles from a stream large enough to float logs. However, after logging roads were built in every part of the Maine woods and commercial demand widened to include many species besides white pine, the old trees became very vulnerable. Fortunately, nearly 20 years ago the descendants of David Pingree, the timber baron who bought

the forest originally in the great public land auctions of the mid-1800s, quietly decided to set it aside as a reserve.

After taking care of the Big Reed Reserve for decades, the Pingree heirs sought a permanent owner for the land, an owner that was in the business of owning and managing conservation lands. They came to the Conservancy, and their request began negotiations that lasted several years and resulted in a three-way exchange among the Pingrees, the state of Maine, and the Conservancy. The Conservancy acquired the 3,800-acre Big Reed Forest Reserve; the state acquired Allagash Mountain and other lands along the Allagash River formerly owned by the Pingrees; and the Pingrees acquired state-owned public lots that were inholdings in their timberlands. A considerable amount of cash also changed hands; the Conservancy's cost for the acquisition and long-term protection of Big Reed was $1.1 million. After a two-year fund-raising campaign, to which thousands of people contributed, the Conservancy completed the acquisition of the 3,800-acre sanctuary in 1987.

LICHENS AND OLD-GROWTH Biologist Steven B. Selva of the University of Maine at Fort Kent has identified more than 180 species of lichens in six forested natural communities at Big Reed. Fifty of these are considered old-growth indicator species.

Lichens are especially sensitive to logging, pollution and other intrusions. Dr. Selva's continuing study includes managed timberlands, and aims to create an index based on the presence and abundance of particular indicator lichen species that can be used to measure degree of historic disturbance in Maine's forest ecosystems.

 The Big Reed Pond Reserve old-growth forest is irreplaceable precisely because it has escaped man's influence. Therefore, the Conservancy has not developed access. There are no signs or trails. The forest is remote and often difficult to traverse; even experienced guides who have visited the area before have gotten "temporarily misplaced." Please contact the Chapter stewardship office before attempting to visit Big Reed. All research projects require prior approval as well.

The Maine Chapter periodically offers guided field trips to Big Reed.

Seboeis River Gorge Preserve

673 acres, T5R7, T6R7 WELS

Just east of Baxter State Park, the Seboeis River runs wild through one of Maine's few major gorges. The forested banks rise over 100 feet above the river.

Racing along in its narrow channel, cascading over steep pitches, the wild Seboeis River flows through eight and half miles of unspoiled shore protected by the Conservancy.

Just below the Seboeis deadwater, the river enters the preserve in a deep gorge. The walls of the gorge rise up to more than 100 feet with slopes approaching 60 degrees. The rapids here are heavy (Class IV), with two sets of falls, Tiger Rips and Godfrey Pitch. The gorge ends, and the surrounding landscape opens up. The river becomes gentler, flowing along with a steady current through milder whitewater and one last set of falls, Grand Pitch.

The preserve and adjacent lands are essentially undeveloped and unpopulated. Most of the forest in this region is actively managed for timber production; a few hunting and fishing camps are the only developed sites.

The gorge is forested, with occasional bare rock outcrops on the steep slopes above the river. Spruce and fir grow on the more precipitous slopes; hardwoods and white pine mix in as the terrain becomes less steep. Near the river, black ashes and white spruces grow along with a few American elms. Alders, sedges and ferns, expecially ostrich fern, are abundant in the low-lying areas that are flooded by the river each year.

The wild, unspoiled river and preserve lands are rich habitat for wildlife. Moose are seen regularly. A major deer wintering yard is located in the southern half of the preserve.

As one of Maine's few major river gorges, the Seboeis is listed on the state Register of Critical Areas.

The Seboeis River Gorge Preserve was donated to the Conservancy in 1976 by the J.M. Huber Corporation.

 Most canoeists run the Seboeis during spring high water, starting at the Grand Lake Road crossing. Above the crossing, the river is Class IV whitewater with several dangerous rapids. It is not recommended for canoeists. (People have died here.) The river below is generally easy going with the notable exception of Grand Pitch, a short set of falls which should be bypassed with a quarter-mile portage. Be ready: the falls are hidden by a left bend in the river. The lower Seboeis makes a popular alternate beginning for trips headed down the East Branch of the Penobscot. Anyone planning to run the river should consult the Appalachian Mountain Club's river guidebook for Maine.

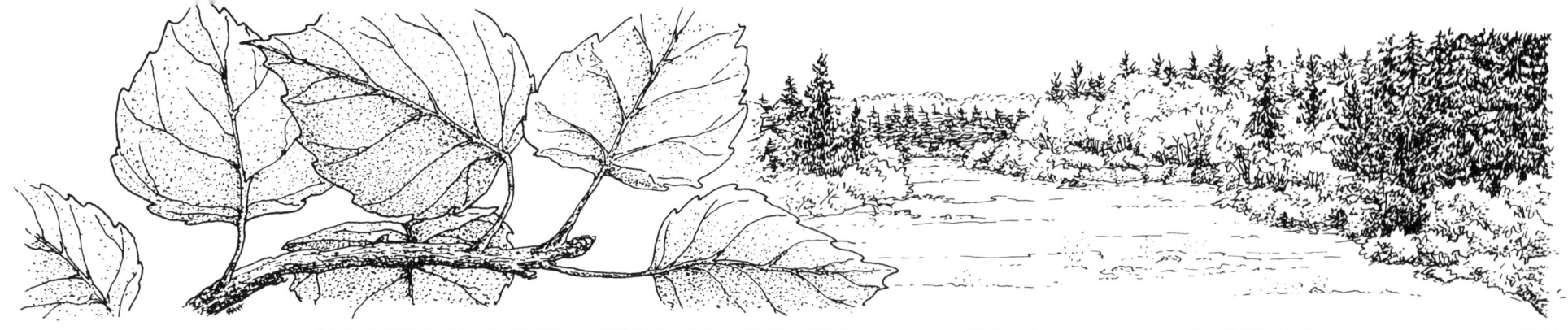

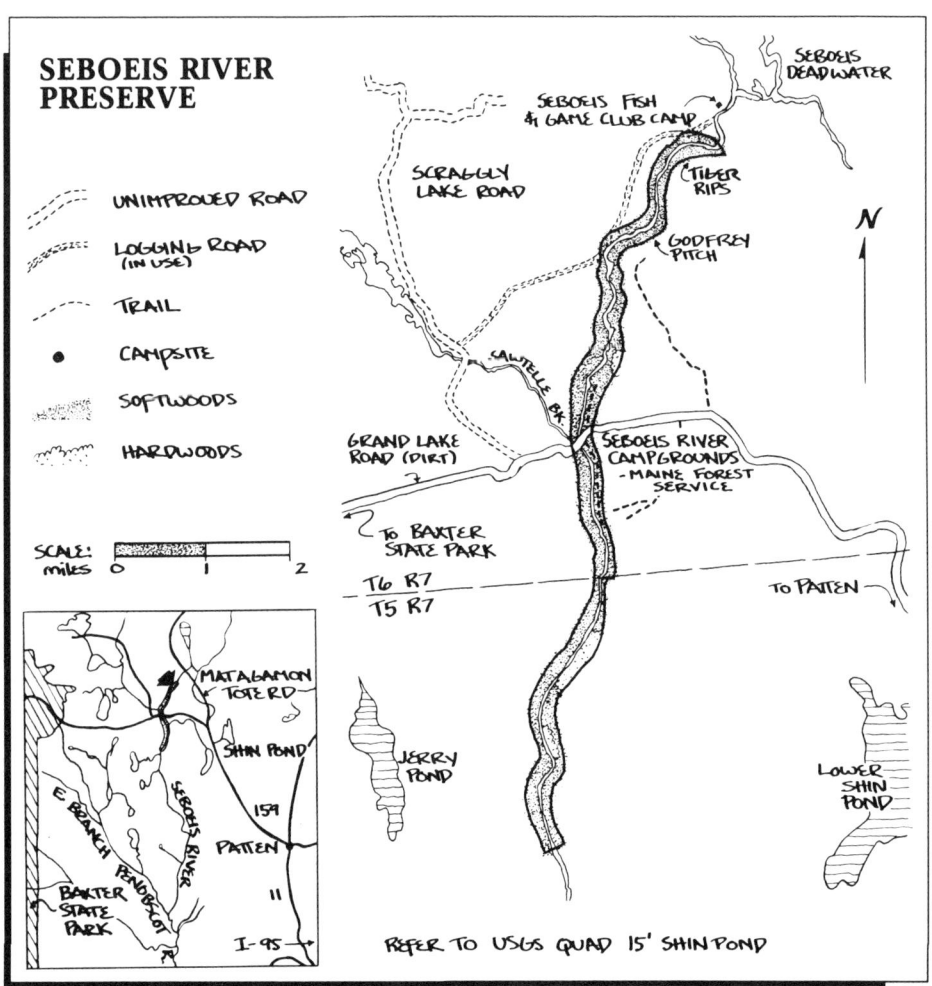

SEBOEIS RIVER PRESERVE

Legend:
- ‑‑‑‑‑ UNIMPROVED ROAD
- ·‑·‑·‑ LOGGING ROAD (IN USE)
- ‑ ‑ ‑ TRAIL
- • CAMPSITE
- SOFTWOODS
- HARDWOODS

SCALE: miles 0   1   2

SEBOEIS DEADWATER

SEBOEIS FISH & GAME CLUB CAMP

SCRAGGLY LAKE ROAD

TIBER RIPS

GODFREY PITCH

N

SALSTELLE BK.

GRAND LAKE ROAD (DIRT)

SEBOEIS RIVER CAMPGROUNDS - MAINE FOREST SERVICE

TO BAXTER STATE PARK

T6 R7
T5 R7

TO PATTEN

JERRY POND

LOWER SHIN POND

MATAGAMON TOTE RD.
SHIN POND
159
PATTEN
11
I-95
E. BRANCH PENOBSCOT
SEBOEIS RIVER
BAXTER STATE PARK

REFER TO USGS QUAD 15' SHIN POND

Most of the preserve land is accessible only by bushwhacking. A few short trails exist, but they are overgrown.

There is a Maine Forest Service campground at the Grand Lake Road crossing, and other MFS campsites along the river, just outside the preserve to the south. Fire permits are required. *Camping and fires are not allowed in the Conservancy preserve.* (For more information on camping and access, please contact the Maine Forest Service in Patten and/or the North Maine Woods Association, P.O. Box 382, Ashland, Maine 04732.)

DIRECTIONS: From Patten, take Route 159 to Shin Pond, and continue on this road (variously known as the Grand Lake, Matagamon or Baxter Park Road) to the crossing over the Seboeis. The crossing is the usual put-in point. Warning: logging trucks have the right of way on private woods roads. Stay alert and give them plenty of room.

Crystal Bog Preserve

4,102 acres, Crystal and Sherman

Crystal Bog, more than six square miles of undisturbed northern peatland near Mount Katahdin, is one of the Conservancy's most ecologically significant preserves in Maine and the nation.

One of the most interesting and important peatlands in eastern North America, Crystal Bog is a complex of several peatland types, with a correspondingly rich and diverse flora. At least 20 of these plants are rare and threatened in Maine; many more are species found only in association with the particular habitats typical of Crystal and similar peatlands of the far north.

Crystal, also known as Thousand Acre Bog, is a National Natural Landmark and is listed on the state Register of Critical Areas. It also has been nominated as an International Biosphere Reserve by the United Nations.

The Crystal Bog complex includes one of the largest sphagnum-heath bogs in the Northeast. The bog is a concentric raised peatland, a type of peatland that forms only where conditions are continually cool and moist.

Over the centuries, countless generations of sphagnum moss and other plants die and contribute their remains, which slowly decompose in the acid, saturated conditions, forming peat. The peat steadily accumulates, raising the bog's surface above its surroundings in a gently sloping dome. Since the bog is now raised above the groundwater by its thick layers of peat, it becomes completely dependent upon atmospheric sources for water and nutrients, and grows increasingly acidic since there is no flowing water to flush away accumulated minerals and products of decomposition. The peat acts like a giant sponge, holding moisture; most raised bogs have small, shallow ponds scattered across the upper level of the dome.

An unusually attractive set of ponds arranged in a concentric pattern occupies the center of Crystal's raised bog. Concentric ponds frequently form in bogs found farther north in Canada and Scandinavia, but are rarely seen in the United States.

The vegetation is typical of northern bogs: an open expanse of shrubs of the heath family interrupted with small stands of black spruce, northern white cedar, tamarack and balsam fir. The whole area is blanketed with a thick, spongy mat of sphagnum moss. Streams flow along the edges of the bog. The uplands around the bog are covered with a forest of spruce and fir, with plenty of northern white cedar and tamaracks occurring in the wetter areas. Northern hardwoods occupy the higher, drier, less exposed ridges.

In the northern and eastern parts of the preserve, the raised bog blends into another type of peatland called a fen. The fen differs from the bog in that the plants growing in it have access to groundwater. Its less-acidic, nutrient-rich, and moist but well-drained peat supports an assemblage of plants that are specifically adapted to its conditions. The fen is an open, "grassy" place, carpeted with a variety of sedges, two of which are officially listed as threatened in Maine. Most of the other exceptionally rare and threatened plants at Crystal are also found here in the fen. It is the only known historic site in Maine for the prairie-fringed orchid (*Platanthera leucophaea*), a plant on the state endangered species list that has also been nominated as a federal threatened species. Two other plants, the linear-leaved and English sundews (*Drosera linearis and D. anglica*), are listed as state endangered. More than a dozen other species are considered to

merit special concern in Maine and the nation. These include northern valerian (*Valerian uliginosa*), American bog rush (*Juncus stygius var. americanus*), dwarf birch (*Betula pumila*), grass-of-Parnassus (*Parnassia glauca*), and several orchids.

The Conservancy has encouraged appropriate research on the preserve, which has led to discoveries of more rarities and to a better understanding of the peatland ecosystems' history and function. All research projects must be approved in advance and are carefully monitored. Permits are required for any collection.

Crystal Bog Preserve was donated to the Conservancy in 1976 by the J.M. Huber Corporation. The company bought the property with the intention of mining it, but reconsidered and abandoned its plans in favor of protecting the peatland and its threatened plants.

Crystal Bog is a very fragile place that is also remote and difficult to reach. To protect the easily damaged peatland and its endangered and threatened plants, humans must remain infrequent guests. All aspiring visitors are asked to contact the Maine Chapter office for permission before attempting to visit Crystal. The best way to see the bog is to join one of the Chapter's periodic guided field trips.

The Crystal Bog stewardship committee has prepared a slide show that features many of the preserve's plants. It is an excellent way to see the peatland's rarities.

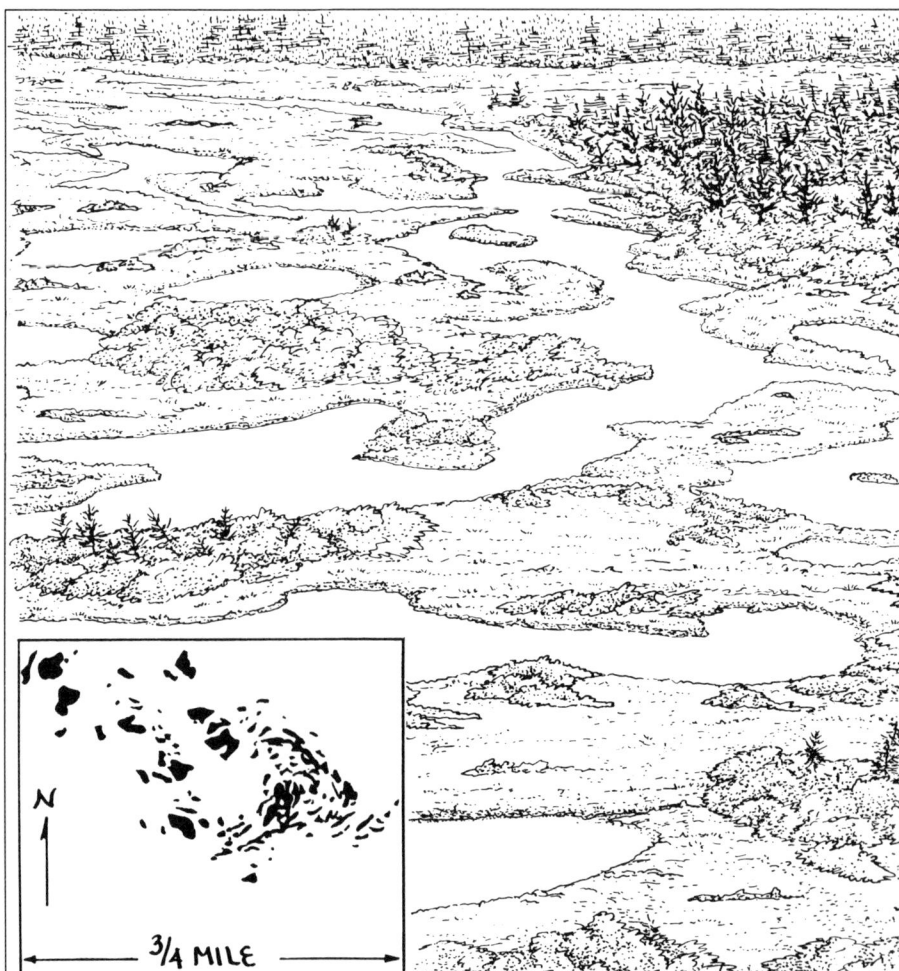

Ponds form concentric rings around the raised portion of Crystal Bog. The insert diagram shows the overall pattern of the ponds as seen from the air.

Woodland Bog Preserve and Perham Bog Preserve

Woodland, 202 acres, Woodland;
Perham, 40 acres, Perham

In the rolling open country of northern Aroostook County, the open fens and dark cedar swamps of Woodland Bog and Perham Bog preserves shelter a collection of threatened plants that are specifically adapted to these particular habitats.

Woodland and Perham bogs are not really bogs. To be precise, they are northern calcareous fens surrounded by northern calcareous seepage swamps. Unlike bogs, fens and swamps receive their moisture from flowing surface and subsurface water.

Both areas lie in the upper drainage of the Aroostook River. In this part of Aroostook County, the topography is open and rolling, with many streams that meander through great expanses of low-lying wetlands. The wetlands may appear level, but water flows steadily through them down to the streams, into the Aroostook River, and east to the St. John.

The bedrock of this northeastern corner of The County is limestone, calcareous sandstone, and shale. The lime-enriched silt loam soil derived from the bedrock is the reason for the region's productive farms. Lime leaches quickly from the soil, however, and must eventually be replaced artificially in croplands. In wetlands like Woodland and Perham, however, the slowly moving groundwater delivers a steady supply of dissolved-lime (calcium carbonate) and other minerals to the plants.

Calcareous fens and their associated plant species are found in less than a half dozen locations in Maine, including Crystal Bog. The fen of Woodland Bog is a 10-acre sedge lawn dominated by sphagnum moss and a variety of sedges, several of which are listed as threatened in the state. Diminutive wildflowers like grass-of-parnassus (*Parnassia glauca*), sticky tofieldia (*Tofieldia glutinosa*) and brook lobelia (*Lobelia kalmii)* fill the opening with white and blue blooms in summer.

Hummocks covered with northern white cedar, black spruce and tamarack along with rare shrubs including hoary willow (*Salix candida*) and swamp-fly honeysuckle (*Lonicera oblongifolia*) are scattered throughout the fen. There are also treacherous sinkholes filled with marl, a mucky mixture of clay and silt.

A dense cedar swamp surrounds the fen. The swamp is habitat for the small round-leaved orchis (*Anerorchis rotundifolia*), a tiny, purple-spotted orchid that grows in the shade of the cedars. One of the rarest orchids in the Northeast, it is found at only four documented sites, all of which are in Maine. The swamp is also home to an even more obscure orchid, white adder's mouth (*Malaxis monophyllous* var. *brachypoda*), which grows in the arctic in open wet meadows, but this far south is found only in cool, limy cedar swamps. Two other orchids, showy lady's slipper (*Cypripedium reginae*) and yellow lady's slipper (*Cypripedium calceolus*) favor openings in the cedar swamp. Northern valerian (*Valeriana uliginosa*), a pink wildflower that resembles its relative, the common garden heliotrope, also prefers open, unshaded spots. Northern valerian is rare throughout its range, and is being considered for inclusion on the federal endangered species list.

Perham Bog shares many of the same plants as Woodland Bog. The threatened small round-leaved orchis grows in its dark cedar swamp. Two other plants that usually grow only in association with northern white cedar also occur here: Lapland buttercup (*Ranunculus lapponicus*), a sub-arctic species found at only three sites in Maine, and calypso or fairy slipper orchid (*Calypso bulbosa*), a tiny pink

flower that often grows right at the base of the trees. Northern valerian and showy lady's slipper, two more plants also found at Woodland in similar habitat, grow in or near the openings in the swamp.

The eastern side of Woodland Bog was farmed until 1957, and logging continued until the early 1970s. Neither activity appears to have harmed the fen and nearby swamp.

In 1983, the Conservancy purchased the Woodland fen and 100 adjacent acres of cedar swamp to protect the rare plants. Unfortunately, ecological boundaries rarely conform to property boundaries, and a significant percentage of the small round-leaved orchis and northern valerian populations spilled over into the adjoining property to the south. The Conservancy acquired an additional 75-acre southern parcel in 1985. Despite the fact that its cedar swamp had been cut over, hundreds of orchids still survived under the cedars left standing. In 1988, the Conservancy acquired another 27 acres of cedar swamp and buffer zone along an abandoned section of the Aroostook Valley Railroad that bisects the preserve.

Perham Bog Preserve was donated to the Conservancy in 1988 by Richard and Susan Clark, who bought the property with the intention of protecting its rare plants.

 Since the saturated fens and cedar swamps are easily damaged by foot traffic, visits to Woodland and Perham bogs are discouraged. It is essential that the plants of the fen and swamps remain undisturbed. Please contact the Chapter office for permission and information before considering a trip to either preserve.

An abandoned section of railroad that crosses the southwestern corner of Woodland Bog Preserve is maintained as a snowmobile trail through a lease agreement with the Conservancy.

The Chapter offers small, guided field trips to study these areas and other northern swamps.

THREATENED NATIVES A 1988 survey by the Center for Plant Conservation found that as many as 680 American plant species could well become extinct in the next 10 years. An estimated 200 native plants have become extinct since the first Europeans arrived. The natural extinction rate is about one species every 1,000 years.

Although the only species in Maine in possible danger of extinction is the small whorled pogonia (found in the southern and western part of the state) a significant number of plant species are considered to be at risk within Maine's borders. Eighty-four species are officially listed by the state as endangered: that is, found recently in just one place, or federally listed as endangered. Another 74 species are listed as state threatened: found in two to four places, or federally listed as threatened.

Rocky Island Preserve

2 acres, T18R10 WELS

Located at the junction of the St. John and St. Francis rivers at the very northern tip of Maine, tiny Rocky Island is home to a riverine natural community with at least six rare plants.

Rocky Island is aptly named; it is formed from a calcareous (limy) ledge that rises some 20 feet above the river. A few spruce and fir trees grow in a small area at the summit that has some soil. The remainder of the island is ledge that is bare on the upriver shore and covered with a variety of shrubs on the downriver sides.

The open ledge supports a plant association distinctive to a few northern New England riverside outcrops. The plants that make up this natural community have adapted to the often harsh seasonal changes that accompany life in rocky crevices at the edge of the longest stretch of free-flowing river on the eastern seaboard. The island's shores are frozen fast in winter; scoured by sheets of ice and floodwaters at spring ice-out; and left high and dry in the summer and fall, barring occasional floods. Seasonal changes and fluctuations in the river's level are the norm for this natural community. If the river is altered by dams or diversions, the plants lose their preferred habitat and competitive edge. Other species, often those which could never survive in such habitats under natural conditions, can invade and displace the original inhabitants.

Because so few rivers remain undammed, thriving examples of these natural riverside communities are not common. Correspondingly, the plant species characteristically found in them are also not common. On Rocky Island, the rarest plants make up a large percentage of the total number of plants in the natural community. The island is listed on the state Register of Critical Areas.

The cut-leaved anemone (*Anemone multifida*), a sub-arctic member of the buttercup family, has been called the rarest plant in New England. It is found at a few sites in Vermont and in several places along the St. John River. The Rocky Island stand is the largest in the eastern United States. The anemone grows with St. John Oxytrope (*Oxytropis campestris var. johannensis*), a tall purple-flowered plant that is found in the United States only along the St. John. Both species are officially listed as threatened in Maine; the oxytrope is also under consideration for listing as threatened on the federal endangered species list. Two other rarities, New England violet (*Viola novae-angliae*) and sweet broom (*Astragalus alpinus var. brunetianus*) also grow in the vertical cracks and crevices of the shore ledges.

The St. John River has an impressive collection of plants that are abundant in its drainage, but that are rare in Maine. Two of these, St. John tansy (*Tanacetum huronense var. johannense*) and northern painted cup (*Castilleja septentrionalis*), grow on the shore ledges and among the shrubs of Rocky Island. The anemone, oxytrope, painted cup and sweet broom are all western species that are usually found in alpine areas of the Rockies and arctic regions of Alaska and Canada.

Rocky Island was donated to the Conservancy in 1984 by Mr. and Mrs. Leonard Pelletier, who continue to act as stewards of the island.

 The rare plants of Rocky Island are sturdy perennial species that have adapted to floods, ice and summer drought and that are able to grow anew from crevices or cobbles each year. However, the adult plants cannot withstand being trampled, picked or burned – any activity that interferes with their ability to store ample reserves in time for winter or that disrupts their successful production of seeds. Therefore, camping and fires are not allowed on the island. Daytime activities, such as swimming and picnicking, are permitted.

DIRECTIONS: Rocky Island is just off the point of land on the western side of the confluence of the St. John and St. Francis rivers. It is a short paddle from St. Francis.

Moose (Alan Hutchinson)

Partners in Conservation

Cooperative projects are an important part of the Nature Conservancy's efforts to preserve Maine's natural diversity and finest lands. Working with and on behalf of others, the Conservancy has protected more than 30,000 acres in addition to the land it owns and manages in its own system of nature preserves.

The relentless rise of land prices, combined with a growing understanding of the need to protect larger ecological systems, has drawn the Conservancy to join with others to leverage each group's respective capabilities through cooperation. The Conservancy works jointly with federal and state agencies, town governments, local land trusts, other conservation groups, and private landowners. These cooperative projects range from agreements that allow it to manage land owned by another group to complex arrangements involving several adjacent parcels of land that are all owned and managed by different parties.

Land purchases often require quicker action than public agencies and legislatures can muster. Government agencies frequently ask the Conservancy for help when they want to acquire a natural area, but don't have authorized funds in hand, or when a negotiation is particularly difficult. The Conservancy buys the land and holds it until the agency is able to repurchase it. Areas protected in this way include Sunkhaze Meadows National Wildlife Refuge (Milford), Wilbur Neck State Wildlife Refuge (Pembroke) and Virginia Lake addition to the White Mountain National Forest (Stoneham, Lovell).

The Conservancy also helps local groups with their land acquisition projects. Nearly two dozen communities now enjoy public parks, town forests, environmental education sites and other natural areas that were preserved with the Conservancy's assistance.

Lands that the Conservancy transfers to the care of another organization are often further protected by deed restrictions that prohibit or limit activities that might harm the natural area. In all cases, the Conservancy checks periodically to make sure that any outstanding biological features are being protected.

By working together, the Conservancy and its partners are able to accomplish far more than any one group could by working alone. The result is a dramatic increase in the amount of land protected for the people of Maine.

Partnerships: Protected lands

The lands described in this section were protected with the help of The Nature Conservancy. They are not owned and managed by the Conservancy, but by a variety of public and private conservation agencies. Most of these places are open to the public, but access policies vary widely among them. For more information, please contact the appropriate owners and/or managers.

Appalachian Trail

1,216 acres; Eliotsville Twp

Owned by the Maine Bureau of Parks and Recreation; managed by the Maine Appalachian Trail Club (Colby College Outing Club)

More than six miles of trail corridor along the Barren Mountain ridge are protected by this tract. The Barren-Chairback ridge has been described as the most difficult section of the trail between Bigelow Mountain and Katahdin, but the views from it are well worth the effort. The protected corridor includes Barren Mountain, Cloud Pond and Slugundy Falls.

The Conservancy accepted a gift of the land from the International Paper Company and held it until the state could assume responsibility for it. The land was transferred to the state with conservation restrictions and provisions for continued monitoring.

Brier Island

1,200 acres; Westport, Nova Scotia

Owned and managed by the Nature Conservancy of Canada

Located at the western tip of Nova Scotia, at the edge of the Gulf of Maine, Brier Island is a major resting and feeding stop for birds migrating along the Atlantic flyway. The island is also a magnet for birders seeking additions to their life lists. More than 150 species, especially pelagic birds like razorbills and phalaropes, have been seen near or on the island. The sanctuary includes forest, fields, marsh, bogs and ponds bordered by more than six miles of undeveloped coastline.

Since the former owner of the sanctuary land was a U.S. citizen and Maine summer resident, the Nature Conservancy of Canada asked the Conservancy's Maine Chapter to negotiate the sale. The owner eventually agreed to sell for well under half the original asking price, and the Chapter resold the land to its Canadian sister organization for the same sum. The acquisition was paid for by a coalition of Canadian agencies and organizations.

Donnell Pond/Black Mountain/Tunk Lake

6,950 acres (acquisition), 489 acres (easement); TDSD, T10SD, Sullivan.

Owned and managed by the Maine Bureau of Public Lands

Donnell Pond is known and cherished for its spectacular mountain scenery and pristine ponds. The protected land includes Black, Caribou, Catherine and Schoodic mountains, as well as Rainbow Pond, Wizard Pond, the western shore of Tunk Lake and most of the shore of Donnell Pond. Access to the region's interior is by canoe and foot only.

For more than 50 years federal and state government officials talked about protecting Donnell Pond, perhaps by including it in Acadia National Park. When the tranquil, unspoiled natural area was threatened by a massive subdivision in 1989, the state asked the Conservancy's help in negotiating a conservation purchase of the land. The project was eventually expanded to include five separate tracts and three landowners. The final result of this complicated public/private transaction was protection of the original 1,500-acre Donnell Pond property and over 5,000 additional acres.

Hurds Pond

Swanville; 100 acres

Owned and managed by the Maine Department of Inland Fisheries and Wildlife

For more than 30 years, the Maine Department of Inland Fisheries and Wildlife viewed Hurds Pond as one of its top acquisition priorities but was unable to acquire it. The 25-acre pond is surrounded by a large sedge meadow and extensive freshwater wetlands. It is used by many species of breeding and migrating waterfowl, including bitterns, ospreys, great blue herons, and ducks such as teals, ringnecks and wood ducks.

The pond, marsh and adjacent woodlands were donated to the Conservancy by Bill and David Hauk. The Hauks were amenable to the idea of a state wildlife refuge, so the Conservancy transferred the property to IF&W.

National Wildlife Refuges

Owned and managed by the U.S. Fish and Wildlife Service

The Conservancy and the U.S. Fish and Wildlife Service have enjoyed a productive working relationship for many years. The Conservancy has helped the USFWS acquire more than

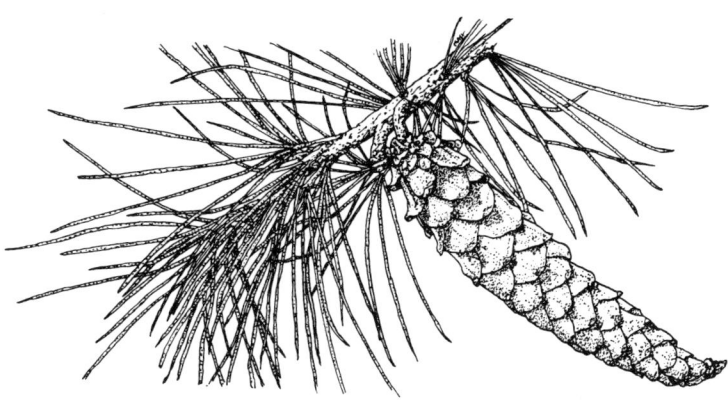

12,000 acres that are now protected in Maine's National Wildlife Refuges, including the state's only new refuge established in decades, Sunkhaze Meadows in Milford.

Moosehorn NWR

Cross Island archipelago: Cross Island, 1,485 acres; Inner Double Head Shot Island, 8 acres; Old Man Island, 6 acres; Scotch Island, 10 acres; Minklet Island, 1 acre; Mink Island, 10 acres. All in Cutler.

Located just south of the Cutler peninsula, the remote archipelago has long been a sanctuary for nesting eagles and seabirds. On Old Man Island, razorbills find the sheltered, inaccessible ledges they require for their unprotected eggs. Old Man was also the site of the only common eider breeding colony left on the Maine coast at the turn of the century. The islands have been used by generations of bald eagles for nesting, roosting and wintering. A small number of black bears live on Cross Island itself.

The islands were given to the Conservancy by Mr. and Mrs. Thomas Cabot with the understanding that they would become part of the National Wildlife Refuge.

Petit Manan NWR

Petit Manan Point, 1,724 acres, Steuben; Bois Bubert and Little Bois Bubert islands, 925 acres, Milbridge.

The refuge lands, Petit Manan Point and nearby Bois Bubert and Little Bois Bubert islands, are habitat for bald eagles. Wooded Bois Bubert Island has a large deer herd. Seals haul out on its ledges, and black ducks and common eiders frequent the waters offshore. Little Bois Bubert Island is covered primarily with cranberry and peat bogs.

Most of Bois Bubert Island and all of Little Bois Bubert Island were donated to the Conservancy by Dr. and Mrs. Lawrence L. Weed, Dr. Harvey Brooks and Mrs. G. Gardiner Brown, with the understanding that the land would become part of the wildlife refuge.

Rachel Carson NWR

145 acres total; Kennebunkport, Wells.

The Rachel Carson refuge includes wetlands and waterfowl habitat in sections strung along the southern Maine coast. The Conservancy has helped acquire several parcels of salt marsh, wetlands and uplands on behalf of the refuge, including the marshlands of the Little River.

Sunkhaze Meadows NWR

9,337 acres; Milford

The Sunkhaze Meadows refuge protects Maine's second largest peatland. The refuge is a wide expanse of bog, marsh and floodplain forest. A network of streams flows through the bog, creating a complex of at least 11 different ecosystems. Nearly 150 bird species have been spotted breeding here or stopping by during migration, including black, ring-necked and wood ducks. In the late 1970s, a energy development company began making serious plans to mine Sunkhaze and burn its peat to generate electricity. After several years of studies and planning, the peat-to-energy project proved to be unprofitable without federal subsidies. Sunkhaze got a reprieve.

Over the years, Sunkhaze Meadows rose to become one of the U.S. Fish and Wildlife Service's top 20 acquisition priorities nationwide. In 1987, the landowner, a major forest products company, put the area on the market. Although Congress had approved the new refuge, it had not yet appropriated the necessary funding. The Conservancy bought the land and held it for nearly a year until the federal funds became available. The Conservancy granted the USFWS a management lease immediately after buying the land, allowing it to manage the wildlife refuge from the start.

Tracy Property

33 acres; South Bristol

Owned and managed by the town of South Bristol

This town park provides public access to 800 feet of shore along the Damariscotta River at Jones Cove. The park includes rocky ledges, cliffs, a small tidal basin, and a small marsh. The land is forested with mixed hardwoods, including some very large red oaks. Two brooks with waterfalls flow through the area.

The land was donated to the Conservancy by Dwight and Mary Tracy with specific instructions that it be transferred to the town so that it could be used for education and recreation by the inhabitants of South Bristol.

Vaughn's Island

35 acres; Kennebunkport

Owned and managed by the Kennebunkport Conservation Trust

This 35-acre island located just off the Kennebunkport shore is used as an outdoor classroom, especially by the York County Extension Service's 4-H program. Educational programs held on the island feature marine ecology and Maine coast culture. Students also learn about no-trace camping and other low-impact wilderness recreation techniques.

Vaughn's Island was acquired in 1969 by the Vaughn's Island Preservation Trust, a group of local citizens who joined together to save the island from development. The trust transferred the island to The Nature Conservancy in 1971. The Conservancy returned the island to the care of another local group, the Kennebunkport Conservation Trust, in 1982.

Virginia Lake and Shirley Valley
Virginia Lake: 1,690-acre acquisition, 25-acre conservation easement; Stoneham, Lovell. Shirley Valley: 1,447 acres
Owned and managed by the U.S. Forest Service, White Mountain National Forest

For many years, conservationists and the U.S. Forest Service sought to add Virginia Lake and its surrounding forest to the White Mountain National Forest. The largest undeveloped lake in the White Mountain region, Virginia Lake is a popular with fishermen, boaters and cross-country skiers. Trails through the wooded hills surrounding the lake connect with an extensive regional trail network.

At the request of the landowners and the Forest Service, the Conservancy agreed to help overcome the obstacles of timing and funding by purchasing the property and holding it until funds could be approved and appropriated by Congress.

MORE LANDS
Allagash Wilderness Waterway
(T7R14 WELS; 1,500 acres; *Maine Bureau of Public Lands*) Allagash Mountain and land along the waterway.

Augusta Nature Center (Augusta; 17 acres; *Augusta Nature Club*) Addition to existing nature preserve.

Baker Island (Cranberry Isles; 74 acres; *Acadia National Park*) Western half of the island.

Benedict Property (Biddeford; 20 acres; *Maine Audubon Society*) Part of East Point Sanctuary. Renowned birding spot.

Colby Marston Bog (Oakland; 21 acres; *Colby College*) Student research area. National Natural Landmark.

Cousins Island Property (Yarmouth; 20 acres; *Town of Yarmouth*) Environmental education area for Yarmouth schools.

Falmouth Foreside Preserve (Falmouth; 34 acres; *Town of Falmouth*) Town park near the Conservancy's Mill Creek Preserve. (*Please see the Mill Creek listing on page 22.*)

Forbes Pond Marsh (Gouldsboro; 25 acres; *Town of Gouldsboro*) Resting and feeding area for bald eagles, ospreys, loons and waterfowl. Managed by the town conservation commission.

Green Island (Steuben; 11 acres; *Me. Dept. Inland Fisheries and Wildlife*) Seabird nesting island. Next to Petit Manan.

Helliwell Property (Beals; 38 acres; *Town of Beals*) Town park near the Conservancy's Great Wass Island Preserve. (*See Great Wass Archipelago preserve listing on page 94.*)

Meadow Mountain (Warren; 259 acres; *Town of Warren*) Town forest.

Mill Cove (South Portland; 31 acres; *City of South Portland*) Tidal flats, salt marsh and small upland frequented by many bird species.

Redin's Island (Kennebunkport; 8 acres; *Kennebunkport Conservation Commission*) Wooded, rocky island.

Ritchey Property (Portland; 60 acres; *Cushing Island Conservation Foundation*) Backshore of Cushing Island. Addition to area held by local land trust.

River Bend Woods (Kennebunk; 13 acres; *Ramanascho Land Preservation Trust*) Forested upland sloping down to freshwater marsh along Mousam River.

Stover Point Marsh (Harpswell; 4 acres; *Harpswell Garden Club*) Beach and salt marsh on Harpswell Harbor.

Wilbur Neck (Pembroke; 230 acres; *Me. Dept Inland Fisheries and Wildlife*) Bald eagle and waterfowl habitat; large intertidal zone. On Dennys Bay.

Wing Property (Lovell; 13 acres; *Greater Lovell Land Trust*) Shorefront on southern end of Kezar Lake.

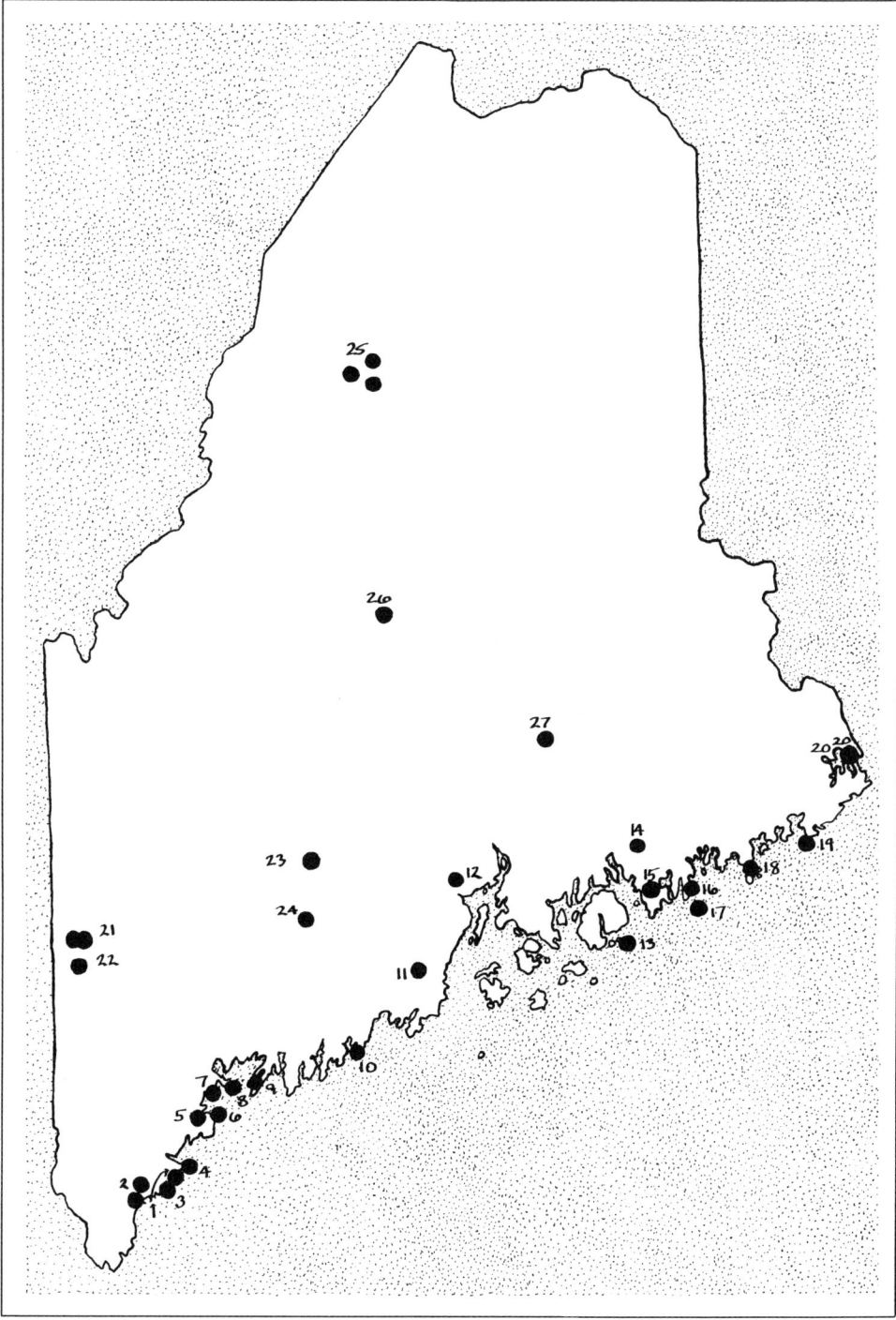

1. Rachel Carson NWR
2. River Bend Woods
3. Vaughn's & Redin's Islands
4. Benedict Property
5. Mill Cove
6. Ritchey Property
7. Falmouth Foreside Preserve
8. Cousin's Island Property
9. Stover Point Marsh
10. Tracy Shore
11. Meadow Mountain
12. Hurds Pond
13. Bakers Island
14. Donnell Pond
15. Forbes Pond Marsh
16. Petit Manan NWR
17. Green Island
18. Helliwell Property
19. Moosehorn NWR
20. Wilbur Neck
21. Virginia Lake & Shirley Valley
22. Wing Property
23. Colby Marston Bog
24. Augusta Nature Center
25. Allagash Wilderness Waterway
26. Appalachian Trail
27. Sunkhaze Meadows NWR

Index

Italic - photograph or illustration
* - detailed listing

THE NATURE CONSERVANCY

The Nature Conservancy is a national nonprofit conservation organization whose resources are devoted solely to the protection of natural areas and the diversity of life they support. The Conservancy preserves lands by:

- systematically identifying lands that contain the best examples of native plant and animal communities.

- protecting these areas through gift, purchase, or by assisting government agencies and other conservation organizations.

- managing Conservancy-owned preserves to insure perpetuation of significant elements of natural diversity and to encourage compatible uses for research, education, and public appreciation.

- increasing public awareness of the need for protection of natural areas.

Contributions, foundation grants, and membership dues support the Conservancy's activities. Membership in The Nature Conservancy is open to anyone. All contributions are tax-deductible.

Please join us in protecting Maine's unique natural heritage by sending us the attached membership card.
For more information, contact:

Maine Chapter
The Nature Conservancy
122 Main Street
P.O. Box 338
Topsham, Maine 04086
(207) 729-5181

YES, I want to help save Maine's distinctive natural heritage. Enroll me as a member of The Nature Conservancy's Maine Chapter.

☐ $1,000 Life   ☐ $50 Supporting   ☐ $25 Family
☐ $100 Acorn   ☐ $35 Contributing   ☐ $15 Subscribing

Enclosed is an extra gift of $ _____ to be used to save more land in Maine.

Name _____

Address _____

City _____ State _____ Zip _____

Dues entitle you to membership in both the Maine Chapter and the National organization. Please make your check payable to: *The Nature Conservancy, Maine Chapter*, and mail to *P.O. Box 338, Topsham, Maine 04086.* Phone: (207) 729-5181.

YES, I want to help save Maine's distinctive natural heritage. Enroll me as a member of The Nature Conservancy's Maine Chapter.

☐ $1,000 Life   ☐ $50 Supporting   ☐ $25 Family
☐ $100 Acorn   ☐ $35 Contributing   ☐ $15 Subscribing

Enclosed is an extra gift of $ _____ to be used to save more land in Maine.

Name _____

Address _____

City _____ State _____ Zip _____

Dues entitle you to membership in both the Maine Chapter and the National organization. Please make your check payable to: *The Nature Conservancy, Maine Chapter*, and mail to *P.O. Box 338, Topsham, Maine 04086.* Phone: (207) 729-5181.

YES, I want to help save Maine's distinctive natural heritage. Enroll me as a member of The Nature Conservancy's Maine Chapter.

☐ $1,000 Life   ☐ $50 Supporting   ☐ $25 Family
☐ $100 Acorn   ☐ $35 Contributing   ☐ $15 Subscribing

Enclosed is an extra gift of $ _____ to be used to save more land in Maine.

Name _____

Address _____

City _____ State _____ Zip _____

Dues entitle you to membership in both the Maine Chapter and the National organization. Please make your check payable to: *The Nature Conservancy, Maine Chapter*, and mail to *P.O. Box 338, Topsham, Maine 04086.* Phone: (207) 729-5181.